Social Work
Career Development

W9-AZR-935

Social Work
Career Development

A Handbook for Job Hunting and Career Planning

Carol Nesslein Doelling

NASW PRESS

National Association of Social Workers
Washington, DC

Josephine A. V. Allen, PhD, ACSW, *President*
Josephine Nieves, MSW, PhD, *Executive Director*

Jane Browning, *Director, Member Services/Publications*
Nancy A. Winchester, *Executive Editor*
Patricia D. Wolf, Wolf Publications, Inc., *Project Manager*
Christina A. Davis, *Senior Editor*
D. D. Verdier, *Copy Editor*
Annette Hansen, *Proofreader*
Louise Goines, *Proofreader*
Sandi Schroeder, *Indexer*

First impression September 1997
Second impression June 1998

Library of Congress Cataloging-in-Publication Data

Doelling, Carol.
    Social work career development / Carol Doelling.
        p.   cm.
    Includes bibliographical references and index.
    ISBN 0-87101-282-0
    1. Social service—Vocational guidance—United States. 2. Job hunting—United States.   I. Title.
    HV10.5.D63 1997
    361.3'2'02373—dc21   97-30573
                                                                 CIP

Printed in the United States of America.

Contents

Acknowledgments

Social Work Career Development could not have been written without the support and insights of family and friends, colleagues, and graduates of the George Warren Brown School of Social Work.

In particular, I would like to thank Shanti Khinduka, dean, for his support of this project and Enola Proctor, April Hamel, Nancy Vosler, Mark Rank, Eric Paulsrud, and Larry Davis for their advice and encouragement.

Several readers provided invaluable feedback on the manuscript. Renee Hill and her colleagues Jane Sommer and Carrie Hemenway of the Career Development Office, Smith College, and Barbara Matz, EdD, of the Graduate School of Social Work and Social Research, Bryn Mawr College, critiqued the complete manuscript. Anne Bowie, Andrhea Fox, David Gillespie, Loretta Haggard, Esq., Eugene Hickey, Arlene Janis, Rochelle K. Kaplan, Esq., Dana Klar, Esq., John Morris, Deborah Paulsrud, William Spitzer, Nancy Vosler, and Sandy Wilkie offered insights for various sections. And, of course, this book would not be possible without the assistance of the staff at the NASW Press, NASW, and the NASW chapter offices, especially Nancy Winchester and Christina Davis for editorial services; Joanne Bryson for advice on benefits; Carolyn Polowy, Esq., for advice on legal issues; Loretta S. Robinson for advice on professional liability insurance; and editing expertise from Patricia Wolf, Donna Daniels Verdier, Karen Cochran, and Cathy Cooper. I would also like to thank Linda Beebe, former associate executive director of communications, for her initial support and guidance.

Several people provided an array of information and support. My thanks to James Lowery, Sandy Wilkie, Ken Schulman, and Tim Collenback for recommendations of people to interview; Louise M. Jones on the executive search industry; Thomas W.

Lauman, CEBS, on benefits; Jeannine Dillon on loan repayment programs; Jessica Engman, Clayton Hicks, and Violet Horvath for Internet guidance; Kathy Steiner-Lang on hiring issues for international students; Andrhea Fox, Kathryn Lane, Amy Stringer, and Amanda Moore for literature searches; Andrhea Fox for excellent proofreading; and Annette Flugstad, Susie Fragale, and Vivian Westbrook for clerical support. The skills lists in appendix 10 were adapted in part from ideas and material provided over the years by Jan Bueker, Theresa Caldwell, Deanna DeBrecht, Melford Ferguson, Pamela Fitch, David Gillespie, Melissa Hensley, Sally Kaplan, Betul Ozmat, Amy Stringer, Nancy Vosler, and meetings with master's and doctoral students. I would also like to thank the Social Work Career Development Group for providing an arena to discuss ideas, the JobPlace listserv for sharing information, and the staff of the St. Louis County Library and the Washington University Social Work and Olin Libraries for research assistance.

This book is a compilation of experience and interviews with social workers and employers who hire them. Many administrators of nonprofit, public, and for-profit organizations provided insights on social services hiring, critiqued my work with students, and discussed various career issues with me. In particular, I would like to thank Beverly Bates, Beth Bostwick, S. Wray Clay, Diana Cohen, Philip Coltoff, William Donley, LaDeana Gamble, Eugene Hickey, Dennis Higbe, Sr., Patricia Johnson, Steve Jones, Doris King, Kathy Mandel, Carol Murphy, Susan Phillips, Ruth Reko, Mark Richardson, Barbara Rigabar, Meg Schnabel, Michelle Shiller-Baker, Bob Sontag, Susan S. Stepleton, Joanne Travis, Marybeth Weinhold, and Janlee Wong. I would also like to thank all the policy and program staff in Washington, DC, who provided details on career issues and expectations for working at the national level. There were also individuals who shared their career paths and job search stories. Specifically, I would like to thank the graduates of social work programs and experienced social workers whose advice, job search stories, and career paths brought life to what would have otherwise been merely a to-do list for job hunters, especially Michelle Adler, Merceda Ares, Rose Ann Ariel, Barbara Bauer, Barbara Cahn, Madeleine Dale, Tammy Delbruegge, Christopher Donovan, Diane Dugard, Kirsten Dunham, Cheryl Edwards, Steven Erikson, Wendy Fishman, Pamela Fitch, Jane Fonville, Sarah French, Sherri Fry, Amy Gifford, Laurie Hall, Sarah Hansen, Lauren Heller, William Johnston-Walsh, Rebecca Jones, Sally Kaplan, Matthew Kawaik, Patricia Kehoe, Jamila Larson, Brian Legate, Suzanne LeLaurin, Kathleen McHugh, Chad Morse, Robin Mulholland, Jennifer Ocon, Leslie Scheuler-Whitaker, David Shaw, David Shimkus, Stephanie Thomas, Clifford Tokuda, Scott Ward,

Kim Weir, Rebecca Wells, Rebecca Jimenez Yoder, Kimberly Zimmerman, and Joan Zlotnick.

Thanks also to the faculty and professional staff of several institutions for sharing their thoughts on master's and doctoral education considerations and on the academic job search and career issues. In particular, I appreciate the input of Enola Proctor, Washington University, and April Hamel, research consultant. Others to whom I am grateful include Ann Bowman, Goshen College; David Cronin, Washington University; Therese J. Dent, Washington University; Jerry Finn, Arizona State University–West; Charles Garvin, University of Michigan; Elizabeth George, Washington University; Grafton Hull, Indiana University; Lowell Jenkins, Colorado State University; Alice Johnson, Case Western Reserve University; Jane Kronick, Bryn Mawr College; Curtis McMillen, Washington University; Susan Murty, University of Iowa; Nancy Kester Neale, Appalachian State University; Ann Nichols-Casebolt, Virginia Commonwealth University; Paula Nurius, University of Washington; Deb Page-Adams, University of Kansas; David Polio, Washington University; Cynthia Rocha, University of Tennessee–Knoxville; Jack Sellers, University of Northern Alabama; Gary Seltzer, University of Wisconsin; and Mark Singer, Case Western Reserve University.

The staff of several associations and centers clarified questions on licensing and professional credentials, trends affecting different fields, and career development issues and connected me with other resource people. My thanks to Jim Baxendale, National Association of Directors of Treatment Centers; Rick Berkobien, The ARC; Karen Brock, Fayetteville Public Schools, Kentucky; Elizabeth Cole, S. Cole Associates; Shirley Pinder Cook, National Resource Center on Family Centered Practice; Donna DeAngelis, American Association of State Social Work Boards; John W. Epperheimer, The Career Action Center; Steven M. Fishbein, Department of Human Services, New Jersey; Gloria R. Gablin, American Association on Mental Retardation; Ashley Harris, Employee Assistance Professionals Association; Sally Hein, Southern Human Resource Department Consortium for Mental Health; Reed Henderson, Family Service America; Vivian Jackson, National Association of Social Workers; Charlotte McCullough, Child Welfare League of America; Galin Miller, National Hospice Organization; Mary Raymer, National Hospice Organization; J. Robin Robb, PhD, National Federation of Societies for Clinical Social Work; Marie Sanchez, Western Interstate Commission for Higher Education Mental Health Program; Eleanor Sargent, National Association of Alcoholism and Drug Abuse Counselors; and Linda Spears, Child Welfare League of America.

Special thanks go to friends and family—my husband Denis and my son Christopher, as well as my parents Rosemary and Bill, my mother-in-law Marge, my brother Mark, and my sister-in-law Carol—who managed without me, pitched in, and encouraged me during this process.

Introduction

*S*ocial Work Career Development is a reference book you can consult from time to time during your job search and throughout the course of your career. Looking for a job or thinking about a new career direction takes time, energy, and fortitude. It also takes information and ideas. When you need to expand your thinking about a search or career direction, revisit these pages.

The book is not meant to be read all at once. Skim the chapter headings and appendixes, read the sections you need now, and mark pages for future reference. Take a look at the "Quick Tips" at the end of chapters 1–6. Use the contents as a springboard to get started or restarted, whether you are defining your next career step, looking for your first job, or seeking to expand your credentials. Note that throughout the book, BSW, MSW, and PhD are used to refer to all social work degrees at those levels.

Chapter 1: Setting a Direction for Your Search

The first chapter will help you make some decisions about your next career move, expand and warm up your vocabulary for a search, and prepare a concise message about your objective and qualifications. The chapter takes you through a series of self-assessment exercises to select the skills and knowledge areas in which you are most confident, identify your accomplishments, and consider what is important to you in your work. The exercises will enable you to write a résumé more quickly, focus the message of your correspondence and interviews more precisely, and evaluate an offer with greater confidence.

Chapter 2: Researching Market and Salary Information

You know it is difficult to solve a problem or assist someone else with a problem unless you first gather some information and assess the situation. The same is true of your search—chapter 2 helps you set the stage. How much you know about the big picture in your field of practice, particularly within your geographic boundaries, will affect what you look for, how long you look, and your ability to negotiate and make a decision on an offer. Think of researching the market as putting together your own resource and referral guide, database, or Rolodex. Instead of developing resource information for clients or constituents, you are preparing it for yourself. Chapter 2 discusses sources of information on potential employers, salary data, and network contacts. Appendixes 1–4 provide detailed information on associations, employer directories, and questions you may want to ask about your field of practice.

Chapter 3: Preparing Résumés, Curricula Vitae, Portfolios, and References

Whether you are updating your résumé or curriculum vitae or starting from scratch with a new format, skim the information in this chapter and take a look at the samples in appendix 6. There are many possibilities for writing an eye-catching résumé. Select the style elements you like and create a résumé that best highlights your experience. If you are pursuing an academic career, review the discussion on the curriculum vitae and the sample in appendix 6. You will find the skills lists in appendix 10 helpful when writing or rewriting your résumé or curriculum vitae. Chapter 3 also discusses references and suggests how you can provide employers with samples of your work.

Chapter 4: Identifying Jobs and Pursuing Leads

You may believe that "who you know" is the best or only way to find a satisfying job. However, social workers have found satisfying jobs through other sources as well. When you need some additional ideas for sources of jobs, take a look at this chapter and at appendix 8. Chapter 4 suggests search strategies for those with a bachelor's or master's degree in social work as well as those looking for an academic job, gives a detailed look at the job-search experience of some social workers, and discusses the value of several job sources for social workers. You will also find suggestions for following up on a job lead, including an outline for cover letters. Sample letters for several situations are in appendix 5.

Chapter 5: Interviewing Effectively

Chapter 5 recommends strategies for approaching the job interview as a two-way discussion between two or more people. When you are preparing to interview for jobs, review the suggestions for setting your agenda and packaging yourself, managing various interview formats, and fielding typical questions. You will find sample interview questions in appendix 7.

Chapter 6: Evaluating Job Offers

Deciding whether to accept a job offer can be difficult, especially when the employer wants a decision quickly. It may be helpful to skim this chapter early in your search so that you can anticipate the information you will need to make a satisfying decision.

Chapter 7: Career Management and Professional Development

Many insist that a professional network is the key to a successful job search and career. Although "who you know" is an important element, keep in mind that "what you know" and "how you perform" are equally important in career management. Chapter 7 raises questions and gives examples for you to consider for managing a career change. You might read this section and the sample career paths once or twice a year to help brainstorm ways in which you might explore new options and expand your qualifications. The second part of the chapter details information on state licensures and certifications, professional certifications, postdegree training, and academic degree options. Appendix 9, which lists special opportunities, and appendix 11, which outlines recommendations for selecting graduate programs, complement chapter 7.

Setting a Direction for Your Search

O ver the past 25 years the number of trade publications on career management has exploded. Some popular literature promises the reward of a dream job with minimum effort, if only you follow its flawless methods. Do not be frustrated if you are not finding that dream job. Some social workers, like people in other fields, find jobs that exceed their expectations, while others find positions that at least meet their highest priorities.

The job market is a complex environment. Your search will be influenced by the geographic target you set, the job requirement levels employers are able to or must meet, the economic and political factors that affect the financial resources of organizations, and the changing nature of practice. Professional decisions and personal factors—your presentation or ability to communicate, your resourcefulness and job-search skills, and your own commitments—will also make a difference.

The better you are at packaging and articulating your qualifications, the greater your chances—even in small, tight markets—of finding work that meets your needs. Preparing a well-thought-out, polished message for the varying circumstances of your search requires hard work, particularly if you are marketing your qualifications to organizations whose staffs have limited views of social workers.

Just as you would when working with any client, organization, or individual, you want to assess the situation and create a plan before you take action. Your assessment will help you define what you want to do, sharpen your vocabulary, enable you to develop arguments for landing positions, and assist you in thinking about a strategy for your job search. One gerontological social worker described this as putting together her own care plan. In this chapter you will begin to put together your care plan, starting with the following exercises, which will prepare you for writing résumés and letters and conducting interviews:

- create lists of your knowledge areas, skills, and other qualifications
- analyze the lists to select your best qualifications
- review work preferences that affect choices
- draft some objectives for your search
- outline your relevant qualifications
- compose brief and full introductions.

These exercises are organized into the four parts that make up this chapter. Part 1 guides you through a self-assessment of your strengths. Part 2 helps you identify your work preferences. Part 3 addresses the needs of social workers who are considering a move across job functions or fields. Part 4 helps you package your objectives and strengths into a statement that you will use throughout your search.

You will find it easier to spread the work of these exercises over a week or longer than to try to complete them in one sitting. It is also helpful to set time limits of 10–15 minutes for each exercise, particularly for each segment of exercise 1, which involves brainstorming. Do not spend extra time looking for the perfect phrasing. You will refine your message as you go through the process of looking for a job or deciding on a new career direction.

Assessing Your Strengths

Part 1 consists of two exercises. Exercise 1 entails listing your knowledge, skills, and accomplishments. Exercise 2 helps you select your greatest strengths from exercise 1.

Exercise 1:   **Assessing Your Knowledge, Skills, and Accomplishments**

First you will want to create a document on diskette or organize a notebook to compile and maintain lists of your skills, knowledge areas, and accomplishments. This is time-consuming work, especially if you are starting from scratch and have years of experience, but it is work that will pay off. There are several reasons you should find the discipline to initiate and maintain this file.

- You will build and warm up the vocabulary you need to articulate your objectives and qualifications succinctly in introductions to new contacts, correspondence with organizations, and telephone conversations and interviews with employers.
- From this material you will develop résumés and letters that establish why employers should hire you for particular positions. In this changing job market, you may need to find a job in a hurry. Even if you update this file only once each year, you will be able to mount a job search quickly and effectively.
- When you are rethinking your career direction, you can use this list to explore interests, identify themes, and identify transferable knowledge and skills. Your analysis will be part of any meeting with a career counselor or executive search consultant.
- When it comes time to write a cover letter or meet with a potential employer, this list will refresh your memory and help you pinpoint those elements of your background that are most closely related to the position.

Use this as a planning document as well as a record. As you brainstorm, you may identify goals and areas that you want to develop further. Ideas on what to include in your qualifications list fall into the categories of knowledge, skills, and accomplishments.

Knowledge

It's helpful to list the subject areas that you have mastered or studied through education, experience, training, reading, and use of technology. This list can be especially pertinent if you are switching fields of practice, planning to work with a new population, interested in weaving together two career histories, or seeking an opportunity to do cutting-edge work. Before you begin brainstorming for the list, identify some categories. You might use the following:

- issues
- interventions
- theories
- policies
- populations
- settings.

If you are a student or recent graduate, do not assume that employers will grasp the range of knowledge you developed through your studies. Employers may know nothing about social work education, or what they do know may be limited to social work programs from a different era. Unless they are relatively recent graduates of your program or are actively involved in your school, they will not be familiar with the particular features of your education.

List your courses, specific topics you studied, and your papers and project topics. If you are a student, you can build your list as you go through the program. List the weekly topics from your course syllabi at the start of each semester. During or at the end of each semester, add papers and projects. Then mark those topics that you are especially comfortable discussing.

Creating your knowledge treasure chest gives you a head start for the next phase of your assessment. When you are creating a list of knowledge areas, you will often find that skills—those elements of how you apply that knowledge—are mixed with other terms. Try to separate your skills from your knowledge list in preparation for the next part of this exercise.

Skills

Your next step is to brainstorm a list of your skills and add them to the skill list you just created from your knowledge list. If you can think of categories for grouping items ahead of time, go ahead and use them. Considering functional areas such as advocacy, consulting, direct practice, supervision, program administration, management, community development, policy, research, and teaching and training—and these categories can be subdivided—might help you think of more skills. For example, do you have skills in evaluation methods or fund-raising? After you have stated your skills in your own words, scan the list of skills in appendix 10 for more ideas. By using your own words first, you are more likely to think of those skills that you can truly "own" and substantiate.

With a list of skills and knowledge you are well on your way to assembling all the elements for making decisions about your search. Now it is time to add specific accomplishments to this skills treasure chest.

Accomplishments

When you are attempting to convince someone that you are qualified to do a job, you will need examples of past performance that demonstrate your ability to put your knowledge and skills into practice. This exercise will help you brainstorm some additional skills and knowledge areas for your list.

First, think about and then list all the things you have done in (1) jobs; (2) the community and professional associations; or

(3) courses, practica, and school activities. What problems have you solved or what projects have you coordinated? Have you earned one or more academic degrees or completed training programs? Have you held leadership positions, contributed to task forces or committees, received awards and honors, or met requirements for licensure or certification? Group your accomplishments according to these three areas.

When recording your projects, list project results as well as titles, and describe the role you played. Increasingly, social work agencies—indeed, all nonprofit organizations—are becoming more outcome driven. However, few social workers are accustomed to quantifying or specifying results. It is surprising how many students write grant proposals during a practicum, complete the practicum before the funder has made a decision, and then, a year later when discussing their qualifications, cannot say whether they have experience writing a successful grant because they never found out whether the grant application was funded. Likewise, if you are a member of a staff that is trying to lower the recidivism rate of clients, can you state how successful you have been?

Although those who are seeking leadership positions must present a history and theme of related accomplishments, individuals in direct practice need to think of their work in this light as well. Accomplishments can demonstrate a theme or direction for your work, a progression of skill building, an approach to self-evaluation, and recognition of your work by others. Think about your accomplishments not only from your perspective but also from the perspectives of supervisors, colleagues, faculty, associations, and community groups. In other words, do not limit them to publicly recognized successes. You may or may not be asked directly about your accomplishments, but you will want to weave them into your responses to interview questions and clearly state them on your résumé. You may have, for example,

- rebuilt the agency's community resource directory
- delivered an in-service training class on prioritizing a caseload during a crisis
- received an excellent grade for an options paper discussing issues of collaboration for a statewide program
- increased by 25 percent the number of volunteers who completed the training program
- decreased, through intensive case management, four homeless families' repeated needs for emergency housing by one-third

- adapted a brief therapy model to work with depressed clients that met program requirements
- prepared a successful grant proposal to the World Renown Foundation for $100,000.

If you are in direct practice, you may not be used to tracking or stating results or even to encountering an interviewer who asks about them. Accountability, however, is becoming increasingly important in all social work environments. Even if you are in direct practice, including clinical practice, you will need to demonstrate an understanding of and an ability to work in an outcomes-driven environment. Although you may not have quantitatively evaluated your work, do try to state an outcome for each accomplishment.

Exercise 2:   **Selecting Your Best Knowledge, Skills, and Accomplishments**

Step 1. Record where you developed each element of your knowledge and skills. These examples are important. You do not want to fool yourself by making assumptions and statements that you cannot back up with experience. For example, you might assume that, like many social workers, you are adept at working with diversity issues, but can you articulate where and how successfully you have done this?

Step 2. Qualify your level of expertise for each knowledge or skill item. Use the following notations: A = advanced, I = intermediate, B = beginning.

Step 3. Create a summary page of your best-developed skills and knowledge areas and sort your list. Add your most important accomplishments to this list.

Deciding on Your Objectives

Now it is time to make some decisions about the type of work you want to seek. Part 2 consists of four exercises. Exercise 3 presents a series of questions regarding your work preferences. In exercise 4 you will list characteristics that will further define the type of work you are seeking. Exercise 5 entails writing three objectives, and in exercise 6 you will summarize your best qualifications for one or more objectives.

Examining Your Work Preferences

In addition to identifying your key knowledge, skills, and accomplishments, you need to consider your work preferences. Knowing what you prefer will steer your search, enable you to judge the fit between you and work opportunities, and help you understand the dynamics of conflicts on the job and the sense of "needing a change." Think about what you would like at this time in your career.

It is easy to assume that how you felt, for instance, two years ago still holds true currently: "Well, of course, it's still important to me to become an executive director someday." Your preferences can change, however, as your needs and interests evolve. If you have been employed for some time, your current work preferences are likely to be quite different from those you held as a student. Do you still want to be an executive director or is your interest in direct practice? Have you discovered that you are more interested in thinking about the big picture and addressing policy change than in working one-on-one with the people affected by policy?

The following questions will help you think about your current work preferences. The idea is to sharpen your thinking about what you want in a position. The clearer your thinking, the better you can identify jobs and organizations that are going to be a successful match for you and the better you will be able to present yourself. Although you are not likely to find a job encompassing all your preferences, you will hopefully have at least two offers, each including some ideal elements. Look at "Deciding among Offers" in chapter 6, pp. 144–146. Each example describes how the individual weighed the strengths of each position against his or her preferences. For an extensive list of questions to consider, see appendix 2.

1. How important is it that you work in an organization that formally recognizes the *NASW Code of Ethics*?
2. Do you prefer work focused on social change, or service delivery?
3. Do you prefer being part of large complex organizations, or small, single-focus organizations?
4. Do you prefer to work primarily with social workers, or with an interdisciplinary team?
5. Do you prefer to work with people who share your religious beliefs or cultural heritage?
6. Do you prefer work settings that allow you to be a generalist, or a specialist?

7. Is your preference to work directly with people, or to manage the resources that others need to work with people?

8. Do you prefer that clients come to your office, or do you prefer going out into the field (homes, schools, community centers)?

Exercise 4:

Choosing Elements That Frame Your Objective

You will find it helpful to first outline some of your interests using the ideas you have generated on knowledge, skills, and work preferences. Start by jotting down some of your choices for each of the following.

**Sidebar 1
Functions**

community development

direct practice: case management, clinical social work

fund-raising

management

policy

program planning/ administration

research leading

supervision

teaching

Function or role (see sidebar 1):

Choice 1   program planning /adm.

Choice 2   management

Choice 3   policy

Field of practice (see sidebar 2 on p. 9):

Choice 1   children services

Choice 2   community development

Choice 3   family services

Issue area (housing, depression, substance abuse, and so on):

Choice 1   adolescence

Choice 2   education

Choice 3   pregnancy / mental health

Sector (nonprofit, for-profit, public):

Choice 1   for profit

Choice 2   public

Choice 3   nonprofit

Type of organization (see the list in appendix 4):

Choice 1 _Community Dev, Govt, Public Policy_

Choice 2 _Children & Family Services._

Choice 3 _____

Population (frail, older adults; homeless people; people with chronic mental illness; or other populations):

Choice 1 _young adults_

Choice 2 _adults_

Choice 3 _adolescents_

Interventions (family therapy, case management, advocacy, and so on):

Choice 1 _advocacy_

Choice 2 _family therapy._

Choice 3 _C.I._

Sidebar 2
Fields of Practice

aging/gerontological
   social work

alcohol or drug
   abuse treatment

children's services

community
   development

criminal justice

developmental
   disabilities

domestic relations

domestic violence

family services

fund-raising

group services

health

mental health

occupational social
   work

public assistance

school social work

Setting Objectives

The first question any contact or employer will ask about you is "What do you want to do?" You also know from your own work that you are much more likely to be successful if you have a goal to motivate you. Your goal or job objective is the theme or mission statement that drives your job-search plan. You will develop introductions, telephone conversations, cover letters, résumés, and interview agendas on the foundation of your objective. State your job objective in writing. The choices you listed earlier should help you. Do this regardless of whether you will use an objective on a résumé.

Stating an Objective

Your objective can include elements of the following: a generic job title, type of organization, applicable skills, and particular interests. Think of it as simply a statement of what you would like to do. Here are some examples:

- Seeking a clinical social work position in an outpatient setting.
- Seeking a program management position in the area of developmental disabilities. Interested in applying eight years of

experience that includes direct services, training, and program planning.

- Seeking a clinical social work position in a pediatric health or mental health care setting working with children, adolescents, and families.
- Seeking a position in fund-raising that focuses on writing grants, researching prospective donors, and organizing special events for a nonprofit organization. Particularly interested in women and children's services.
- Seeking a position in research and policy using experience in quantitative and qualitative analysis. Particularly interested in health care, Medicaid, and AIDS.

Exercise 5:   **Developing Three Job Objectives**

Unless the job market in your target community is unusually strong, prepare three objectives, one for your ideal job (a job for which there is intense competition), one for your best bet or most likely job (a job for which you have the qualifications and would be happy to take), and one for a fall-back job (a job for which you are qualified or may be overqualified but one that would at least pay your dues and bills—this might be a job at an agency with a high turnover rate for staff, for example). Particularly if you take a fall-back job, read chapter 7 for ideas on enhancing your position in the organization and other possibilities for developing your career.

Exercise 6:   **Outlining Your Qualifications for Your Objectives**

The following exercise will help you begin packaging your qualifications for your objectives and others as you need them.

Step 1. At the top of a sheet of paper or a new document file, write one objective. Under the objective list the knowledge and skills important to the type of work you are seeking. If possible, divide the list into those qualifications that are required and those that are desirable. If you are using this exercise to prepare an application for a particular job, use the exact wording of the employer.

Step 2. Then review the summary list of best knowledge, skills, and accomplishments that you determined in exercise 2. How well does the list of requirements for the objective (step 1) match your best assets? You will find it helpful to write down your related qualifications across from or under each item in step 1.

Samples of Key Qualifications for an Objective

Seeking a clinical social work position in a pediatric health or mental health care setting working with children, adolescents, and families.

- have neonatal and pediatric intensive care experience
- have emergency room experience
- handled assessments with families
- provided individual and family therapy
- handled crises and made referrals
- designed a children's program at a shelter
- completed an MSW and certificate in play therapy
- studied and wrote on domestic violence, divorce and children, and crisis management.

Seeking an executive position with a social services agency focused on aging.

- have a strong fund-raising record, including several successful grants
- managed a department with clinical and research functions
- supervised multidisciplinary teams
- initiated and supported collaborative efforts across departments and institutions
- led a reorganization resulting in [insert dollar amount] savings
- directed a team in restructuring services and information management to meet requirements for outcome measures.

Step 3. Your answers to the following questions will help you fine-tune your objectives and qualifications.

- Do you need to learn more about what employers require and expect? How specific or extensive was your list for step 1? What do you still need to learn about this type of work? How is this work changing? What is known about the future of this work?
- If you do not have the experience or credentials to cover all of the qualifications for your target position, what questions could the employer raise about your background? How can you compensate for those missing qualifications? If you decide to pursue this work, these missing items can be the basis of your response to the interview question, "What are your weaknesses?" (see p. 112 in chapter 5).
- What would people from other academic disciplines or with other training have to offer?
- What can you offer that others, particularly those from other academic disciplines, cannot offer?
- Does your objective entail a move across functions, fields, populations, settings, and so on?

If you are satisfied with the match between your objectives and qualifications, go to part 4 of this chapter to prepare your message for employers. If you found that you have difficulty stating specific requirements for a position or that there is a gap between the job requirements and your background, read part 3, "Making Transitions."

Making Transitions

Your next career move may entail taking your skills and knowledge into a new arena. At a minimum you will need to learn about that new area. A major transition will require careful consideration and a strategy.

Educating Yourself on New Areas

Unless you want to make a lateral move within the same field of practice, you are likely to be pursuing positions in settings with which you need to become more familiar. Look over the work settings, job titles, associations, and questions listed in appendix 4 and the skills listed by function in appendix 10. These should help you expand your vocabulary and identify associations that could be resources for you. If you do not have associates working in your interest area whom you could tap for information, check with your NASW chapter office for names of its members or get the names of alumni from your alma mater. If you are near a university library or have access to interlibrary loan services, you will want to read the practice literature. Internet listservs are another way to educate yourself on other fields or issues (see appendix 8).

Information interviewing, popularized by Richard Bolles (*What Color Is Your Parachute?*, 1997), is another option for educating yourself. The purpose of information interviews is to give you an opportunity to explore a career field with a seasoned professional. You can gather information on trends in services, particulars of the systems involved, political and economic factors affecting the work, and practice issues.

It is best to begin with someone you already know, who can then suggest other names. Alternatively, you can call an organization and ask to speak with the social services director, clinical director, program director, or a social worker. Introduce yourself. If you are a student, indicate that you are looking for information that will help you target your studies and plan a career in social work. If you are a social worker, indicate the area in which you now work and say what your new interest is—for example, "I have been working in family preservation for some time, and now I am exploring options. I understand that you work in domestic relations at the court, which is something I would like to learn more about. My reading in this area has prompted several questions. Would it be possible to arrange a time to meet with you?"

You might also be interested in learning more about preparing for a goal. For example: "My long-term goal is to be an executive director of a service for families and children. Right now, I need advice on how to build on my direct service and advocacy experience, add to my skill base, and position myself to compete for those opportunities. Jean Lowe suggested I contact you. Would you be willing to discuss this with me?" Or, "I have been involved in advocacy around family issues and domestic violence for several years. I am now thinking about a move into politics. Would you be willing to help me explore that idea?" Or, "I have been the executive director over several functions of a large research hospital for several years. At this point, I want to shift gears. I would like to remain in an executive role, but I want to work in a social services organization. Would you be willing to discuss this type of transition with me?" You can also send a letter requesting an information interview and follow up with a telephone call—do not ask the person to call you to set up an interview.

You may need to assure your contact that the sole purpose of the interview is to gather information and that you are not looking for a job. Remember to ask your contact for a business card and to send a thank-you note.

Sample questions for the information interview follow. Use information in appendixes 4 and 10 to tailor your inquiries so that you can obtain the details that could help you decide whether to pursue this work.

- What are common titles for this type of position?
- What tasks do you perform? Or, what work is done by this department? Is this work handled similarly in other organizations, or are there other models?
- What skills or abilities are critical to your success in this work? Might new trends require other skills?
- Do you work with a team? How does the team operate? With what groups or types of individuals outside your organization do you interact, refer to, or consult?
- What kinds of career paths are there in the type of work you do?
- What advice do you have for someone who is preparing to work in your field of social work? What are common mistakes people make in planning their careers in this field?
- Can you suggest other people I might contact?

Moving across Functions and Fields

Look carefully at your list of knowledge and skills and compare it to the list of requirements for the work you want to do. Certainly there are shared knowledge and skills across the lists, but what are the unique aspects of your new direction and are they on the list? Do you know what they are? What will it take for you to build that second list to a level strong enough to compete for positions? Are there elements of your background—knowledge of evaluation, outcomes-driven practice, or technology—that would be an asset in the new environment or role? If you were in that new role, how would you think differently about management, policy, or practice? Do you know what the difference is? How well do you know the culture, issues, and language of the new arena? How well can you envision yourself in the next role, and can you present yourself as confident and knowledgeable—in other words, do you appear ready to assume that role? To help you analyze your readiness to make a transition, add the following category to exercise 6.

Transitions: Comparing and Contrasting Your Background with Your Goal

Go back to the end of exercise 6 and prepare an analysis divided into five headings: (1) skills, (2) knowledge, (3) technology, (4) culture and expectations, and (5) credentials. Under each heading list detailed statements under the subheadings of "comparable items" and "contrasting items." Your analysis of what your background and the new job goal have in common will result in comparable items. Those items in the job goal that you identify as different or perhaps missing from your background will result in contrasting items. Use the following questions to think through this process.

- What skills are required in the goal job that are part of your demonstrated skill list? What skills are different?
- What knowledge is required in the goal job that is part of your knowledge list? What knowledge is different?
- What technologies that are used in the goal job are part of your background? What uses of technology will be different?
- What work culture and expectations are part of the goal environment and parallel to your experience? How are these different?
- What legal or professional credentials that are required or desired for the goal job are part of your qualifications? What credentials may be different?

This step will help you determine how well prepared you are to make a case for your target job. The more definitive your statements, the more realistic your choice of a new goal will be.

What Will It Take to Make a Transition across Fields or Functions?

What enables people to change directions in their careers? A successful career transition calls for two things: motivation and a link from one job to the other.

To move from point A to point C, you need to find link B. You might think of this link as a stepping-stone or a bridge. You may already have a link or asset, such as skills, knowledge, credentials, or contacts that would be of value to an organization outside your field. Look at your summary from exercise 2 and brainstorm other fields and settings that use similar skills, address the same issues or will need to address those issues in the future, or serve the same population. If you need ideas, visit a library or bookstore and browse through magazines and journals unrelated to your work. You may discover something in your background that you can use to make a transition.

- Specialized skills such as a second language, a new practice method, ability to work with diverse populations, or experience with a particular computer package or program language might be the deciding qualification for an employer who is willing to train you in other aspects of the job. For example, an investment firm hired a social worker in the human resources department because she had the ability to work with diverse populations.
- Knowledge about a particular cultural or ethnic perspective, for example, or about diversity issues, aging, service delivery systems, or resource development, may be the common factor that enables you to move across fields of practice.
- A new credential—a degree, professional certificate, or training program, for example—could strengthen your qualifications for another field and create the bridge you need.
- Your contact network itself may be key to a transition. For instance, an information systems company that wanted to do business with state governments hired a social worker who knew administrators in many state social services departments.

If your review of your background or qualifications does not turn up a strong link, then pursue a new experience that will strengthen your case. You might volunteer for a special project at your present place of employment or in an association or get some training that would develop skills. You could make a lateral move in or out of your organization to a position that requires your primary skills but also enables you to stretch your experience in a new area. This could be the interim job or pivotal position that creates the link to your next major career move.

Can you identify the motivation or value that will sustain you through the transition? For the transition to succeed, your motivation—an intense desire or need to accomplish a goal (other than attaining a job) or to achieve some other value (money, prestige, freedom) must be strong.

A major career change is difficult. The weaker the link and the motivation, the less likely the change will occur. You are more likely to succeed if you look at the areas most closely related to your current work or background strengths and make incremental moves, small steps outside your experience base. As you build new skills and knowledge and connect with associations and others in the new area, your identity will shift internally and externally toward a new goal. To learn more about making career transitions, read *What Color Is Your Parachute?* by Richard Bolles (1997); *Wishcraft: How to Get What You Really Want*, by Barbara Sher (1979); or *Career Change*, by D. P. Hefland (1995).

Preparing Your Message

Now that you have listed your qualifications for your objective(s), begin preparing introductions. You will use these in telephone conversations, meetings with contacts, letters, and interviews. These samples are written for various audiences and circumstances. If a friend is introducing you to neighbors at a block party, your sound bite will be different from the one you would use with an exhibitor at a conference. Note that the introductions for Lisa Denton match sample résumés in appendix 6 and sample letters in appendix 5.

Brief Introduction

Take advantage of any opportunity to introduce yourself and tell someone what you are seeking. You can weave a brief message about your interest—a tag line or a sound bite—into a conversation almost anywhere. If you are already in the habit of doing this, great. If not, you will find it helpful to think precisely about a brief message that fits your job-search needs. Here are a few examples where the tag line follows the name immediately in a conversation, but this will not always be the case.

> *Hi, I'm Lisa Denton. I've just moved back to Dallas and I'm looking for a job as a clinical social worker.*

> *Hi, I'm Lisa Denton. I'm a clinical social worker looking for a job. My experience is in health and mental health work with kids and families.*

Hi, I'm Lisa Denton. I'm moving back to the Dallas/Fort Worth area in June and I hope to find a clinical social work position working with children and families.

Full Introduction

You can add several sentences to your brief introduction to create a full introduction that states your objective and its related qualifications. This paragraph will become the basis for cover letters and responses to the interview questions "Tell me about yourself," and "Why should we consider you for this position?" This message, which you will tailor for specific circumstances, will serve as a theme for your interviews.

Hi, I'm Maria Gonzalez. I have a bachelor's degree in social work and work experience, and I am looking for a case management position. My recent experience includes home visits, goal setting with clients, and assessments and referrals with emergency shelters, transitional-living programs, and homeless services. Before returning to school, I managed apartments—I worked with HUD guidelines, managed staff, dealt with tenant crises, and prepared the budget.

Hi, I'm Lisa Denton. I'm moving back to the Dallas/Fort Worth area in June, and I'm looking for a clinical social work position working with children and families. In May I will get my master's degree from My University, where I did two field placements. One was in medical social work in the neonatal and pediatric intensive care units; the other was in day treatment with a residential center. Before that I spent two years working with a children's program for the Women's Shelter in Dallas.

Hi, I'm Lisa Denton. I'm returning to the Dallas/Fort Worth area in June. I have nearly four years' experience working with children and families. I spent two years working as an advocate and volunteer coordinator for the children's program at the Women's Shelter in Dallas. I have recently had training in medical social work for neonatal and pediatric care units and day treatment at a residential center. Now I am looking for an opportunity to work with children and families in a health or mental health setting.

Hello, I'm Caroline Demer. I am a doctoral candidate at Mountain University; I am looking for a tenure-track position beginning in the fall. My teaching interests are in program planning and policy. My research interests center around the frail elderly population, caregiver stress, alternative care, and housing. By June I expect to defend my dissertation, which is on [name the subject]. I have had the opportunity to work with several faculty members on research projects and to teach as well.

Hi, I'm Clayton Winter. I have been directing a multi-disciplinary family outreach program at a large teaching hospital for nine years. The program encompasses an assessment center, parent training, counseling and family therapy, a school-based clinic, and pastoral care. Through grants and collaborative alliances, I have doubled the number of families served. Through my board work, collaborative efforts, and fund-raising, I have developed an interest in the work of foundations and resource allocations.

Moving On

You have assessed your background and set a primary and perhaps secondary objective for your search, or at least you have some ideas. With this focus you can begin researching your market, identifying leads, and pursuing opportunities. The next few chapters will help show you how.

References

Bolles, R. N. (1997). *What color is your parachute? A practical manual for job-hunters and career-changers.* Berkeley, CA: Ten Speed Press.

Hefland, D. P. (1995). *Career change: Everything you need to know to meet new challenges and take control of your career.* Chicago: VGM Horizons.

Sher, B. (1979). *Wishcraft: How to get what you really want.* New York: Ballantine Books.

Career Transition Tools

Listed below are common tools used by social workers making career transitions. Identify which ones will work for you. Be careful about using more than one at a time with one person. Doing so will create confusion or, at best, a poor impression.

- **Interviewing for information:** When you are exploring career options and need to learn about a new field of practice, function, or trends in social work, conduct information interviews. See the section earlier in this chapter on educating yourself on new areas.

- **Seeking advice:** When you have decided what you want to do and need advice on seeking work in a particular geographic location or specialty in multiple geographic targets, seek advice on the job market and job-search resources. See the section in chapter 2 on seeking advice from key contacts.

- **Making cold calls:** When you want to know quickly whether an organization has an opening, simply make a cold call to ask whether there are openings, as discussed in chapter 4.

- **Networking with contacts:** When you want to expand the list of people you know who may hear of jobs or know something about the organizations in your field of practice or policy or those potential employers you have targeted, ask colleagues, friends, and other contacts whether they can refer you to others.

CHAPTER 1 QUICK TIPS: Setting Your Direction

- Brainstorm 5–10 skills you want to use on a job, 5–10 knowledge areas you have, and 3–10 accomplishments you can discuss.

- Next to each skill and knowledge item describe where you used or learned that attribute.

- List two types of organizations you like to work in and two job functions you would consider.

- Write a sentence describing what you are looking for.

- Add four sentences to create a paragraph that concisely states what you would like to do and outlines key qualifications, skills, knowledge, accomplishments, experience, and credentials.

Chapter 2

Researching Market and Salary Information

A man with a master's degree in social work and five years of experience in fund-raising and political campaign management in California moved to Indianapolis to be with his fiancée. While juggling wedding planning with job hunting, he discovered an opening, applied, and was offered the job. It was a great job—he would work closely with a range of organizations in the local community. This experience would prove helpful when he was ready to change jobs or pursue some entrepreneurial ideas in the back of his mind. Of course, there was a catch. Accepting the offer meant a cut in salary. Efforts to negotiate did not close the gap. Having researched the market for only a short period, he did not have enough information to determine whether he should take the job offer in hand or chance the possibility of a better opportunity. As it turned out, he accepted the position, which proved an excellent career move for him.

The dilemma just described is a common one for social workers. When you decide to look for a job, you naturally apply for any appealing opening you come across. This makes sense—you certainly do not want to pass up an opportunity. If you also take time to become familiar with the market, you can make better-informed decisions and be more efficient with your time.

If you are able to anticipate a job search because you will be graduating, moving, or completing a project, consider yourself lucky and do some advance planning. For instance, if you are a student, designate an hour every week during your second-to-last semester to study your market. No matter how busy you are, you can find at least an hour each week to surf the Internet, clip items from a newspaper, scan organization directories, or make some calls. Even if you lose your job suddenly, you can improve your chances of securing a good position by spending part of your time learning more about the market.

Researching the market is especially important for social work generalists and those who are changing careers. To find a good match between your abilities and an organization's needs, you must know the details that affect organizations (see appendix 4). This information will help you tailor your message for the needs of the field and compete better against those with specific experience.

Your goal for researching the market is to answer the following questions:

- Which organizations engage in the type of work I want to do?
- Do these organizations hire people with my qualifications? What other qualifications do they require?
- How long should I expect to look?
- What is the salary range for the work I want to do?
- What trends or events might affect the market?

In this research phase you want to gather information, not inquire about positions. Concentrate on two tasks: (1) compiling information on employers, salaries, and licensure laws and (2) seeking advice from a network of contacts.

You may find this beginning step in the search fun, frustrating, or a good excuse for putting off decisions and action. The suggestions posed in this section are not meant to overwhelm you. You need to have a realistic picture of the market, but you may also need to set limits on how much information you gather.

The Printed and Electronic Word: What to Look for before You Seek Advice

Before you seek advice from your network contacts, do some background research on your own. The more knowledgeable you are, the more specific your questions can be and the more productive your discussions with contacts will be. Here are some suggestions.

Update Your Memberships

If you are not a member of NASW, join. If you are a member who will be moving to another state, change your membership as soon as possible so you can begin to receive the local chapter's newsletter and learn about social work in that state. Or contact the NASW chapter in the new state and ask for a couple of newsletters. There may be a small charge for this service, but it is worth it to learn of job opportunities and the names and activities of leaders in your new social work community. To change your NASW membership, call 800-638-8799; have your membership number ready. Chapter addresses and telephone numbers are available at the NASW home page: http://www.naswdc.org or by calling the number listed above. There may be other professional societies or organizations that you may want to join. Some societies list job openings in their newsletters, hold conferences and job fairs, maintain home pages on the Internet, or offer referral services (see appendix 1).

Check Licensure, Certification, and Reimbursement Regulations

If you are interested in direct or clinical practice—particularly at the master's level—licensure, certification, and reimbursement regulations will affect your search. Find out what licensure levels or certifications exist in your target state and determine whether you qualify to practice there. You also will need to know about state regulations for reimbursement for your work—some states have complicated vendor laws regarding reimbursement. Will you be required to have supervision? From whom? How independent will you be? Will you also need professional certification for reimbursement at a particular level (personal communication with J. Robin Robb, PhD, research chair and vice president for professional development, National Federation of Societies for Clinical Social Work, Arlington, VA, June 13, 1996)?

Request a licensure packet from the social work board for your target state. Contact the American Association of State Social Work Boards (see appendix 1) to obtain a telephone number for your state board. If you are interested in school social work, you should contact the state's department of education. Substance abuse certification varies by state; contact the state department that handles professional licensing for information. Administrative, advocacy, and policy positions do not usually require licenses. However, it would be wise to put this on your list of questions to discuss with local contacts. See chapter 7 for an overview of credentials.

Compile a List of Target and Potential Employers

In any community, a finite number of organizations do the specific type of work you want to do. If you have not set geographic limits but instead are looking for a good opportunity to use your specialty, you can be more selective about choosing those organizations that match your mission, serve as models, have experts on staff, and are known for training.

Start by compiling a list of those organizations that do exactly what you want to do; bearing in mind the size of your geographic target, expand your list from there. If your first love is pediatric social work and you are looking in only one community, children's hospitals will be the focus of your search. Unless your community has several children's hospitals and the job market is strong, however, you will need to identify other potential employers. Conversely, an exhaustive list of children's organizations in a large city would take too long to compile and would contain agencies of little interest to you.

Break your list of employers into groups of organizations that do exactly what you want to do, those that address some of your interests, and those that do something related to your interests. Research these organizations through directories, news publications, the Internet, and your contact network. You may discover that some of the organizations doing exactly what you would like to do hire staff with credentials beyond yours, rarely have openings, or perhaps are merging with other organizations. Or you may learn that an employer in your third-tier group has just gotten a grant to initiate a new project or has received a recognition award from a national organization. Your research efforts will allow you to reorganize your list into target, potential, and fallback organizations.

Bury Your Nose in Printed or Online Directories

An easy way to begin identifying potential employers is to use printed or online directories that list organizations by purpose, service, and location. If you are looking for a position in direct practice or in planning or management in social services, the local community services directory and telephone book will cover most potential employers in your target community. If you are now in direct services or social services management, you already use a local community services directory and may have access to an online regional resource database. Otherwise, purchase a directory, borrow one from a friend, or use the copy in the local library. To purchase a community services directory in another city, call United Way, which can connect you with the office or organization that publishes the local directory. See appendix 3 for addresses of publishers for community services directories for major cities.

You may discover through networking that a local interest group has printed its own resource directory. For example, someone interested in working in AIDS services was making exploratory long-distance calls to Massachusetts. She discovered that an AIDS task force had printed a local resource guide on HIV and AIDS services. The contact person offered to send the job hunter a free copy.

For a search that covers several geographic areas, you will have to access national directories for types of services (for example, community mental health centers, hospice programs, adoption services, and family services). Associations, publishing companies, and the federal government publish these directories of programs, which are usually arranged by state. Examples include the Child Welfare League of America's *Directory of Member Agencies*, Family Service America's *Directory of Member Agencies in the US and Canada*, *United Way of America Membership Directory*, Congressional Quarterly's *Washington Information Directory*, and *The Adoption Resource Guide* by Julia L. Posner and James Guilianelli. See appendix 3 for a list of directories. Look under the international heading for directories of organizations that work abroad. You can also ask a reference librarian to show you *Books in Print*, which lists all published books and other job-search resources available at your local library. Membership directories of associations you belong to are also good sources. Some association membership lists are for sale, although they can be expensive.

Surf the Internet

You will find that some social services agencies, large nonprofit or international organizations, universities, and many hospitals have home pages on the Internet. These may include descriptions of services, projects, products, and reports; lists of staff; job openings; and an e-mail address for correspondence. Some well-known organizations with home pages are American Red Cross, Children's Defense Fund, World Bank, and the United Nations. You will also find Web sites that provide data and other material on issues in social services. If you do not have access to the Internet, check with your public library. Many library reference services offer Internet access and instruction on its use. See appendix 8 for a list of Internet sites.

Scan Publications Regularly

While visiting the Minneapolis/St. Paul area, one student noticed a series of newspaper articles on services for older adults; the reports named organizations and quoted professionals in the field. She asked a friend to save each week's article. The following year, six months before moving to the Twin Cities, she launched her search with information from the series and landed a job about a month after graduation.

If you know a job search will be on your agenda, start saving want ads and articles from newspapers, newsletters such as *NASW News*, other publications, and the Internet. They will give you specific information about new services, changes in personnel, and turnover in particular agencies, all of which are valuable details for your research file.

Gather Information on Specific Organizations

As you compile a list of organizations, keep notes on information you come across and begin researching specific organizations. You can request newsletters, annual reports, and brochures; speak with contacts; use the Internet; and search publications for articles. Talk with the reference staff of your library about online services and directories concerning nonprofit, public, and for-profit organizations. You should look for the following basic information:

- whom to contact (name, address, and telephone number)
- the purpose of the organization (for example, direct services, research, advocacy, education, program planning, fund-raising, community development, philanthropy, or organizing)
- the types of services or projects carried out by the organization (primary or traditional services or innovative programs, for example)
- the organizational setting (public, nonprofit, or for-profit)
- the affiliation of the organization (for example, religious, university, or foundation)
- the organization's staff size.

After obtaining these facts, you may want to check with your contacts and resources to get further information. Although it would be inappropriate to ask some of the following questions regarding particular organizations, keep the ideas in mind as you gather information:

- What are the organization's strengths? For what is it well known?
- Is the organization in a starting phase, growing phase, or well-maintained state, or has it become overgrown and stagnant?
- Who leads the organization? Does it have a strong leader, a capable management team, and a supportive and active board?
- Who makes up the management team? What are the different roles?
- What are the goals of the organization? How have the goals changed? How might they change in the future?
- Has this organization merged, downsized, or expanded recently?
- Considering the factors in this list, how does this organization compare with its counterparts?

- Do professionals and organizations with which this entity interacts respect its philosophy and staff?
- How do salaries in this organization compare with those of similar institutions?

If you have been part of a management team, you are already familiar with accreditation standards and can assess the quality of a direct-services organization. If you are not familiar with the accreditation standards for the types of organizations you are researching, discuss standards and their effect on agencies with people in your contact network.

These are some questions you may want to ask about nonprofit organizations:

- What are the funding sources and what proportion of the budget does each provide? Is the organization dependent on one primary funding source? Does the board raise money and, if so, how effectively?
- How heavily does the organization rely on volunteers and what roles do they play?
- Is this organization part of a larger umbrella organization? If yes, what is the relationship between them? Is the umbrella organization headquartered out of town?

You will want to know the following about public institutions:

- Does this public unit have a positive reputation among constituents, or has it been a political "hot potato"?
- Compared with similar departments in other jurisdictions, is this department considered average, cutting edge, or behind the times?
- Is the political appointee heading the department interested in and committed to the agency's mission, biding his or her time, or even hostile toward the agency's work?
- Is the experience or education of the members of the administration related to the department's service?

Find out the following about for-profit organizations:

- Is the company publicly held? Does it sell shares and publish an annual report?
- What is the size of this organization in terms of number of clients, revenue, number of facilities, and number of employees?
- How does it compare with its competitors?
- Does this company have a parent company or subsidiaries?
- Where is each located?

Example of Using Research in an Interview

"I think what made my interview stand out the most was the fact that I had researched the company before I came in and thus showed that I was very interested in their company. Also, I spent a lot of time before the interview thinking about what I had to offer the organization that was different from what other people would have to offer. The most important thing that I came up with was the ability to evaluate the programs and put mechanisms into place that could monitor the programs. I also expressed an interest in what the future held for their clients and employees. We discussed in the interview various things that could be accomplished in the future. I believe this was helpful in putting the idea in the interviewer's mind that I was already a part of the organization."

Collect Salary Data

Of course, you will have to consider salaries and the cost of living when you are searching for a job. Look at these variables carefully—in many cases they will affect your decision to take a position.

Set a Salary Goal

People in human resources and career development generally advise that you plan on spending one month seeking a position for every $10,000 you wish to earn. This formula assumes that you have the qualifications to compete for your preferred job; that the job market in your target community is at least moderately strong; and that you conduct an aggressive, efficient search and present yourself well. If you are switching fields or functions, lack familiarity with your target community, or cannot meet the criteria mentioned in the previous statement, you should plan on a longer search.

Think carefully about the salary you think is appropriate for your qualifications, about your expenses, and about the salary figure you are willing to accept. Salaries will be influenced by the following six factors:

1. *Geographic location:* Salaries and the cost of living on the eastern and western seaboards are higher than in the central part of the country. According to 1995 NASW salary data, the highest incomes were reported by members in the Pacific, Middle Atlantic, New England, and South Atlantic states (Gibelman & Schervish, 1997). If you are comparing job

opportunities in two communities, you will find the following
reference books and Web site helpful: *American Cost of Living
Survey* by A. J. Darnay and H. S. Fisher; *ACCRA Cost of Living
Index*, published by the American Chamber of Commerce Researchers Association; and *U.S. Cost of Living Comparisons for
399 U.S. Job Markets* (http://www.datamasters.com/cgi-bin/
col.pl).

2. *Economic sector:* In general, for-profit organizations pay higher
   salaries than do nonprofit or public organizations. In the nonprofit arena, organizations that do not have religious affiliations tend to pay higher than those that do. Salary levels for
   nonprofit and public institutions depend on the location, department, government level, and field of practice. NASW
   membership data for 1995 indicated that public-sector members usually were paid better than their nonprofit counterparts.
   NASW members with the federal government, including the
   military, reported higher incomes than those employed at other
   government levels. (Gibelman & Schervish, 1997) At the state
   level, Illinois public child welfare positions usually pay better
   than nonprofit opportunities; this is not true in all states,
   however.

3. *Field of service:* Jobs in health care usually pay better than those
   in children's services or mental health services. Unfortunately,
   salaries in women's services, daycare centers for children, and
   agencies for homeless people often reflect the low priority and
   poor funding that these segments receive.

4. *Size of organization:* Salary may vary according to organization
   size. Salaries at a small, single-service nonprofit organization
   are likely to be lower than those at a large teaching hospital,
   public school system, or managed-care company. Nevertheless, be aware that large size and wide reputation are not always indicators of higher salaries.

5. *Job function:* In general, management, policy analysis, fund-
   raising, consulting, and tenure-track faculty positions pay better than direct practice jobs.

6. *Qualifications:* Academic degrees, licensure, certifications, experience, skills, and specialized knowledge all play a part in an
   employer's decision about salaries to offer.

Local Salary Data

Your best sources of salary information in your target location are
the same people you will contact for a sense of the market: local
social workers, nonprofit managers, officers of local chapters of

professional associations, and staff of groups that study and fund social services. Once again, be sure you talk with several people; not everyone has up-to-date information on salaries around the community. Of course, you would not ask someone what his or her salary was; instead, you would ask what salary range you might expect. Some schools of social work routinely collect employment data on recent alumni and may be willing to give you salary ranges for particular types of services over the telephone. Be sure you know how recent the figures are.

Sometimes cold calls to employers work well, too. One person who was looking at positions working with older adults, including medical social work, called human resources offices at several hospitals; some of those offices provided her with salary ranges for someone at her level of experience.

National and Regional Salary Data

Various groups collect salary data that may be useful to you. Often their reports are published and can be purchased. If you find that an organization does not make its report available to the public, perhaps people in your network will be willing to share information they receive as members of the society or association. These reports come from several sources.

Some professional societies, including NASW and the Association of Baccalaureate Social Work Program Directors, collect national and regional salary data; state chapters may also have membership-based salary information.

Associations to which organizations belong, including the National Council for Behavioral Community Healthcare, Family Service America, and the Child Welfare League of America, also collect salary data (see appendix 1).

Nonprofit management assistance centers, United Way offices, regional think tanks, universities, and state departments of labor and economic development also may collect salary data.

National data are valuable but very broad—you should look at compilations carefully. For example, data classified by area of practice will include those in entry-level positions as well as experienced directors, unless otherwise stated. The data may or may not reflect geographic differences, economic sectors, or academic degrees. Often salaries are identified by distinct job types or titles such as executive director, but at lower levels many titles are less clear. The size of an organization can also affect salary; in a pool of executive directors you will find those running operations with budgets of $100,000 as well as those with budgets of several million dollars.

- *BPD Outcomes Instrument*, a project of the Association of Baccalaureate Social Work Program Directors, includes nationwide data on first-time social work employment for those with a bachelor's degree in social work. Authors are Grafton H. Hull, Jr., JoAnn Ray, John Rogers, and Marshall Smith. (The report is not published regularly. To obtain information about the latest version of the report, visit the association's Web site at http://www.rit.edu/~694www/bpd.htm.)
- *Who We Are*, by Margaret Gibelman and Philip H. Schervish (1997), is a detailed profile of the NASW membership in 1995. A chapter analyzing salary data looks at primary income by highest degree earned, years of experience, gender, ethnicity, age, primary practice area, setting, auspices, primary function, and geographic region.
- *The MSW Job Market*, a pilot project, collects salary data on new graduates of MSW programs; however, only a small number of MSW programs are participating at this time. Coordinators are Carol Doelling of Washington University in St. Louis, Missouri, and Barbara Matz of Bryn Mawr College, Bryn Mawr, Pennsylvania.
- *Statistics on Social Work Education in the United States* is an annual Council on Social Work Education publication prepared by Todd M. Lennon (1997); it includes data on faculty salaries by rank, geographic region, program type, gender, and ethnicity.

NASW-Recommended Salaries and Salary Data
NASW has set recommended starting salaries for degreed social workers, with the understanding that these figures are subject to geographic differences. The NASW recommendation for a social worker with a bachelor's degree is $23,320; for a master's degree holder, $29,150; for one who holds a master's degree in social work or Academy of Certified Social Workers (ACSW) certification with two years of experience, $34,980; and for an advanced professional, $52,741.

The Human Element: Building a Contact Network

Although you will find some useful information in print, people in your target community or specialty will be your best sources of information about your market. Like composing a list of potential employers, creating a list of potential contacts with whom you could network is a valuable step in the preparation process. Seeking advice from some of these contacts is the next step.

Create a List of Potential Contacts

Write down or enter in the computer possible names for a contact network. You will use the network to get advice and job leads for your search. To get started, brainstorm a list of people who are knowledgeable about your field of social work, your potential employers, and your target community (if you are looking in a specific location). Remember that people in your current location may have information on contacts, employers, professional societies, and advocacy groups in your new target community. To create your list, start with people you already know—coworkers, fellow committee members, classmates, practicum supervisors, former professors, friends, and family members. Check your Rolodex, address file, the resource referral list you use on the job or in practicum, your alumni directory, and membership directories from your professional associations. Do not overlook leaders of the social work community and others who work closely with professional and community issues, particularly if you are looking at the market for community development, advocacy, policy, and management. Consider contacting the following people:

- officers of local, state, and national professional associations (NASW, for example, or the American Association for Marriage and Family Therapy)
- staff at United Way offices and other organizations that consult with or study nonprofit organizations; one executive director suggests that you consult United Way for the number, demographics, size, scope of services, and history of private agencies
- volunteers and staff of civic groups such as the Urban League or researchers at regional think tanks
- facilitators of local collaborations, task forces, or coalitions
- faculty and staff at schools of social work
- people whose work you have read or heard about
- state legislators who are particularly interested in your field (contact them when the legislature is not in session)
- chairs and participants of NASW committees, agency networks, and so on.

Seek Advice from Key Contacts

Identify three to five people in the field who can give you advice about conducting a job search in your target community or a national job search in your specialty. This step is especially important if you are moving to a new location, are inexperienced in job hunting, are unclear about the strength of the market, or if you have not looked for a job in a long time.

Think of who might have a good overview of the field, services, and the local community or market you are exploring. If you are a doctoral student planning an academic career, you will want to meet with your adviser, members of your dissertation committee, and other faculty to talk specifically about a nationwide academic search.

This conscious effort to seek advice on a search is pertinent for those who hold a BSW as well as for those with an MSW. For instance, a student interested in program planning for children wished to relocate in Boston. Six months before graduation with an MSW, she called three agencies in Boston and asked to speak with the program directors. Although she was able to reach only one person on the first try, he scheduled a time when she could call him back to get his ideas on looking for a program-planning job. When you seek advice, keep these specific purposes in mind:

- to get thoughts on your list of potential employers
- to learn of any trends, legislation, or events that could affect your search
- to build relationships with a few key advisers whom you can consult about your search when necessary
- to make your name and professional interests familiar to others involved in your field.

Guidelines on Contacting People for Advice

After you have identified key contacts and before you pick up the telephone to seek advice for your search, think through your approach. Here are some suggestions.

Determine What Information You Need

Do your homework first. Learn about the community from printed and online sources. Write down questions you want to ask, including any broader issues that could affect your search. Some ideas follow. See appendix 4 for questions specific to broad areas of service. Ask yourself

- Is there a task force addressing my interest area that I should know about and get involved in—for example, a communitywide collaboration on family violence?
- How is managed care affecting various local agencies, hospitals, and so on?
- Will recent public policies affect my job? Are the licensure laws changing? Is there a referendum on taxes being discussed?
- Who are the individuals in this community who know the most about services, new developments, and policies in my field—for example, aging, home health, children's advocacy?

- Are there state or local regulations that make services here different from those where I now work? For example, are all school districts required to have school social workers?
- What organizations have merged recently or may merge? What has been the impact on social work jobs?
- With what professional and advocacy groups do social workers or those specializing in this field affiliate? Who is the contact person?
- What organizations will hire individuals with my level of experience? (Be familiar enough with your list of potential employers that you can recognize or mention organization names. For example, you could say, "I have a list of five residential treatment centers for adolescents, which are [state the names of the centers]. Are there any others I should add to that list?")
- What salary range is realistic for someone with my level of education and experience?

Prepare a Concise Introduction

Be sure you know how you are going to introduce yourself. If you do not already know the person you are asking for information, explain how you got his or her name. Explain the purpose of the call or letter (see sample letter 1 in appendix 5). Ask whether he or she has a few minutes to talk or find out when it would be convenient to talk in person or over the telephone.

Start with People You Know

Even if you are moving to an area where you have no contacts, start talking with those in your present community. They can give you advice on your next career move, and they may know social workers or be familiar with organizations in your target community. Of course, you will want to be selective in making contacts (for example, you may not want coworkers to know that you are looking for a new position).

Starting your efforts with people you know will prepare you for contacting those you have not met. You need to be prepared for all of these calls and meetings, but you especially want to be prepared for a conversation with someone you do not know. The higher the position the person holds, the less time you are likely to have with him or her and the more precise your questions need to be.

Focus on Advice, Not Job Openings

During this research phase, the focus of your networking should be advice on how to go about finding the type of social work position you want in that community. In the course of a conversation someone may tell you about an opening, but do not use these conversations to identify openings. At this point you are introducing yourself to other professionals and getting ideas on appropriate job-search strategies in the market.

Keep Your Call or Visit Brief

Part of a successful network effort is pacing your conversations. Strive to limit telephone calls to five minutes and visits to 15. However, be prepared to spend more time should you encounter a particularly conversant contact.

Remember Propriety and Protocol

If someone says, "I can refer you to Ms. Jones, but I want to call her first," be sure to respect your contact's wishes. When someone refers you to a colleague, always ask whether you can use his or her name when you follow up with that colleague.

In some cases, if a potential contact is located in another community or is at an executive level, you may want to write a letter introducing yourself and indicating that you will call. See sample letters 1 and 6 in appendix 5.

Record Detailed Notes from the Conversation

Be sure to take some notes during your conversations; immediately after the conversation, record as many details as you remember.

Thank Your Contact

Immediately after your conversation, send a brief handwritten or typed thank-you letter (see sample letters 7 and 8 in appendix 5). Do not send a résumé unless the person asked for one. Again, keep this initial contact focused on advice. Later, after you have assimilated the pieces of advice you solicited and you actually begin pursuing leads, you can write to particularly helpful contacts a second time. See the section "Contacts and Networking" in chapter 4.

What to Do If All You Hear Is Discouraging News

As you research your target market, you may find that people in the field discourage you from looking for the job you really want. If this happens, ask yourself these questions:

- Have I talked with a variety of people in nonprofit, public, and, if applicable, for-profit settings?
- What is their information based on? Have they come into contact with many social workers with my experience who are looking

for the same type of job? Have they been frustrated in their own work or in their attempts at changing jobs or careers?

- Do I have a comprehensive list of employers for my primary and secondary interests?
- Do I know which organizations are likely to hire someone with my background?

In other words, be certain that you have covered all the bases to obtain a balanced picture of the opportunities. It is not uncommon to encounter someone whose personal experience makes him or her overly negative; your background and experience with the market could be very different.

Yet the community of your choice may indeed be saturated with qualified professionals—this often happens in college towns and popular cities. You may nonetheless find a position if you extend the length of your search, expand your objective, or take a job where you will pay your dues to the profession. Vigorous networking will be the key in that situation.

For example, if you are a new MSW graduate your chances of finding a job with an employee assistance program (EAP) may be slim. You may decide to take a job in a substance abuse treatment center, get a few years of experience while earning your clinical license and substance abuse certification, and become a member of the Academy of Certified Social Workers. You can simultaneously become involved in the professional community and network with individuals in EAPs. Then you will be better positioned to look for your preferred job.

References

American Chamber of Commerce Researchers Association. (1997). *ACCRA cost of living index*. Louisville, KY: Author.

Darnay, A. J., & Fisher, H. S. (1994). *American cost of living survey*. Detroit: Gale Research.

Gibelman, M., & Schervish, P. H. (1997). *Who we are: A second look*. Washington, DC: NASW Press.

Lennon, T. M. (1997). *Statistics on social work education in the United States: 1996*. Alexandria, VA: Council on Social Work Education.

U.S. cost of living comparisons for 399 U.S. job markets. Available online at http://www.datamasters.com/cgi-bin/col.pl.

CHAPTER 2 QUICK TIPS: Researching the Market

- Obtain licensure or certification information from your target state.
- List 5–10 organizations doing the work you want to do. Consult printed directories and online information.
- List 5–10 organizations doing some type of work related to what you want to do.
- Brainstorm a list of people (2–5 of them) you know who could give you advice on your search and current issues in your field of social work.
- Talk with the NASW chapter and fellow alumni in the area or make cold calls to organizations to determine the salary range for the type of position you are seeking.

Preparing Résumés, Curricula Vitae, Portfolios, and References

S ome social workers find jobs without résumés, but chances are that you will need one some time during your job search. Even if you use your résumé only once, the process of composing your document is a good exercise in recalling your accomplishments, clarifying your career direction, refining your presentation of skills and knowledge, and setting goals for the future. You may sometimes hear the terms "vita" or "curriculum vitae" (CV). Generally speaking, a CV is the academic version of a résumé. CVs are used primarily in academic and research environments, whereas agencies and businesses usually ask for résumés. A portfolio, which is a compilation of materials that demonstrate your knowledge and skills, might also prove useful in your search; it could include published or unpublished documents to which you have contributed, a videotape of a presentation that you made, or other evidence of your accomplishments. No matter what form your submission to a potential employer takes, be sure that you can back it up with references if you are asked to provide them.

Résumés

There are about as many ideas on effective résumés as there are career counselors, interviewers, and job hunters, and any library or bookstore is likely to have several texts on résumé writing. More difficult to find are specific suggestions for social workers, which is what this chapter will give you.

Before You Start

Everyone has a unique set of credentials and personal goals, and your résumé should be individually designed to reflect yours. Compose your own. You might be tempted to use the résumé template—a preformatted layout—in your computer's word processing program or to purchase a résumé package. Be aware that templates do not offer the flexibility of simple word-processing, which allows social workers to highlight their unique mix of work, training, and public service assets. Also note that résumés written by professional résumé writers or friends often do not use social work language accurately, nor do they highlight your job-related strengths. They are likely to focus on generic skills and lack content specific to social work. To help outline a strategy for presenting your best qualifications, answer the questions in this section; then complete exercises 1, 2, and 5 in chapter 1 or complete the exercise that follows the questions.

What Is the Purpose of This Résumé?

Will you use the résumé to look for a job, to apply for graduate school or training programs, to explore consulting or speaking opportunities, to update your employer or board on your professional activities for public relations purposes, or simply to keep your own records organized? The format and qualifications you choose for the résumé will depend on your answer. If you are applying to graduate school, you might emphasize your research assistantship. If you are keeping a record of your experiences, you will probably use a chronological format.

Who Is Your Audience?

Are the people who will read your résumé in your field or are they trained in other disciplines? The language you use in your résumé will depend on your readers' background. "Absolutely, but some language, such as 'facilitate implementation,' is too fuzzy," cautions one employer. What criteria will your audience use to review résumés? Do you know what your audience is looking for? Although it is important, be aware that catering to a particular audience may not always convey the message you intend. States a director for psychiatric social work: "There is a fundamental difference between applying for a job to do tasks and being a member of a profession pursuing a career. Deprofessionalization of human services, the incorporation of health care, etcetera, are factors underlying the issue of different audiences and the need to respond to them while being clear about who we are as a profession."

What Is Your Objective?

Regardless of whether you state your objective on your résumé, write a sentence about what you want for yourself. What are you looking for? This theme statement will help you organize your information. Of all the elements in your background, which are the most relevant to your objective? The answer to this question will help you formulate a strategy for drawing the reader's attention to your best qualifications for your current objective.

Comparing Your Objective with Your Qualifications

If you completed the exercises in chapter 1, you can skip this exercise. At the top of a sheet of paper marked "Worksheet A," write your job objective or a statement of what you would like to do. Under the objective, list the knowledge and skills important to the type of work you are seeking.

On a second sheet marked "Worksheet B," list all of your key experience, degrees, and accomplishments, including those not related to your objective. Then prioritize those items as they relate to your objective. The items high on the list will be the ones you emphasize on your résumé. In other words, you have identified the best cards you have to play.

Compare worksheets A and B. Do the high-priority items on worksheet B address the knowledge and skills listed on worksheet A? If you do not have experience or credentials to cover all of the qualifications on worksheet A, you can anticipate what questions an employer could raise about your background; review all of the items on worksheet B to find out whether some of your skills and experience might compensate for those missing qualifications. Let your qualifications and those elements that are important to the work you want to do determine the format you choose for your résumé.

Choosing a Format

Increasingly, we hear that employers like one-page résumés that they can skim quickly. This does not mean that a strong two-page résumé will eliminate you from consideration, but it does mean that you must select your words and format carefully. Anyone skimming your résumé should be able to pick out your key qualifications. Whether one page or two, the résumé must be a stand-alone document. Do not count on a cover letter to fill in missing information. You could be in a situation in which you simply hand someone the résumé, or the résumé might be copied and distributed to a search committee or staff without a companion letter.

Résumés are usually chronological or functional, or some combination of those forms. The one you choose will depend on your personal preference and the nature of your qualifications. A chronological résumé lists all employment and unpaid experience in reverse chronological order. A functional one outlines experience according to skill areas and states an objective; this format is sometimes used when changing careers, because it highlights abilities rather than particular job titles or dates. (If you use a functional résumé, you should also prepare one with a chronological format, in case an employer requests it.) A combination format includes elements of both chronological and functional résumés, often according to personal preference and background; a combination résumé often includes an objective or a section called qualifications, accomplishments, or skills.

You may need to prepare more than one résumé. For example,

- you may need résumés for different purposes
- you may prefer to write a résumé for a specific opening
- you may be looking at more than one type of job
- you may be sending résumés to large organizations that select résumés to review based on keyword searches
- you may be sending résumés through electronic mail.

Résumés for Different Media

Ask yourself how you will be using your résumé. Will you be handing it to contacts, sending it through regular mail, sending it by fax or e-mail, or entering it into a database, perhaps on the Internet? In most cases you will use a résumé that stresses action and accomplishments through verb phrases (see appendix 10 for examples). However, if you know that your résumé will become part of a database in a human resources department or professional association career service or entered in an Internet résumé database, you will need a résumé that focuses on nouns (see sample 13 in appendix 6). When employers search a résumé database, they use certain nouns, or key words, to narrow their search for qualified applicants.

The use of technology for a job search also affects the format you choose. If you are sending your letters and résumés electronically, you must format them differently than if you send them through the mail. In general, if you plan to send your résumé to an employer via e-mail, you must save your résumé file as a text document, which removes any special formatting (italics, bullets, and so forth), edit it, and test it by sending it to yourself or a friend. If you learn that an organization will be scanning the résumé into a database, print it without bullets, italics, boldface, and other design features, which some scanners are not able to read. To learn more about electronic résumés, see *The Guide to Internet Job Searching* (Riley, Roehm, & Osennan, 1996) or *Electronic Resume Revolution* (Kennedy & Morrow, 1995). On the Internet, visit *The Riley Guide* at http://www.dbm.com/jobguide/.

Format Strategies for Different Stages of Experience

Whether you are a new graduate, career changer, or experienced social worker does not determine which format you can use. In general, however, those with more experience are in a better position to use the functional and combination formats, simply because they have more to say. The following notes will help you determine how you might organize your material using the headings described later in this chapter.

New Graduates

Your most important credential is your degree. Therefore, put the education section at the top of the résumé after your objective, if you choose to use one, or after the summary or qualifications section if you are using a combination résumé. For a new graduate without job experience, your practica will be your second key credential. A section on professional development that describes your leadership, affiliation, workshops, and so on can be used to demonstrate additional accomplishments and commitment to the field. If your extracurricular activities, volunteer or part-time work, or college honors are significant in terms of skill development or levels of responsibility, describe them. Try to keep your résumé to one page. See appendix 6 for sample résumés.

Career Changers

You want your mental shift—a commitment to your new career—to be evident on paper. If you are a career changer, you will want to state your objective and probably use a qualifications summary. Emphasize your social services experience, and put it early in the résumé. Without diminishing your accomplishments, streamline information on your previous career. Retain the major elements of your work—such as "supervised 25 people"—and those elements related to your new goal—"coordinated team-building exercises to reduce stress" and "experience with analysis, communication, and problem solving." If community and social work professional activities are your strong suit, they should dominate your résumé. Take a look at your draft. If you were an accountant, homemaker, volunteer, nurse, or teacher and are just beginning your social work career, what gets the most attention on your résumé? Your first occupation or the experience related to your new career? To which audience does your résumé speak?

If you are taking your traditional social work experience into a nontraditional arena, you also will need to demonstrate a commitment and potential for success in your new target career. In this case, you will convert social work–specific language into terms commonly used in your new field. You will also add to your résumé those elements that may not have special relevance to your current social work career, but are important in your target arena. If you are looking at government opportunities, public service might be one of those items.

Experienced Social Workers
Your postdegree experience and license (if appropriate) are now your most important qualifications. In a chronological format, professional experience should precede academic degrees; practica experience will diminish in importance, if indeed you mention it at all. Professional development should focus on recent and major career accomplishments. Only outstanding college and graduate school awards and activities, such as Phi Beta Kappa or president of the student council, will remain, if at all. For clinical social workers and other direct practitioners, licensure and certifications are very important. In this case, add LCSW (licensed clinical social worker or your state's equivalent) and ACSW (Academy of Certified Social Workers) or any other professional credential you have behind your name if appropriate for the work you seek. It is not uncommon for someone at the executive level to have a résumé several pages long.

Sections and Sample Headings

Résumé content can be organized in many ways. A sample list of section headings and ideas for each follow. Select those sections that are most appropriate for your unique background.

Objectives and Summary Statements
There are a number of optional devices that you can use to alert the reader to your goals, interests, accomplishments, and skills. These techniques enable you to convey your message, rather than leaving the interpretation of your background to the reader. Some of the choices you have follow.

Key Words
A summary paragraph of key words or terms is recommended if your résumé will go into a database. Note that employers using some computer systems see only the keyword summary and only if it is in plain type (no boldface) (Kennedy & Morrow, 1995). See sample 13 in appendix 6.

Objective, Job Objective, or Career Objective

A statement of your objective is optional if you are using a chronological format. However, it is helpful to use it or a qualifications summary in functional or combination résumés to explain your purpose. Write a brief objective. In one or two sentences you can include a job title, type of organization, skills to be used, and a particular interest area (see part 2 of chapter 1).

If you have easy access to a computer and wish to use an objective, tailor your résumé each time you need it. If you do not have easy access to a computer but have a specific job objective, write a specific résumé using the job objective as a theme statement. At the same time, prepare a general résumé as a backup that can be used for unexpected opportunities that do not fit your objective. If you don't have a specific objective in mind, write a general résumé without a job objective and incorporate your job objective in the cover letter (see samples 2 and 4 in appendix 6).

Professional Summary, Qualifications, Special Accomplishments, or Professional Accomplishments

Select three to five statements representing your key accomplishments, experiences, or skill sets that highlight your background and convey your message (see samples 6, 10, 11, and 12 in appendix 6).

Skills

You can use this heading with any résumé format. Use it to highlight skill sets or to list those skills not stated elsewhere ("fluent in Spanish" or "computer skills," for example). When used in functional résumés, divide the skills section into two to four subheadings, such as direct practice, clinical social work, administration, management, program planning, research, or fund-raising. Under each subhead describe your relevant experience in concrete terms (see samples 5, 8, and 10 in appendix 6).

Education

Education is a standard heading, although some social workers combine it with professional credentials. If you choose this combination, be sure that your credentials are easy to find. Employers skim résumés, so put your highest degree first. You can use initials (for example, MSW, BSW) or write out the words (Master of Social Work, Bachelor of Social Work). If you are moving, think about whether the name of your university or the name of your particular school of social work is more likely to be recognized and list them in that order.

If you are a student, do not list courses unless you need to show a connection between what you studied and the position. For example, you may be applying for a position that is not usually held by social workers and need to stress your knowledge of budgeting, statistics, policy analysis, and program evaluation. Usually, stating your concentration, method, and specialization or briefly indicating your academic emphasis is sufficient.

Experience

You have a number of options for listing your paid, training, and volunteer experience. Using the exercise at the beginning of this chapter or the work you did in chapter 1, select the heading that works best for your background mix. Besides the headings below, you may be able to use descriptive headings, which tell a story and get attention, like those in appendix 6, sample 9. This works best for people whose types of experience fall into neat chronological sequences.

Professional experience. If you have full-time experience in the field, list it in this section, which will go at the top of the résumé if it is postdegree experience and after the section on education if it precedes the degree. You might use the heading "professional experience and training." This arrangement will work if your recent field training is more closely related to your job goal than your previous experience. A combined section of "professional and volunteer experience" is a practical choice when your volunteer positions are stronger than or equal to your work experiences or you are a student whose work and volunteer experience is important but secondary to accomplishments in practica.

Experience or related experience. These headings are alternatives for people whose experience does not fall easily into another, more descriptive heading. If you use "related experience," your résumé should have a job objective. The word "related" must refer to something, and in this case it is the objective.

Professional training. If you are a student without prior full-time work experience in the field, your best cards to play, second to your degree, are your practica. Set them apart in a section entitled "professional training," placed just after the section on education. This section should describe each field placement as if it were a job, and it should dominate the page. Use descriptive titles such as "social work intern" or "medical social work intern." Many graduating students list field placements as professional experience; however, some employers prefer to see practica separated from full-time postdegree experience. The choice is yours as long as you make the context of the experience clear through position titles or headings.

Community experience or volunteer experience. Volunteer experience can be an important asset in your search. You need to assess its importance, like that of all other information, to the position you are seeking. If you founded an organization, served as an officer or on the board, had responsibility for a major project, or coordinated a team effort, you will probably want to describe these activities in detail, similar to the way you describe your jobs if it is equal to or more important than your work experience. If you have extensive community work, consider the heading "community activities" or "public service." Like titles for internships, use descriptive terms such as "special events volunteer" or "volunteer tutor," especially if you combine volunteer work with other experience.

Leadership and Professional Development
For some social workers, professional and community leadership roles and other professional activities are among their most important assets. Here are a couple of alternatives for presenting them.

Professional development. This heading is good for grouping additional items that indicate commitment, particularly to the profession. Use subheads such as presentations, publications, leadership, research, grants, affiliations or memberships, training, licensure or certification, language or computer skills, and community or volunteer work. These sections must be brief. If you have many presentations or publications, put them on a separate sheet.

If you are a direct practitioner, you have probably attended many in-service training sessions, workshops, and continuing education seminars. Do not list each of these on your résumé. You might give a very brief statement listing the topics, such as "1993–96 attended workshops on ethics, family-centered practice, and interventions with blended families." If you completed an extensive training program by a recognized organization or expert and you have space, give the title, date, and location.

If your experience is extensive in one of these subheadings under "professional development," it may warrant its own section in the résumé. Leadership is one example. If this is the case, you might consider using the heading that follows.

Leadership and professional development. If leadership is a strong asset for you, consider adding it to the heading "professional development" and lead off this section with your leadership roles. The same can be done with other subheadings under professional development (see samples 2 and 3 in appendix 6).

Describing Your Experience

Regardless of which format or headings you choose, keep the following points in mind when describing your experience,

...ading leadership positions and major community or profes-
...al activities.

*...lude Your Major Job Functions (Counseling, Training, Data
...nalysis) and Major Accomplishments*
...tate specifically how you contributed to each project, service, program, or outcome. Use brief, uncomplicated verb phrases for résumés that will be read and not scanned. A verb phrase is a statement without a subject. Write "Organized local chapter," not "I
organized the local chapter." For students, sometimes what was
learned in a position is more relevant to the objective than what
was done. For example, maybe you had a job as an administrative
assistant for a nursing home where you learned about insurance,
regulations, and issues facing older adults and families. Try using a
"learn" statement, for example, "Learned about alternative care
options for older adults."

*Write for Your Audience, and Use a Language Style Appropriate for
Different Media*

- To convince a supervisor that you would make a good clinical
  therapist, use clinical social work terminology: psychosocial
  assessments, *Diagnostic and Statistical Manual of Mental Disorders*
  (DSM), treatment planning, brief strategic therapy, cognitive
  behavioral therapy, treatment evaluation, and so forth. Or, to get
  the attention of the assistant superintendent reviewing résumés
  for a school social work position use such terms as "multidisciplinary team planning," "group work," "parent and teacher
  relationships," "prevention programs," and "at-risk children."
- If you are looking at positions not usually held by social workers,
  adopt the language of the role and organizations that you are
  considering.
- If you are submitting your résumé to a database, whether on the
  Internet or not, you will need to shift from an emphasis on verb
  phrases to an emphasis on nouns. The nouns or terms such as
  policy analysis, project management, case management, and grant
  writing are key words used in searchable databases.

*Consider the Knowledge You Gained on Policies, Cutting-Edge Issues,
Funding Streams, Political Feasibility, and the Use of Technology*
Depending on your purpose, include specific experience with and
knowledge of

- populations (older adults, young children, homeless families)
- issues (job training, eating disorders)
- methods (group work, community organizing, advocacy)
- skills (data analysis, SPSS and other computer packages).

Quantify Your Accomplishments in a Way Appropriate to the Job You Are Seeking

Many authors of résumé books stress the importance of quantifying accomplishments, for example, "increased sales by 60 percent." This approach is important for administrators of programs, managers of social services, and fund-raisers. Quantifying accomplishments in direct practice can be difficult, however, even though there is now a greater emphasis on outcomes. Handle accomplishments in direct practice differently by shifting the emphasis: for example, "follow-up interviews indicated that interventions were still effective after three months" or "invited to give an in-service training session for the multidisciplinary team." Note that it is likely that even those in direct practice will increasingly need to be able to quantify results in the future.

Put All Experiences within a Section in Reverse Chronological Order

The examples in appendix 6 list dates close to the content to emphasize content and minimize distraction. Condense information on short-term or part-time jobs and other experiences into one statement: "1993–96 Held a variety of part-time, temporary, and summer jobs as a cashier in a retail store, assistant in a library, and data-entry clerk for an insurance company." Do not list this information unless you need to demonstrate responsibility, account for time, or have limited experience.

Content Details

Keep the following details in mind as you prepare your résumé (or résumés).

- Your name should be in caps and boldface unless you are sending the résumé by e-mail or it is being scanned for inclusion in a database. Be sure that your telephone number is listed as well as an e-mail address if you have one.
- Delete unimportant data such as the word "résumé" at the top of the page, high school information, and hobbies unless they spark conversation and you have space.
- Do not include reasons for terminating employment or personal information such as marital or family status, gender, or age.
- A statement that says your references and writing samples are available upon request is not necessary. If interviewers want them, they will ask for them. (The section in this chapter on "Letters of Reference" suggests some options.)
- If you are concerned about listing politically sensitive subjects on your résumé, consider creating two résumés, or do not list these items at all.

- Do not include street addresses and names of supervisors. If they agree to be references, this information can go on a separate reference page independent of the résumé.

Final Preparation

Before you seek several opinions on your résumé, be sure that the content and visual presentation are balanced. Relevant experience should be the focal point or dominant section. After you prepare your draft, look at the amount of space you have allotted to each item. Do your related qualifications stand out more than the less-related position in which you spent more time?

- Ask someone who has not seen your résumé to scan it in 30 seconds. Then ask him or her to summarize the key points. Are those the points you wanted to get across?
- Check and recheck for spelling and grammar. Do not rely on your computer program's spellcheck feature.
- In addition to capitalizing and using boldface type for your name and headings, try doing the same with job titles or names of organizations. Don't overuse boldface, however—use it only for items that deserve emphasis. (Note that it should not be used for electronic résumés.)

If your descriptions are too wordy, do the following:

- Turn phrases into adjectives modifying nouns—use "a teen pregnancy program" instead of "a program addressing pregnancy among teenagers."
- Break up long sentences (use phrases, not sentences).
- Delete information on lower-level skills and minor parts of the job.
- Remove "in-house" titles of programs and replace them with generic terms.

Do not feel you must purchase a computer or camp out at a computer center. Many social workers find jobs with one résumé duplicated on quality paper. Start with a small number of copies on 8-1/2 x 11–inch paper in a conservative color, either white, ivory, tan, or light gray. As you use them, you will find items that you will want to change.

Curricula Vitae

The CV is a detailed document that stresses teaching, research, grant awards, publications, and presentations. If you are planning a career in academia, you will use a CV instead of a résumé. Sometimes the CV is also used for research positions in nonacademic institutions, but a résumé is often preferred.

Before You Begin

Before you begin writing or revising your CV, think first about its immediate purpose and your strengths. Are you applying for tenure, looking for a job, or recording your work? Your answer to that question will determine how you organize your material and the tone you set.

Applying for Tenure

If you are submitting your CV as part of your package for tenure, organize the sections according to the criteria for tenure. For many faculty members, those criteria would call for grants and publications to immediately follow education in the front of the document.

Looking for an Academic Job

If you are looking at tenure-track positions, what are the priorities of the faculty at those institutions? Do they focus on teaching and community service, or on research and teaching? The priority you give to teaching in your CV may be higher in the former situation than it would be in the latter. How important is practice experience for the positions? If practice experience is important and your experience is varied, you may want to use subheadings such as clinical practice and program development. The level of detail you use to describe experience and skills should reflect the priorities of the positions and institutions that interest you. If you are having difficulty writing the CV, think again about the fit between each position and institution and your strengths.

If you are looking for a tenure-track position, you will want personnel committees to be able to determine the following from your CV:

- a theme linking your research, publications, and presentations
- a strong dissertation related to a faculty project (doctoral students)
- your teaching interests and experience
- whom you have worked with
- level of your research skills.

Recording Your Work

The CV is a handy tool for keeping track of your work and providing others, such as funders, conference sponsors, or public relations staff, background on your accomplishments. If you are using the CV for public relations, keep education, honors, and awards up front and place long lists of publications and presentations toward the back. If you are seeking funding, your emphasis will be on grants, research, and publications.

Doctoral Students: Converting Your Résumé to a CV

Like the résumé, your CV conveys the theme of your work. Unlike the résumé, which presents the highlights of your theme-related experience in usually one or two pages, the CV describes all of your experience and has no specified or recommended length. You will use the CV document itself to keep track of all your accomplishments.

In the résumé, practice experience related to your goal dominates the page, and professional development experiences such as presentations, publications, teaching, and research projects play supporting roles. These roles reverse in the CV. Those items that once were listed together under the single heading "professional development" become their own sections, often with subheadings.

Use every opportunity to convey your knowledge areas and skills. Do not assume that personnel committees will recognize your level of ability through position titles alone. For example, unlike experienced faculty members, you will want to include details that describe your role in research projects.

Brainstorm a list of the strengths of your academic program, which in turn will expand your thinking about what you have to offer.

Format and Headings

Once you have selected section headings and subheadings, list each item under the headings in reverse chronological order. Then order the sections to fit the interests of your readers and highlight your strengths. If you have received grant awards and know that this track record is important for your purpose, then you will place the grants section early in your CV. If you are looking for your first academic position, you will probably put your teaching and research interests on page 1.

Tailor headings to fit your material, and use subheadings if you have many items for a section. Keep like items together. Although you may have several subsections on presentations, do not mix them with sections on grants and publications.

Unless an item has two distinct components, it should appear only once on the CV. An exception is a paper that you both published and presented. Or perhaps you were selected for an honor associated with your job. In one case, a doctoral student had been selected to be an executive on loan to United Way while working for a corporation. Because this distinction was related to social work, she listed it in the community service section.

Sections and Sample Headings

Education
This will be your first heading. Under it list each degree, program title, institution, city, state or country, and year, beginning with your doctoral degree and working backward. If you are in a doctoral program, include your dissertation title and adviser's name. If you have completed your requirements for candidacy, indicate "advanced to candidacy" and an anticipated completion date; otherwise, state that you are a doctoral student.

Honors
Set off all academic honors, fellowships, and dissertation awards in one section. Include the name of the award, sponsoring institution, and date. Add a brief descriptive phrase if the honor is not self-explanatory. List papers selected for recognition here, unless they are listed elsewhere. If you were selected among others to attend a conference, include a descriptive phrase, particularly if the program is not widely known—for example, "One of 12 doctoral students selected nationwide to participate in the symposium." If you have one or two honors, consider listing them under the degree in the education section. Other headings you might use are "academic honors"; "academic fellowships"; "academic honors and awards"; "scholastic honors and awards"; and "honors, fellowships, and awards."

Grants
When listing grants, state the funding source, project title, names of investigators, dates, and dollar amounts. Listings in this section should not include fellowship or dissertation material, which are in the education and honors sections. Other headings might be grant development or funded research.

Teaching Interests and Research Interests
You will probably want to create separate sections using each of these titles. These sections speak directly to the immediate interests of the institution's personnel committee members, who are looking for a good fit between prospective faculty members and the school. Particularly if you are seeking your first teaching position, list every course area in which you have taught, assisted, and developed a knowledge base or for which you have an interest. Make it easy for the personnel committee to identify the subjects you can

teach—instead of the specific course title used at your institution, use language that parallels the accreditation standards of the Council on Social Work Education on curriculum content. Under research interests, simply list your subject areas.

Professional Experience

Organize your experience into teaching, research, and practice. Depending on how much practice experience you have and on what you want to emphasize, you may divide your practice items into like categories. For instance, if you wanted to stress your clinical practice experience, you would create a section just for that work.

If you worked in another country, explain the U.S. equivalent of job titles and other terms in parentheses. For example, a school principal in one country may be the equivalent of a dean in another country. A U.S. reader who is not familiar with another country's terminology may not fully appreciate the impact or value of a position you held.

Teaching experience. If you were a teaching assistant, list in reverse chronological order each position you held, along with the name of the professor you assisted and the course title, name of the institution and its location (city and state or country), and semester and year you taught. If you taught several courses at the same institution, just name the university, city, and state or country once and then list the course information underneath. You may also find it helpful to organize teaching experience by position titles: part-time faculty, lecturer, or teaching assistant, for example. Headings you might use include "teaching experience," "teaching and curriculum development," "courses taught," and "lectureships."

Research experience. When presenting your research experience, include the sponsoring organization or funder, project title, principal investigators, and your project title. If you are a doctoral student, describe your role in brief verb phrases: "designed a questionnaire" or "coded, entered, and analyzed data." Briefly state the purpose of research projects, without giving an abstract, when project titles are not self-explanatory. Projects you conducted independently can also be listed in this section. If you are a student and sought advice from a faculty member on a project, you can state "Consulted with Jan Doe, PhD" at the end of the description.

Practice experience. For each direct practice, administrative, or management position, include the name of the organization or institution, city, state or country, position title, and dates. Describe your principal tasks, skills used, and accomplishments. Begin each descriptive phrase with a verb to give your work a vivid, active voice. If you held more than one position with one organization, list the agency, city, and state or country once; under that information list each position title and put the dates next to the title. For practica experiences, put the word "intern" in the title or designate the experience as a practicum. Some headings you might consider are "professional experience," "clinical social work experience," "administrative experience," "management experience," and "program experience."

Previous career experience. If you were employed full-time in a field other than social work, list this experience if it is relevant to your current work or if it accounts for a significant period of time. Include brief descriptions of primary accomplishments and contributions, particularly if they are pertinent to your knowledge and skills.

Publications

List all published and unpublished manuscripts. Use the American Psychological Association (1994) style. If a paper is accepted but not yet published, list it under "journals" and state that it is in press or forthcoming. Unpublished finished manuscripts can go into a manuscript subsection. Some people also list work in process, but others caution that it is better to list only finished work. If you are a doctoral student who has a paper nearly ready to submit to a journal, then consider listing it. This is important if you, like many doctoral students, have not yet had material published.

Use subsection headings to draw attention to your work and to make it easy on the reader to identify types of publications. Some subheadings you might use are books, chapters, journal articles, monographs and final reports, book reviews, peer review publications, papers under review, manuscripts, service to journals and publishers, and papers or work in process.

Presentations

List all presentations. For each include the title of the paper, coauthors, sponsoring organization, city, state or country, and date. Do not overlook presentations that you have made at your institution, such as one in a colloquium series, particularly if you are beginning your career. As in the publications section, you may want subheadings in this section, which might include papers presented at conferences, oral presentations, poster presentations, and workshops or in-service training.

Additional Training

This section is another opportunity for describing your knowledge areas and skill sets. If you completed a certificate program or participated in an intensive, well-recognized training program, give specifics: title, sponsor, city, state or country, and dates. If you have attended several one-session workshops or lectures that supplemented your formal education, you can summarize them in a paragraph; for example, "Between 1990 and 1994 attended training sessions on family preservation, grant writing, clinical supervision, and managed care." Possible headings or subheadings are "continuing education," "supplemental training," and "certificates."

Community, Professional, and University Services

Briefly list all your community and professional activities, including elected and appointed leadership positions, board positions, guest appearances on radio and television, and task force appointments or memberships. List the name of the group or professional society, your role, and dates. If you have done consultations or had contract jobs—for example, to conduct a program evaluation—you can list them under community service or practice experience. Include any university committee or task force on which you have served and responsibilities you have had for advising or field education liaison work. University work demonstrates commitment, contributions, and a knowledge of teaching and campus life issues. Headings you might use are "community service," "professional service," "university service," "university committees," and "community and university service."

Skills

Although it is better to show than to tell, you can use a skills section to summarize sets of skills, draw attention to skills, or list skills not covered elsewhere. This section is particularly important for doctoral students and those early in their careers. Do not assume that readers will review other sections of your CV to discover all your skills. For example, this section is where you want to state the specific computer packages you have used. If you are bilingual or fluent in a second or multiple languages, list them. Headings or subheadings might include "computer skills," "languages," "research skills," and "special skills."

Visa Status

If you are from another country, you might choose to state your visa status on the CV. It is legal for employers to ask you about your visa status.

Memberships

Give names of organizations to which you currently belong. Dates of membership are optional. This section can go toward the end of the CV. Headings you might use are "professional associations," "professional memberships," "professional affiliations," and "organizations."

References

Prepare a reference sheet that can be attached to your CV; put your name, address, and telephone number at the top. Tailor the reference sheet to the position.

Final Details

Be sure that you are not overlooking any of your experiences, especially if you are on the academic job market for the first time. Have you been an academic adviser, consultant to an agency on program evaluation, a clinical supervisor, statistics workshop instructor, or study group leader? Have you reviewed manuscripts, moderated panels, led training on interventions or discussions on the integration of theory and practice? Have you provided consultation to faculty members on a computer package?

Keep in mind these details:

- Put your name in bold letters at the top of page 1, followed by your address and telephone numbers. List your name in the top right corner or bottom of each succeeding page.
- Although some people put "Curriculum Vitae" at the top of the first page, it is not necessary.
- Number the pages, except for page 1.
- If you update your CV regularly or create different versions of it, you could put a date in small print at the bottom of the last page.
- Do not list personal information such as birth date, social security number, marital status, number of children, or citizenship. You may put visa status on the last page if you wish.
- Finally, ask two people to review your document, one who knows your work and one who does not. They will help you identify missing items, inconsistencies, and confusing elements.
- Be sure to proofread several times.

The CV as a Professional Development Tool

Update your CV at least once each year or, better yet, add each new accomplishment as it occurs. Review the organization of your material annually and think about what you would want to see on the CV in the coming year. Maybe the theme of your work is shifting. Is your new direction evident? Perhaps you've developed new curriculum and teaching techniques and then trained others. Do you need to reorganize the sections or add new material under special skills to reflect your current efforts?

ꜱlios

heard of portfolios used by artists to demonstrate their
ꜱal workers can do the same thing.

ꜱꜱnat Is a Portfolio?

A portfolio is a set of materials—documents or videotapes, for
example—that make up a sort of three-dimensional résumé. The
contents of your portfolio demonstrate your clinical, writing, research, analytic, creative, and problem-solving skills. You can as-
semble samples and use them individually or organize several
pieces in a file or other attractive cover with your name and address on it.

Just about any item you've worked on that demonstrates your
knowledge and skills can be included in a portfolio. Sample material might include

- unpublished documents such as agency reports, internal studies,
  grant proposals, policy statements, program proposals, option
  papers, treatment plans, or academic papers
- videotapes or audiotapes of interpersonal counseling (individual,
  family, or group), case presentations, and conference and other
  oral presentations
- published documents such as journal, magazine, newsletter, or
  newspaper articles
- printed materials such as brochures, news releases, or
  presentation handouts.
            (George Warren Brown School of Social Work, 1996)

Develop the habit of building your portfolio: As soon as a project
or phase of work is completed, put at least one copy in a file. You
might also plan a project—a demonstration tape, for example—
that depicts your clinical intervention skills. If you collect a large
number of pieces, select items for the portfolio that are most relevant to your audience.

Refamiliarize yourself from time to time with all the items in
your portfolio. Practice presenting your portfolio by preparing a
one- or two-sentence statement about each piece.

How to Use a Portfolio

You might use a portfolio as part of an application for a job or
fellowship, or you might take it with you to show an interviewer or
send it as a follow-up to an interview—increasingly, social services
employers are requesting writing samples. Or, if an employer

expresses concern or doubt about a particular ability—your writing skill, for example—you can pick a good example from your portfolio, send a copy, and then follow up with a telephone call. The portfolio also might be useful when you meet with contacts to seek advice about career choices. Obviously, however, you must exercise good judgment. If you have only 15 minutes to spend with a contact, you are not going to ask that person to bring out a VCR so you can show a videotape.

A portfolio is always reused. Usually, you show it in person and take it with you when you leave. If the employer asks to keep it, make specific arrangements to pick it up or provide a self-addressed, stamped envelope. If you drop off a portfolio, make sure you get it back.

Important Considerations for Portfolios

- Be certain that you are not breaking confidentiality by using a particular piece.
- Be certain that you have permission to use an item you developed for an agency.
- Note that using video and audio samples poses certain confidentiality issues and that the equipment can be impractical. However, for interviews for upper-level positions that might involve making presentations, a videotape may be useful. Note that you should have release statements from subjects on the tape.
- All portfolio materials must be your work or demonstrate parts of an effort for which you were the responsible team member.
- Items for your portfolio should reflect your best work. If a document has a misspelling, correct it or leave it out.
- Ideally, printed materials should be on agency letterhead or carry the agency name and should include your name when possible.

Letters of Reference

Employers often ask job candidates for references. You have three options:

1. *List of references:* The simplest option is to keep a list of names, titles, addresses, and telephone numbers of those people who have agreed to be references. Then give the list to employers when requested, or contact the individuals yourself when necessary. As on your résumé, your name, address, telephone number, and e-mail address heads this sheet.

2. *References on the résumé:* You can put the same information at the bottom of your résumé. However, you may not know when a reference is being contacted or by whom.
3. *Generic letters:* Another option is to ask your references to write nonconfidential "to whom it may concern" letters. You can make copies for employers. Then if you lose contact with a reference, you will still have a letter outlining his or her comments. You will have the security of a written statement and the option of asking the reference to tailor the letter for a specific employer. A supervisor in a children's health care center recommends using general letters to avoid the off chance that a reference might say more than you wish.

If your school offers a reference service that holds letters of reference and compiles reference portfolios at your request to send to employers on your behalf, take advantage of that opportunity.

Timing

Regardless of which option you choose, make certain that you have either a letter or a current address for each person who knows your work. Although you may not need a recommendation in the near future, in several years it could be very important.

The best time to get a letter of reference, especially for students, is shortly before or after a job, volunteer project, practicum, or class is completed. Recommendations written at this time will be stronger and more detailed because the information is fresh.

Choosing References

Choose your references carefully. When asking someone to write one, ask directly whether he or she can write a positive statement. This person should be up-front with you if there are any reservations about your work. If you have any doubts, reconsider.

Discuss your goals and experience with your references. Give them a current résumé for more information; it's especially handy for them to have when talking to employers or graduate schools on the telephone. Recommenders usually appreciate your thoughts on what to include in the letter. If you want references to emphasize something, such as knowledge of grant writing, skills in family therapy, or your academic record, ask them to do so. Sometimes you will be asked to draft the letter.

If you think a particular employer will contact references soon, alert them. Keep your references informed of your progress—they are often good contacts and advisers.

Content of a Reference Letter

A letter of recommendation should contain the following:

- name of the candidate
- how and for how long the writer has known the candidate
- description of the work, project, or class in which the candidate participated
- specific contributions or accomplishments of the candidate
- candidate's strengths: skills, knowledge areas, work habits, and personality characteristics
- candidate's readiness for a position or graduate program
- summary statement.

Some reference letters also include a statement of areas to be improved or learned.

Confidential Letters

Some recommenders prefer to write confidential letters, meaning that you will never see the recommendations. Do not take this to mean that they do not think well of your accomplishments and work habits. It may simply be a personal preference regarding the integrity of a reference; some feel that a letter of recommendation that is not seen by the subject of the letter is more powerful. Others will automatically send you a copy of the letter for your own file. If you have any doubts about what someone might say in a letter, request a copy; if the request is refused, choose another reference.

References to Avoid

If you have had a negative experience with supervisors, coworkers, or faculty members—it is not an uncommon occurrence—you do not need to offer them as references.

When you are applying for a position, ask the employer about the process and timetable. Employers do not usually check references until shortly before or after making an offer. If you advance in the selection process, you may need to explain why you do not have a particular reference. It is essential that you present your explanation in a professional manner. Keep your statements as positive and as brief as possible. If there was a personality conflict or difference in approach, say so and leave it at that. For example, you might explain the situation thus:

1. *"My supervisor and I had different approaches. Although we maintained a working relationship that did not affect services, the situa-*

tion was never entirely comfortable. That is why I asked the director of the agency to be a reference."

2. *"Our staff accepts and uses a variety of clinical approaches. It happens that my direct supervisor and I have different clinical styles. Although we respect each other's work, I think there are other members of the staff who can give you a better picture of my abilities."*

3. *"Unfortunately, I was in over my head in this particular practicum, but I didn't want to admit it. A situation arose in which I used poor judgment and did not alert my supervisor. In short, I was let go. It was a difficult but important learning experience. Two semesters later I completed another practicum without any problems. In fact, it was quite successful."*

When References Are Not Available

For legal reasons, some organizations have policies that prevent staff from providing written or verbal references. In this case, the organization's human resources office provides confirmation of the dates of employment. You might also face a situation in which you have lost contact with a reference for one reason or another. Keeping complimentary memos or letters, performance reviews, and field practicum evaluations will enable you to fill the gap should you be missing a reference.

References

American Psychological Association. (1994). *Publication manual of the American Psychological Association* (4th ed.). Washington, DC: Author.

George Warren Brown School of Social Work. (1996). *Student handbook.* St. Louis: Author.

Kennedy, J. L., & Morrow, T. J. (1995). *Electronic resume revolution: Creating a resume for the new world of job searching* (2nd ed.). New York: John Wiley & Sons.

Riley, M., Roehm, F., & Osennan, S. (1996). *The guide to Internet job searching.* Chicago: VGM Horizons.

The Riley guide. Available online at http://www.dbm.com/jobguide/.

CHAPTER 3 QUICK TIPS: Résumés, Curricula Vitae, Portfolios, and References

- Make á list of 3–5 of your most important assets or qualifications (particular experiences, license, degree, and so on) and put them in rank order.

- Select a sample résumé in appendix 6 or another style you like, and follow that format for your own document.

- Draft your résumé and ask someone to review it. Read it carefully for errors and make 5–10 copies on good paper to start.

- Ask three people who know your work to be references.

- Select 2–3 items (reports, seminar outlines, papers) of no more than three pages each that represent your work, are not confidential, and would be suitable for showing a prospective employer.

Chapter 4

Identifying Jobs and Pursuing Leads

The easiest way to get a new job is for an employer to call you. Maybe an employer will see your work and recruit you. It does happen, but you can't count on it. If you are like most people, you will need to use several sources to identify job openings. This chapter outlines sources of jobs and evaluates their usefulness for a job search in social work. Then it suggests how you can screen job leads and compose cover letters targeted for specific openings.

We do not yet know a great deal about how social workers at all levels of experience find jobs. Many schools of social work survey their graduates on employment issues at least every few years. However, that information is not collected in a systematic way across institutions to give us an annual picture of the job market that new graduates enter. If you are looking in a geographic location where many of your fellow alumni live, check with your alma mater on the job sources reported by graduates.

The Association of Baccalaureate Social Work Program Directors (BPD) sponsors a survey of graduates with the BSW degree. The BPD Outcomes Instrument reports on salaries, types of positions, sources of jobs, and length of job searches, among other employment details, as well as on the graduates' satisfaction with their education. Local and national publications and contacts through the media, field work, friends, or family accounted for most job sources of new BSWs whose job search lasted one to three months (median length of time) following graduation (Hull, Ray, Rogers, & Smith, 1992).

In a 1994 pilot project, Doelling and Matz collected data (C. Doelling and B. Matz, unpublished data, 1994) on job sources used by graduates completing an MSW in 1993. They repeated the project in 1995, 1996, and 1997, collecting data on the previous year's class of MSW graduates but, unfortunately, most schools of social work do not collect such annual data. Although the pilot project relies on aggregated data and the sample sizes for each year have been too small to report results, the responses did give indications about how some new graduates are finding jobs. Newspapers, unsolicited letters to employers, networking, and practicum were the most commonly reported sources of jobs.

Job-search strategists recommend that you read or scan books on job hunting as you prepare and go through the search process. Most bookstores and libraries have well-stocked sections on careers and job hunting.

Many authors of job-hunting guides divide job-search strategies into two groups: traditional and what some call "targeted" strategies. The traditional approach entails completing applications for personnel departments, responding to ads, and sending unsolicited letters and résumés in a widespread mailing campaign to employers. The targeted approach entails first researching potential employers and identifying those of particular interest to you; second, using a network of contacts and printed resources to detail those problems in the organization that you can solve and to identify the person in the organization with the power to hire you; and third, in a face-to-face meeting convincing that person to hire you.

People do still get jobs using the traditional method, but many job-search experts now downplay that approach. In a competitive job market, authors encourage job hunters to use the more assertive targeted search. Many feel that this proactive approach increases one's chances of a good job fit, greater job stability, and higher salary.

You can use elements of both methods. If convincing an employer—especially one that does not have an opening—that you should be hired based on your ideas and abilities to solve problems is an intimidating prospect, you probably do not want to put that strategy high on your list of approaches.

Some books you may want to read *What Color is Your Parachute?* (Bolles, 1997), *Through the Brick Wall Job Finder* (Wendleton, 1993), *We Are All Self-Employed* (Hakim, 1995), *Career Change* (Hefland, 1995), and *The New Rules of the Job Search Game* (Larson & Comstock, 1994).

Job-Search Strategies

Job-search strategies need not be thought of as just traditional or targeted. The following six approaches are another way you might conceive of your job search. The job sources for each approach are detailed later in this section.

1. Apply for openings identified through newspapers, newsletters, online postings, job information services, job hotlines, and telephone calls.
2. Use career services available through colleges, executive search firms, job fairs, résumé databases, and registries.
3. File unsolicited applications: submit employer applications, get on government registers, and conduct a mailing campaign.
4. Network and gain visibility through current contacts, professional and community associations, temporary and volunteer work, and position-wanted ads, for example.
5. Target organizations.
6. Create an organization.

Job-Search Strategy for BSW Graduates

Like most social workers at any level of experience, the BSW holder needs to develop a message that highlights knowledge and skills and educates employers on the quality of the BSW degree (Boyd, 1996).

- Make a written list of your knowledge areas and skills (see chapter 1). Assume that you will need to educate others on what you know. One BSW graduate says to sell your degree—that is, your knowledge of service delivery systems, the systems and person-in-environment approaches, and specific populations and your internship.
- Think about trends and policy changes. Welfare reform is changing the demands on state workers, who must work proactively with complex family situations. What do you have to offer in this changing environment? One BSW recommends working for a state government, where you can get good experience.
- Research your target geographic market well. Make an extensive list of all the organizations doing any work related to your interests. Call them to find out how they use people with a BSW. The Revised BPD Outcomes Study reports that approximately half of the BSW respondents found their first jobs in the public sector and half in the private sector (Hull et al., 1992).
- Put yourself in situations, especially professional activities, that allow you to meet new people in the field (see the section on "Contacts and Networking" in this chapter). Let everyone know what type of work you want to do, or at least educate them about your interests.

- Put applications on file and make cold calls to agencies to identify openings; follow up.
- Be creative in your job search. BSW graduates have found jobs through summer jobs, field work, newspaper ads, professional activities, and tips from practicum staff and classmates; they have filed applications, done volunteer work, contacted state offices for employment security, talked to neighbors, and sent unsolicited résumés and letters.
- Be persistent, start looking early, be prepared to relocate, and market your degree.

A BSW Graduate's Job Search

A student who would receive her BSW in May had been accepted for graduate school in a distant city where she had no social work connections; her family lived 30 miles away. She needed a full-time job while working on her MSW, so she made plans to conduct a search.

> *Phase 1: As part of her senior seminar she prepared a ré-sumé. About five weeks before graduation in May, she re-quested that her college career center send a letter of reciproc-ity for services to the university career service center where she had been accepted for graduate school. As a result, the gradu-ate school sent her a job list. She had also done her field place-ment at a social services organization with locations through-out the United States. She applied to the affiliate in her target location, but nothing came of the connection until midsum-mer, when the agency called her for an interview.*

> *Phase 2: She moved to her target location in late May and began delivering her résumé to agencies by hand. She thought that, because her experience was limited, at least introducing herself in person to staff would put her ahead of the competi-tion. After three weeks of crisscrossing the town, she stopped. No one had responded, and staff did not have time to meet her or were unavailable; besides, gas and parking were too expen-sive to keep up this effort.*

> *Phase 3: Frustrated by her attempts to apply in person, she launched a mailing campaign, using a list of practicum sites from her future graduate program, the local United Way di-rectory of community services, and classified ads in the news-paper. Over the next three weeks, she sent out 300 letters and résumés in response to ads or as unsolicited inquiries. It was not unusual for her to use a word processor to prepare and send 60–75 form letters in one day. She did tailor slightly the*

letters in response to ads, although she thought she lacked the experience to tailor the letters particularly well. The campaign yielded about a 10 percent response rate in the form of six or seven calls a day. This was encouraging until she discovered through a few interviews that most of the jobs did not pay a living wage.

Phase 4: That's when she began screening jobs over the telephone by saying, "I believe your time is valuable and so is mine. I don't want to waste your time or mine in an interview for a position I know I will not take. If your position pays less than $18,000 a year, it does not meet my needs." Employers appreciated her honesty. In the end, her screening process resulted in four opportunities that met her minimum salary requirement.

Phase 5: Two organizations, a circuit attorney's office and a homeless youth shelter, called her back for a second interview. A school system and a hospital notified her that they were interested in interviewing her again and would be in touch soon to set a time. She accepted a job before either contacted her, and she told both that she had already accepted an offer. She said she appreciated their time, but she believed she had found a position well-suited for her. "They seemed happy for me and apologized for not having been able to move faster in the decision-making process," she reported.

Before she went on second interviews, however, she met with a contact for advice. That person persuaded her that she was underselling her background, particularly her previous work experience. When she went to the second interviews, she detailed how her earlier work, education, and training fit each position. Before entering the BSW program, she had worked for 10 years as an apartment manager—collecting bills, dealing with evictions, making referrals to social agencies, dealing with situations of domestic violence, and consoling victims of crime and family members confronted with tragedies. In her undergraduate program, she had completed several papers and projects on homelessness.

The homeless youth shelter, which initially interviewed her for a position below her minimum salary requirement, called her back, this time to interview for a program director position that had recently opened. During the first interview the agency staff recognized that she had the skills to take on more responsibility. As it turned out, her experience working with renters to collect rent matched their need to help youths with

*budgeting, her experience evicting renters matched their need
for someone who could do the tough job of turning away youths
who did not fit the shelter's program, and her academic work
on homelessness matched their need for someone who under-
stood the issues. They also were interested in the fact that she
was enrolling in a graduate program. Although they had originally intended to hire someone with an MSW, they offered
her the job, and she accepted it.*

*At the same time, she knew the circuit attorney's office
wanted to offer her a position working with victims; however,
their funding was not secure, nor could they set a starting
date. A week after she was on the job at the shelter, the circuit
attorney's office called to offer her a job. They too liked her
knowledge of systems and her previous experience in apartment management. Although the position paid more, she would
have had to pay for parking and a professional wardrobe, which
was not the case at the shelter.*

*Phase 6: With a second offer in hand, she spoke with the
executive director of the shelter, explaining that she had un-
dersold herself in the interview and feared she would resent
her decision in the future because money would be tighter with
this job. She said that she already felt invested in her job, however, and did not want to leave. She asked whether the agency
could do anything to help her. The executive director, persuaded
by her arguments, got approval to increase the salary by
$2,500.*

The first key to this graduate's search was recognizing and articulating what she had to offer—her message, in other words. Early
on, when she was preparing to move and look for a job, people told
her that her work before she received her BSW was irrelevant to
her search. She did not therefore approach the task of finding a job
with confidence. It was not until well into the process that she began
to link those earlier skills, as well as her BSW education, specifically to the opportunities she found. She did not rely on interviewers to discover the connections. She interpreted her background in
terms of each position. "Initially, I was projecting confidence, pre-
tending it was there. Later, I was sincerely presenting confidence
in what I had to offer."

The second key was to identify those organizations that met her
interests, and most of those offered only minimum pay. She dared
to do something different: she screened for salary information when
employers called. Handling this issue in a professional manner saved
time for her and the employer.

When she moved to her target city, she went to a couple of chapter meetings of NASW, where she met supportive people in her field. They told her that a salary of $18,000 was appropriate in that community for a new BSW and gave her some job leads and advice. It was during these conversations that she began to think she was underselling her background.

Seeking advice on her search helped her target her message and salary goal. Of course, she could have used this technique initially to narrow the list of organizations she contacted, which would have saved effort, postage, and some frustration. Beginning at phase 3, her 300 applications generated 40 calls, four interviews in her desired salary range, and two offers. Much of the early work delivering résumés and mailing applications could have been eliminated through more research.

Like many job hunters, this BSW graduate found the job search process to be an emotional one. She had left a career paying much more than $6.00 an hour, plus benefits, to do social work, which she wanted to do so much, but early efforts to find a well-paying job failed. Perseverance and advice-seeking were essential to the success of her search.

Another Example

A second BSW student graduating in December describes her search as follows.

> *My heart was set on advocating for children. I started the job search late because I was so overwhelmed with the demands of my senior year. There was a particular organization that I had really wanted to work for. As I was mentioning my dream to a staff person at my college, I found out that she had a connection to the organization. She connected me with her friend, and I called her early in January. I asked a million questions, which she graciously answered, and then she gave me the names of several people she knew at the organization. Although she didn't know whether they had any jobs, she suggested I just send them a cover letter and résumé, making sure to mention her name. I had previously called the organization's job hotline, but none of the officially open positions met my qualifications or interests.*

> *So I put together as attractive a package as I could, not even knowing if these connections had or knew of a job opening. In addition to the standard cover letter and résumé, I decided to add a photocopy of an award I had just received and a writing sample, even though I didn't know if one was required. I had*

learned through my college experience that what gets you ahead is going above and beyond what is expected of you.

It's indeed why I am here today, as program assistant in a national advocacy organization and with only a BSW. A week after I sent in the packets, I got a call from a staff member who set up an interview with me over the telephone. She offered me a temporary internship position (paid) for six months working on a specific grant-funded project. What made all the difference in the world for me, for the launching of my career, was my creation of a volunteer student organization while I was in college. This was the key to getting such a good job right out of school. As my internship was nearing completion, I started talking with people again, . . . this time after developing a network of relationships with staff in the organization. By the time I decided to stay and postpone graduate school, I had four job offers, none of them published outside of the building.

Job-Search Strategy for an MSW Graduate

Think broadly about looking for a job. Use a range of job sources outlined in this chapter. Experienced social workers and new graduates can find jobs through many sources.

- Develop a presence in your target community; expand your contact network. If you are moving to a new community, get involved in a task force or committee, preferably one that gives you a broad overview of the field and organizations of interest to you. See the "Contacts and Networking" section in this chapter.
- Look into licensure early. With the multiplicity of licensure and certification regulations, you may need more than one. One new graduate recommends that "if your state allows it, take the licensure exam ASAP. It will help to keep you busy, and refreshing your memory will boost your confidence. It will also enable you to get it out of the way. It may be difficult for you to juggle studying and worrying about the exam with job searching. I think, though, that studying really is part of the job-search process, as it helps you refine your knowledge and build the confidence that you will need for the search." Note that passing a licensing exam is an asset that others might not have. If you have completed part of the licensing process, indicate that in your letters and on your résumé.
- Volunteer, particularly in communitywide advocacy, planning, and evaluation efforts to gain visibility for your work. See the section "Temporary or Volunteer Work" in this chapter and the one on "Visibility" in chapter 7.

- Although unlicensed MSW degree holders seeking positions in direct practice are less likely to find jobs on the Internet than are social workers with macro interests, it is still worth using the Internet on a regular basis (see "Online Job Sources" in this chapter). The same can be said for many association newsletters.
- File applications with select organizations; human resources staff do check their files when a position opens.
- Consider targeting organizations. You may or may not want to set up a meeting to discuss mutual interests and try convincing a manager that he or she should create a position to capitalize on your skills. However, the process of researching organizations and thinking about how you can sell your skill sets will definitely strengthen your search skills.

A New MSW Graduate's Job Search

This is the experience of a new MSW graduate who planned to relocate across the country after graduating in December. She began actively researching her target market one year before her graduation. During this time she researched and competed for a practicum abroad and maintained contact with sources; she also completed the practicum, graduated, and moved to her new home. This person's search may seem unusually long, but she wanted to explore a broad range of interests before determining the type of work she wanted to pursue and finding a job that combined several of those interests. Outside the time she spent completing her graduate education, exploring career options, researching her market, and settling in her new community, she spent 2½ months looking for a full-time job before receiving an offer.

> *December: I came to the area [target location] during winter break of my second year [of graduate school] and started making some telephone calls based on the organizations I had written down from career books and publications such as* Community Jobs *and* Opportunities in Public Affairs *[see appendix 8]. I also visited a local university career center. I simply wrote down organizations that sounded interesting to me. Since I had several interests, I prioritized them first in terms of work in prevention and education, children's advocacy, and international social work. I began to narrow my focus when I realized that school-based social work combined my interests in prevention, education, and children's advocacy. I ruled out working in international social work, because I found that there were not many jobs available to social workers—many organizations seem to prefer PhD-level candidates. A bilingual position was important, too. I made a lot of cold calls at*

that time and followed up on some personal contacts that my relatives gave me. The people I talked to were very friendly and helpful. It was at that time that I made a contact at the county department of family resources, who ended up sending out my résumé on her own to several people she thought might be hiring. Ultimately, the job I was offered and accepted had something to do with her help—I never would have gotten to know a lot of people in school social work had she not put my name out there.

January–May: I kept up telephone conversations and letters to the contacts I made over winter break. I also started sending "cold letters," which ended up getting me nowhere. When I talked with the director of the career center about it, she suggested that I contact organizations first by telephone and then follow up with a letter. This definitely brought more results, because then they were expecting my letter and résumé. I also wrote to all of the listed alumni in the area. Although I think that was a good idea, I did not get much of a response, probably because I didn't have a local telephone number.

May–October: By May, I had received two calls from organizations that were interested in interviewing me. I interviewed in July before I left to do my practicum in Mexico. The director from one of those organizations, an adult and child services center, became a very important contact. I went to Mexico and wrote her once I was there. She was not able to offer me a position; however, when I came back and called her, she gave me some great contacts in the field of school-based social work. After four months in Mexico, I returned, took two weeks' vacation, and then moved to [target location].

November–December: I started contacting the names my last contact had given me. Two of those people gave me several good leads. After the first call I made to each of them, I sent follow-up letters thanking them for their help. I developed a kind of mentor relationship with them. One thing that helped me was that my aunt knew one contact, so when I sent her a thank-you letter, I mentioned my aunt's name. I continued to contact them when I needed more leads (I think I talked to them three or four times each throughout my job search). I also applied with the state to be listed as eligible for a Social Work I position.

December–March: I contacted the state chapter of NASW (I joined when I was still a student). They sent me their job bulletin for the next four months. Although I applied for a few of the positions, I didn't get very far with them. I also kept up with the newspaper classifieds. I did get one interview through letters I sent in response to ads. For the number of letters I sent out, that's not a great track record! I kept up with some graduate school friends who were in the area, and they gave me some contacts, which led to at least one interview. I also contacted some of the alumni who had responded to my initial letters. One got me an interview, but I wasn't interested in the position. I also joined a local women's job network and applied for some jobs through their information resources.

February–March: By this time, I knew that I wanted to focus on community-based programs, especially school-based social work. I accepted a part-time contract position with the county department of family resources. The job involved staffing a leadership group, which included all of the major collaborators in an exciting new school social work program. I met all of the people I had been talking to since the start of my job search, for many of them were connected to this collaboration. That of course helped me tremendously—I saw them on a regular basis and continued to build relationships with them. Another important factor was that there was a great need in the schools for bilingual social workers. I began to work with some of the directors of these school-based programs through the county department of family resources. Thus, I interviewed with three different agencies that had federal and state contracts to work in the public schools. These became viable job contacts in school-based social work; one was a family services agency, one a community psychiatric clinic, and one a mental health association. I ended up getting job offers from two, as well as one from a Latino organization providing job development. I accepted an offer from the family services agency, which contracts with schools, because it fit my preference of working in an elementary school within a largely Latino community. It also fit my salary requirements. The offer I got from the Latino organization was way below what first-year social workers earn on average. At the end of March I began directing a day care center at an elementary school, an interim position, because the permanent position would not be vacant for another three months. In June, as planned, they moved me into a bilingual school social worker position, conducting groups for children and doing case management and counseling with parents and children at an elementary school.

This job hunter offers the following advice:

- Call contacts first and ask whether you can send a résumé. They get so much mail that your material will be overlooked otherwise. Then send a letter and résumé. This way they will recognize it when it arrives.
- Focus on your commitment to issues, not to a job function. Various roles might fit your commitment.
- Use a name from a referral when contacting a new person, if possible.
- People are very busy—refine your message. When you reach a contact, get the important parts of your message across quickly— for example, that you have an MSW degree, you are bilingual, and you are new to the area and are researching it.
- If you say that you are bilingual, expect to conduct interviews in your second language.
- If the networking process seems to get bogged down, go back to earlier contacts for more advice.

Another New MSW's Search
This is the job-search story of a May MSW graduate who planned to move across the country to the West Coast, where she was from. During her final spring semester, she juggled job hunting with two courses, a practicum, two part-time jobs, and research on a trip she wanted to take to Central America to refresh her Spanish language skills before starting a new job. To keep focused on her goals, she scheduled four hours a week for researching options for her trip and a job. Her full-time job for two years before graduate school had been in a town of 100,000, where it was easy to get into the action—that is, to see how agency boards operate and observe the politics. This experience gave her a broad view and increased her confidence.

> *November: She had not planned to start the job-search process until February, but a deadline for the school's career services' mailing to alumni encouraged her to begin earlier. She used community resource and national directories to identify community development organizations, then narrowed the list to those specifically doing employment training. She eliminated some agencies because their focus was on first-time home ownership and low-income housing development. She knew that self-employment training was the new trend and that money from the federal government was targeted toward it.*

December: She sent letters to the organizations on her list to request information on their self-employment training that was taking place in her target city.

Winter break: She followed up with calls to the same organizations and met with an agency focused on housing and employment issues for women. The staff gave her lots of information and mentioned one agency in particular. She had four contacts (one in person and three over the phone) with different agencies over the break.

January–March: She continued to follow up with more agencies. This included telephone contact with all agencies on her list and with those identified in initial research meetings. This was her introduction: "I am working in microenterprise in [city] and will be moving to [city] in the summer. I am beginning to investigate what projects are going on in [city]." Note that she had been working in microenterprise development through a practicum and a part-time job.

In February, she spoke (a long-distance cold call) with a staff member of one agency, who spoke highly of the agency and recommended she talk with the director. For a couple of weeks she tried unsuccessfully to get in touch with the director for advice.

In late March, she talked with the career services director at her institution about her frustration with telephone tag. As a result, she sent a résumé with a letter stating that she was working in microenterprise development and giving the approximate date that she was moving to the city. She said that two contacts (from her earlier follow-up calls), whom she named, recommended the agency and that she would like to know more about the agency. She did not ask for an opportunity to seek advice, or whether they had job openings.

A week and half later, when the student called to follow up on her letter, the director was available on the first try. The director, who had sent the letter to the agency training coordinator, said she would pass a message to the training coordinator to call the student. The training coordinator called back in 15 minutes and said, "We want to interview you." The student indicated that she would be at a conference in the region in late April. They arranged to interview at the conference.

April: The student met with the staff several times at the conference and later received an offer, which she accepted two days before graduation. See page 128 for a detailed description of her interviews.

From the beginning, this MSW student defined herself as a professional. She treated her internships as professional experience. She marketed herself as a young professional with four years of experience (two years' work before getting her MSW, plus her field experience) and a master's degree. She determined what type of work she wanted first, rather than looking at what was available. She identified organizations, researched their work, and thought about the fit between their functions and her qualifications. Her research gave her leverage. She had done the homework, knew what was going on in the community, and where she could fit in. The research was like doing a needs assessment. She did not look at newspaper ads. She recommends that students do more self-assessment.

An International Job Search

One MSW graduate, a program officer for an international organization, is working in Eastern Europe to strengthen a network of local nongovernmental organizations (NGOs). He helps determine which projects his organization will fund, conducts outreach efforts, assists NGOs with organizational development and fund-raising, plans and coordinates seminars and workshops led by outside experts, and monitors subgrantee organizations, among other responsibilities. Earlier, he had been a volunteer with an NGO in a Central American country, a volunteer intern on a mental health team for an international organization working with refugees in Central America, and a volunteer with a second refugee service in Latin America. Contacts made through his work on the mental health team project led him to his current job.

> *In my opinion, and because of my personal experiences, I would have to say that it is difficult to find paid international work in the social work field. People with skills in financial management, construction, medicine, public health, agriculture, and engineering probably have a much easier time finding employment abroad. So I suggest that first-time international job seekers really review their abilities and consider what other skills they will need to become marketable. Some valuable skills are foreign language ability (especially Spanish, Portuguese, French, or Russian), project management, and other skills that are not readily available in the country where you're thinking about working.*

Like any job search, connections and personal contacts are crucial for success. Try to get to know international NGOs and subscribe to publications that list job opportunities. A lot of this information is available on the Internet. Volunteering abroad is also a good way to get some work experience that will eventually help in locating a paid position. Apart from this practical advice, luck is a big factor in locating a job.

I hope this is helpful. It's really tough entering this field, but for me it was worth the effort.

Job-Search Strategy for an Experienced Professional and Other Specialized Searches

The basics of job hunting change little over time—many of the things you did to find a job when you were first starting out will be the same things you do when you have many years of experience. Nevertheless, some elements of your job-search strategy are more important now that you are a seasoned professional.

- Assessing your values and honing your message will take more time than before, because you have more work experience to filter, especially if you are moving across fields or functions. You will have more endearing experiences to let go of and synthesize for new audiences, particularly those outside traditional social work arenas.
- If you have focused on your work without building new skill sets or developing your contact network, you may need to spend more time in a preparation phase. See chapters 1 and 7.
- Your range of acquaintances, particularly at upper levels and in a variety of organizations, will be a key factor in your search. The reputation you have developed and the visibility of your work will also affect the pace of your search.
- More than ever before, you will want to research your market and target organizations that interest you. If you are staying in your field, you know what to look for in organizations. If you want to sell yourself in a new field, function, or industry, you will have considerably more background work to do.
- You are more likely than a first-time searcher to find appropriate positions announced on the Internet, perhaps because positions at your level require experience and licensure or certification or because the Internet is being used more to recruit hard-to-find candidates. See the section "Online Job Sources" in this chapter for other ideas on using the Internet for a search.

- Take advantage of résumé databases and registries that professional and trade associations offer. They are usually focused on upper-level positions. See appendix 1.
- Contact executive search firms if you are looking for management positions. See the section "Executive Search Firms" in this chapter.
- If you are interested in positions at universities, read the section "Academic Job Search" in this chapter.
- If you have not looked for a position in a long time, use your support network. Job hunting can be an exhilarating experience if you have a strong support system.
- Expect potential employers to do a background check on you. They will speak with others in the profession and community; they may hire a firm to do this.
- At this level, expect employers to request supplemental materials, such as a very detailed résumé, samples of publications, a proposal for their project, or responses to a list of questions they provide. For an executive position, such questions might address leadership, program development, accountability, and fund management issues.

Search for a Job in Policy and Research

This is the job-search experience of a doctoral graduate who began searching in the spring, defended her dissertation in late summer, and then moved to Washington, DC, to find a position in policy and research, preferably in health care.

> *First of all, my first contact here was a person who is "well connected," as they say in this town. That means that she knows lots of people who have authority, power, or whatever you want to call it, and she also knows what is going on in the government. I found this person through her daughter, who was a student in my social policy class and the first person who asked me whether I had considered locating in DC and doing research there. I also had a contact in a consulting firm, and I knew that a former faculty member was in DC. It turned out that both had changed jobs. This was not a problem, because at each place they told me where the people had gone and gave me a telephone number where I could reach them. My original contact gave me several names of people to contact, about five; with some of them I could use her name, and with some I could not.*
>
> *All but one of these people had a background in child welfare. One was with the Public Health Service and one led a*

division on health care research within the organization. These two contacts opened the doors on two different sectors: consulting firms and associations. There are possibilities in the public sector at the federal level, in the executive branch (Department of Health and Human Services) and legislative branch (House and Senate committees); in the private sector, there are associations (Child Welfare League of America or the American Hospital Association), consulting firms, and think tanks (Brookings Institution or Urban Institute). I pursued all but the legislative branch—I never got that far, although I added names there to a list for cold mailings. The person with the Public Health Service sent me a fax of his contractors, listing contacts' names and telephone numbers, and that is how I got to my job. One of my original contacts also sent me a long list of contractors that I was going to use as a source of blind calls, but I never got around to that, although I did get it on my computer, and I was trying to decide about the best time to send out cold letters.

Then I started networking, making telephone calls to the people whose names I had. An amazing number of these people returned my calls. The approach that I used on these calls was to call first and say that so-and-so had suggested I talk with them. My pitch was that I was finishing my PhD in social work or had just completed the requirements for my PhD and was interested in doing health care research or health care policy research, and that so-and-so had suggested that I talk with them because they would know of openings or of other people I could talk with. After a while, I started asking whether the person had voice mail so I could leave a message—I didn't want secretaries or clerks screening me out. If they did have voice mail, then I left the pitch about being a new PhD. I emphasized that I had heavy methodological training and four-plus years' experience as a research assistant with a longitudinal study. Some people asked me to fax my résumé, although most people had me send my résumé, which they would pass around or keep in an open file. And they really did this. Although I thought that this might be a dodge, several people called me to tell me that so-and-so gave them my résumé; in one case, the person mailed a copy of my résumé to an organization that was looking for a research analyst. Several people explained about the timing of consulting work: The responses to federal RFPs (requests for proposals) generally are completed in the summer and then the contracts are awarded September 30. After the contracts are awarded, the firms then know what their staffing needs are. Generally, only really big firms with more than 100 research professionals on staff hire on a regular basis. The smaller contract firms hire based on the contracts they have been awarded.

After my conversation with each person, I sent a thank-you letter with a copy of my résumé. Although I never got to this point, I planned on sending a résumé after follow-up calls, too. The résumé (no one ever called it a "vita") would have been better as a one-pager, but I could not get it down to that point. Some firms wanted a writing sample as well as the résumé, but I did not have one that I thought was appropriate—short (not more than 12 or 15 pages), sole authorship, and empirically based. I would recommend that people looking for research positions or other positions for which writing is important have something like this ready to send out to those who ask for writing samples.

I also tried sending the résumé with an introductory letter saying so-and-so suggested that I talk with them and telling them that I would follow up in a week. I only did this with a few people, and it was fairly successful, as far as I could tell.

Actually, the success ratio for this type of job search is probably much higher than for the want-ad route. I did not hear from one firm to which I responded as a result of a want ad, other than the form letter they send out to acknowledge receipt of the résumé.

Most of the people that I contacted were in the long-term care area of health care. When I stopped searching, I was just starting to get names from the maternal and child care segment of the market. One thing that was apparent early on is that there are segments within segments, based on specialty. It appears to be pretty easy to get slotted into one particular area, and it is not clear to me how easy it is to move from one area of expertise to another.

There is no doubt that being in DC made a big difference in the search. It is just so hard to do a search long distance, and it's expensive, too. Of course, it is scary to do it the other way—just pick up and go. The perfect solution would be to have someone to stay with while looking for a job, but I don't know too many people who welcome house guests for months and months.

In DC, people were astonishing in their willingness to refer me to people. A number of people went through their Rolodexes while we were on the telephone, giving me names and numbers and letting me use their names as door openers. I cannot say that it will be that way everywhere, and I know that it is not that way in all of academia. People here do not use their titles, do not appear to be into status; they are very open and giving of their time. I would not expect that everywhere. A lot of people work temporary assignments while looking for a job. It is tough to make all the telephone calls that way, but at least it puts some food on the table.

As far as I can figure out, I spoke with approximately 100 people here, both before moving and after I had relocated. It's hard for me to figure out how many names I have in addition, but most people did return my calls, even though some of this work was done in August, when many in DC take a vacation. My records do not indicate when I made the first telephone call, but I talked to [name of firm whose offer she accepted] at the end of April for the first time and faxed my résumé the next day. The first interview with the firm was at the end of May. The second interview was at the end of July. I am convinced that the assigning [awarding] of contracts and September 30 timing of that has a lot to do with the quickness of getting a job.

Academic Job Search

The job market for social workers with doctoral degrees who are seeking academic positions has been quite strong for several years. If you are in the academic job market, you are more likely than social workers looking for other types of work to find positions advertised, partly because it is a candidate's market and universities typically seek to recruit the best from a diverse pool of candidates. Although some academic programs hire master's-level faculty for teaching positions, the trend is toward all full-time faculty having doctorates. Some characteristics of your search are listed below.

- Chances are that your current environment is an academic one. This makes your research phase less complicated, at least initially. You have ready access to people and information about potential institutions.
- Background information on your potential employers is easy to obtain. Sources include Internet home pages, including faculty profiles, reference material such as Peterson's guides, admission bulletins and brochures, alumni newsletters, and annual reports.

- You have the distinct advantage of being able to review faculty publications and attend faculty presentations at conferences.
- Be familiar with the accreditation standards of the Council on Social Work Education (CSWE). Broaden your knowledge of academic programs, and tailor your message on teaching interests to the course content required of all schools.
- The academic world of social work is a close-knit one. If you are a doctoral student, seek the advice of your adviser and other faculty with whom you have worked. Your adviser and committee will be significant players in your search.
- Like all job hunters, research your market to identify those schools whose faculty and programs best match your teaching and research interests and whose cultures offer the best working environment for you. This process mirrors the one you followed in selecting a doctoral program.
- If you are a student, you will be competing for tenure-track positions at institutions whose academic programs are of similar quality or standing to your doctoral program. It is unlikely that you will compete effectively for positions in higher-tier schools.
- You will go through an extensive interview process, usually lasting more than a day. This will include a presentation, usually on your dissertation. See chapter 5.
- Your written and verbal communications must reflect the theme of your work and your ability and promise to produce scholarly work.
- If you are a doctoral student, your search is likely to begin $1\frac{1}{2}$ years ahead of your projected graduation date. This is largely because of the academic calendar, the recruiting schedule of selection committees, the timing of conferences, and the competition for qualified candidates.
- In addition to your teaching, research, and practice experience, your products and products in process will be critical elements of your search. If you are a doctoral student, you will probably have at least one publication before graduation and other papers under review. Ideally, you will also make a conference presentation during the year that you are actively searching—this provides good visibility. Plan ahead: At least two years before your graduation, make a list of conference submission deadlines.
- In social work education, there is one focal conference—the Annual Program Meeting of CSWE—where school search committees typically conduct screening interviews. Both candidates and search committee members attend one another's presentations, and schools invite candidates to attend their evening receptions for an informal round of mutual scrutinizing.

- Participate in the CSWE Teachers Registry and Information Service, which provides candidates with information on openings and school search committees with information on candidates. See the CSWE entry in appendix 1.
- In addition to the criteria you used when you were considering doctoral programs, inquire about the mission of the program; structure of the curriculum, including field education; expectations for teaching loads, committees, and community work; tenure process and timeline; faculty roles in field education, advising, admissions, and student services; relationship of the school to the community, including government units; the school's resources and track record regarding grant applications; and demographic composition of the faculty, including proportion of those tenured.
- Expect your expenses for travel to interviews to be covered by the institutions, but always confirm this.

An Example of an Academic Search
One doctoral candidate took a research position that would become a postdoctoral appointment after she defended her dissertation in December and would last until midsummer. This enabled her to postpone the search and concentrate on her dissertation. She began the search immediately after defending the dissertation. This timing gave her the advantage of giving a job talk on a finished piece rather than a work in process, publishing two coauthored articles, and making presentations at several conferences. Few people, however, have the option of postponing a search until after the defense.

She started by identifying a list of institutions that met her interests. Her sources were the *GADE Guide* (from the Group for the Advancement of Doctoral Education), which lists doctoral programs in social work, and recent articles that ranked social work academic programs, although she did not look specifically at the ranking. She also looked at announcements listed on her department's bulletin board, in *NASW News*, and through the CSWE registry. She did not choose to have her information sent to institutions through the CSWE registry (although this is an important search tool for many, she thought it would complicate the process too much for her). To create the list, she set some geographic limits and decided that she wanted to work at a school with a doctoral program.

Once she had identified those institutions that best matched her interests, about 20–25 of them, she sent packets to each in December and January. In retrospect, this was too many schools—10–12 would have been adequate with her credentials, given the strong market. The packets consisted of a letter, which detailed her practice experience between the MSW and PhD degrees, and her research agenda; a vita; copies of her two published articles; and a reference list. Most schools asked for three to five references, so she listed five on the reference list. Some schools were also very interested in teaching evaluations. Before the packets went in the mail, she received a couple of calls from schools, one of which had gotten her name from a fellow doctoral student who knew faculty at that institution.

Before the Annual Program Meeting of CSWE that February, she exchanged several calls with institutions interested in setting up interviews at the conference. Over the course of two days at the conference, she had 13 interviews. This would have been a wild schedule for any candidate—she could have been more selective. After the conference, she narrowed her list of potential institutions. This entailed even canceling some site visits, which had been offered during the initial interviews.

She visited nine institutions. The first visit was within two weeks of the CSWE meeting. This travel schedule was a logistical challenge that she would not recommend. Three to five site visits would have been adequate. By the week after her first site visit, she had received her first offer.

The site interviews typically consisted of dinner with faculty shortly after arriving, and then a series of interviews the next day and a presentation of her colloquium (job talk). The colloquia were scheduled to run between 45 minutes and $1\frac{1}{2}$ hours. Her typical colloquium followed this outline:

1. She described the steps that led her to these research questions, the theoretical and practice foundation for the study.
2. She presented the study, including two or three highlights or key findings.
3. She discussed the practice and policy implications. For this, she made it a point to talk in practice and policy terms.
4. Finally, she responded to questions from faculty on the study and its implications.

She found it helpful to summarize her points on overhead transparencies; she used five of them, and she recommends not using more than seven. On one occasion she was asked to tailor the talk to the institution, and she therefore focused about 10 minutes of her presentation on their interests.

She thought specifically about how to address the needs of all faculty members with whom she met. That entailed speaking in broader or general terms with those who were not statisticians and using research terms with the quantitative research faculty.

Individual and group interview questions during the visits covered the following areas:

- There were many questions about what she could teach and what she had taught. Faculty were particularly concerned with their teaching needs for next year.
- There were questions about how she handled various situations in classes: the overly verbal student and the nonparticipant, confrontations with students, and the need to value diversity.
- Beyond the details of her research experience, there were questions about the impact she wanted to have on social work education and the field in five to 10 years and what expertise she wanted to develop.
- Faculty also wanted to know with whom she had worked on research projects and who was on her committee.

The timing of appointment offers was not ideal. Her first offer came between the first and second site visits and six weeks before the last interview. She decided to set her own deadline for a decision. She told the faculty from the institution making the first offer that the school was high on her list, which it was. In the end, she had five offers. She was fortunate that the school making the first offer was willing to wait until she had completed her interviews. Many institutions are not this flexible. She accepted this first offer.

Her acceptance of the offer was based on the following factors.

- The institution had a doctoral program, and it appeared that she would be able to begin working with doctoral students fairly soon.
- She would be bringing a contribution to the faculty, both in terms of her substantive areas and her methodological interests.
- She would be able to teach in a couple of areas, namely, policy and administration.
- This institution handled the selection process efficiently, and it effectively followed through. During the visit, the school arranged for a realtor to drive her around the community just to become acquainted with it, not to look for houses. Every week a different faculty member called to discuss a project or talk about textbooks she had used. They also sent the local newspaper.
- The school made an offer quickly after the site visit.
- The faculty were warm and open.
- The cost of living was reasonable.
- The geographic location was fine for her and her family.

If the market is good for applicants, you can be more selective in the number and types of institutions to which you apply. However, you need to be realistic about your chances of being hired by particular schools. You might select five that would be your top choices and five that would be satisfactory.

The job searcher described above advises that it is a good idea to have a research project in process that is relatively pressing—in the analysis stage or with a publication deadline—so that your research agenda can continue to be a priority through your adjustment period on the job. Otherwise, your time might be consumed with course preparation, committee work, and the development of new relationships. Certainly that schedule of activities is important, but it also means a cold start for your research agenda.

Do not underestimate the time and energy necessary to keep a successful search organized. Do not feel that you cannot begin the search if you do not already have articles published; published work is not essential. You can put sections entitled "under review" and "works in process" in your vita.

Keep your lists of presentations and publications in balance: If you have many presentations that have not turned into publications, then simplify your list of presentations. If you do not have computerized reports, summarize comments from your teaching evaluations. Finally, do not wear yourself out by traveling with too much luggage: Pack light and carry everything on board if you can, but be sure to take extra copies of your vita and syllabi for the courses you have taught.

Sources of Jobs

"It's who you know" is a common refrain among job hunters. Although a contact network is a great asset to any job search, it is not the only way to find a job. Your strategy should include a number of sources; some are in the following sections. Which resources you use will depend on the sort of job you are seeking, your qualifications, and your research on the market.

Applications

Individual supervisors and human resources offices usually keep résumés and application forms on file for future reference. Particularly if you are applying to large institutions such as hospitals and school systems, send a résumé and letter to the director of social services and complete an application form for the human resources office (or personnel or employment office). For school systems, you will send a résumé to the student support services or pupil personnel services offices and an application to the personnel offices. This way, regardless of where the hiring process begins, you will have material on file. You may encounter a few organizations that charge applicants a fee. In that case, you may want to wait until you know for sure that an opening exists. Some human resources offices will mail you an application.

When filling out an application, use descriptive, detailed language, including social work terminology, to explain how your experience is directly related to the job you are seeking. For example, if you are a psychiatric social worker you will want to use DSM (*Diagnostic and Statistical Manual of Mental Disorders*) terminology. If you do not have experience that is directly related to the position, then describe what you have learned and accomplished as it applies to the job. Often there is no space on application forms specifically for practica or volunteer experience. Describe these positions like jobs in the work experience section. Include the words "intern" and "volunteer" in your title (for example, medical social work intern, research assistant intern, or volunteer fund-raiser); in the salary box state "unpaid."

Applying in Person

The advantages of dropping off résumés are knowing that your material arrived, seeing the location and at least the external physical environment, and possibly being able to talk with someone. Disadvantages are the amount of time and gas spent, perhaps not having all the information you need to complete the application, and the real possibility that the person making the hiring decision is too busy to see you. Going directly to an agency, particularly a large employer, may make sense if you are looking for an entry-level position or if using the mail would not ensure that your letter and résumé arrived on time; however, it is not appropriate for advanced positions. Generally speaking, you can use your time more efficiently. If you are going to personnel offices to complete applications, one student recommends taking a copy of a completed application with you so that you do not have to rely on your memory for details.

An exception is looking for positions on Capitol Hill. It is quite common for people looking for positions in congressional offices and on congressional committees to carry résumés by hand to offices.

Associations

Professional associations and national advocacy organizations provide several avenues for learning about jobs. Professional associations, such as NASW, are made up of individual members. Membership services may include a newsletter or hotline listing job openings and position-wanted ads, job fairs at conferences, and résumé databanks. If you are a student, be sure to inquire about student membership rates and any discount on registration for students who volunteer at conferences.

National advocacy organizations, also called trade associations, usually are made up of institutional members, although they may have individual members as well. The Child Welfare League of America is an example of a national advocacy organization. As a service to their member institutions, such organizations may list jobs in a newsletter; maintain a résumé databank; and consult with organizations on their human resources needs, particularly at the executive level. Some national advocacy organizations also sell a directory of their member agencies. See appendix 1 for information on career services offered by specific associations.

In addition to offering career or personnel services, associations provide a way to meet colleagues with interests similar to your own. Get involved in a committee or group concerned with your interests. This is the best way to develop long-term relationships and probably the most comfortable way of meeting people. Ask officers and committee chairs how to join committees.

Attend association conferences (see appendix 1 for associations' meeting dates). Local, state, and regional conferences are less expensive than national meetings and probably more cost-effective when you are job hunting in a specific geographic location. You usually will not find job fairs at these meetings, but you can find opportunities to expand your network. Contact the society's national office or state chapter for information. Details on hunting at job fairs are explained later in this section.

Colleges

Schools of social work often post job openings on bulletin boards, which you can see by simply visiting the school. You might find that the college's career center also posts job announcements on boards, although they are more likely to post them on a universitywide computer network or home page, which may or may not be open to the public.

Some social work programs offer job referral services, job newsletters, career planning and job-search workshops, a collection of community service and other directories, an alumni network directory, job or career fairs, job clubs, and individual career counseling for students and alumni (Boston University, 1996). If you are a student, participate in programs offered by your college career services office early in your academic program, and definitely start working with the staff early in your last year. If you are part of a student social work organization or alumni association, talk with members about cosponsoring career information and job-search programs or services with your school and career center. If you are a graduate, inquire about alumni services.

Contacts and Networking

Contacts are considered a cornerstone of any job search but are particularly important for social workers seeking advanced positions, moving across fields or functions, or looking for work outside traditional social work settings and roles. You have already identified a list of people you know and others who are knowledgeable about issues and organizations related to your interests (see chapter 2). You have also sought advice from a few of these individuals. At this point, you want to let everyone on your contact list know that you are starting your search. When you contact people you know, briefly explain what types of positions interest you and ask whether they know of possible openings. In some cases you will want to give them a résumé. Selectively, call or follow up with a brief letter every three or four weeks to remind people that you are still looking, to inform them of any changes in your plans, and to see whether they have any additional suggestions. For guidelines on contacting individuals, see chapter 2.

Ask the people on your contact list for suggestions about whom else you should contact. In addition, begin thinking about functions you can attend and groups you can get involved with to meet new people.

International, national, regional, state, and local conferences for professional associations and collaboration groups, or special events sponsored by local task forces, can be productive meeting places. Ask your contacts about upcoming meetings. When you participate, make a conscious effort to meet people, including speakers, before and after workshops and while visiting conference exhibits, sitting at luncheons, attending receptions, and standing in line. You are more likely to make these efforts when you are not accompanied by friends, so sit with people you do not know when you attend a luncheon. If you are new to an association, attend any orientation sessions, receptions for new members, or training workshops specifically for beginners. Newcomers like yourself will be interested in meeting other new people.

Making the effort to get involved in committees can have added benefits as well. For example, a BSW graduate who was serving as a student representative on the school's self-study committee met some social work representatives from the community. When she saw a classified ad placed by an agency at which two committee members worked, she applied and mentioned her application to the representatives. As it turned out, both committee members were on the interview team for the position. The student had made a good impression in committee meetings and she received an interview and got the job.

Create an Organization

Through your research, you may have identified a service need that you can provide and thus create your own job. You might establish your own for-profit consulting or contractual business or a nonprofit entity. You will have to study the environment carefully, create a business plan, have your own consultants in place, and probably begin on a part-time basis. If you want to consider this approach to creating a job, take a look at *Zen and the Art of Making a Living* (Boldt, 1993). Books such as *The Nonprofit Handbook* (Grobman, 1997) will help you tackle the nitty-gritty of starting a new nonprofit.

Current Organization

The work you do—your accomplishments on the job or in practica— may result in an invitation to apply for a job or in a promotion. As you assess the potential of your current work setting for new opportunities, it may be helpful to talk with someone who has a broad or different perspective on your organization. Besides considering whether there is an opportunity for a promotion or full-time employment, is there a possibility for a transfer or for an interim position that could lead to something permanent? Look carefully at the needs and problems of your current employer. Could you propose the creation of a new position to address their problems? Could you propose a project, perhaps an entrepreneurial effort or collaborative project, with the potential for creating a job? Could you write a grant that creates a position to address a particular need?

Executive Search Firms

Like corporations, some public, nonprofit, and for-profit health and social services contract with executive search firms to hunt

nationwide for candidates for positions such as chief executive officer or chief operating officer, and occasionally for vice-presiden-
tial or middle-management positions. Large nonprofit boards often
hire search firms to locate executive directors, and for-profit health
care companies have used them to identify managers for psychiatric units. Search firms look for potential candidates by asking for
suggestions from people in the field (for example, executive directors of similar agencies and professional and trade associations, as
well as university faculty and administrators). Your visibility and
reputation could lead a colleague to suggest your name when an
executive recruiter calls.

There are two types of executive search firms: retained and contingency. Retained firms have ongoing contracts with companies
to consult on long-term and immediate hiring issues for only top-
level positions. In contrast, contingency firm business depends on
filling positions for employers as they occur. In addition to filling
positions at uppermost levels, some contingency firms locate candidates for middle-management positions. Note that executive
search firms work for the employer. They are not in the business of
locating jobs for individuals.

Although search firm business originates with employers and
recruiters aggressively look for top-quality candidates, it is not
unheard of for individual job hunters to initiate contact with executive search firms. To identify firms that have worked with health
and social services organizations, check your library reference desk
for *The Directory of Executive Recruiters* (Burke, 1997). You will find
pertinent organizations listed by industry, function, and geographic
region. If you choose to explore this source, check with the local
Better Business Bureau and your contacts to be sure you are working with a reputable firm. When working with search firms, expect
all fees to be covered by the hiring organization.

Government Registers

Regulations usually require public agencies at the local and state
levels to use government registers to fill positions. A register is a
list of applicants whom departments can consider for employment.
This personnel practice parallels the one used by nonprofit and
for-profit agencies, whereby résumés or applications are kept on
file for consideration for future openings. However, some government units allow people to register at any time, while others accept
registrations only when there are openings. The formal registration process can be an effective tool for identifying openings, but
networking among your contacts to learn about government openings is equally, if not more, important. When inquiring about

public agency jobs, be sure to ask whether you need to live within that jurisdiction once hired, and find out how difficult it is to be considered for positions if you are not already living there.

In many states students can register with the state merit or civil service system before graduation; check with the local employment security office or state personnel office for applications. To learn about opportunities with state agencies, call the state personnel office and the agencies themselves, which are listed in the telephone book. Look at the state's manual to learn about state departments and services; any public library will have a copy of its own state manual and possibly other government directories. You will also find government entities on the Internet (see appendix 8 for details).

Visit the federal government's local Office of Personnel Management home page for federal openings at http://www.usajobs.opm.gov/. Federal offices are no longer required to use the laborious SF-171 application form but instead can accept résumés. Use the Internet and the *United States Government Manual* (1996), an annual you will find in most public libraries, and other publications to learn about federal government agencies.

Job Fairs

Associations, colleges, and some companies sponsor job fairs. Associations such as the Council of Jewish Federations, American Public Health Association, National Association of Black Social Workers, and NASW routinely or occasionally hold job fairs at their conferences (see appendix 1). College consortia, individual colleges, and some schools of social work organize job fairs for their students. Sometimes a job fair open to the public is announced in the local newspaper. These public events, which may involve a fee, are usually for technical, business, and health care fields.

Weighing the Cost of Travel

Job fairs held in conjunction with national conferences can be a good source of leads, particularly for social workers willing to relocate, but they can be expensive. Before you spend a lot of money to attend a national job fair, ask enough questions of the conference planners to know whether the trip is worth the cost. If a job fair is your sole purpose for attending the conference, get specifics ahead of time, such as the following:

• What is the structure of the event?
• Is it an exhibit format, in which you walk around introducing yourself?

- Do you submit résumés in response to jobs listed in a booklet you receive at the event, and then wait to hear from employers who want to interview you?
- Are onsite interviews arranged ahead of the event, so that you can judge whether the trip might be cost-effective?
- How many employers are expected to participate?
- What types of employers participate?
- What types of positions do employers list? Can you see the list in advance?
- Where are the employers located? Are most of these in the community near the conference site?

Surviving a Job Fair

People who have participated in job interviews at conferences can tell you that these are stressful experiences. When many job hunters are in a confined space waiting for an interview or a message from an employer, you can feel the tension. Here is some advice for increasing the benefits and reducing the stress.

- Approach the fair with a realistic attitude; do not count on the fair as your primary source of job opportunities but as one of several.
- Plan ahead. Research the organizations and try to arrange interviews in advance.
- Take extra résumés or vitae with you, paper for writing quick notes, and paperclips.
- Do not spend all of your time around the job fair; go to the sessions, participate in other conference activities, go to your room for a catnap, have coffee breaks with friends or read a good book, and leave the conference hall for meals and walks.
- Do not schedule too many interviews or back-to-back interviews. You'll wear yourself out.
- Pace yourself—it takes a lot of energy to be "on" all day.
- Get advice from others who have been through the process.

Job Hotlines

There are two national job hotlines specific to social work: NASW JobLink and DirecTree list a range of social work positions (see appendix 8).

Some large organizations, such as medical centers, government departments, and corporations, have job hotlines listing current openings. Call the employment office for the number or check a book that lists job hotlines, such as *The 1997 National Job Hotline Directory*, by Marcia P. Williams and Sue A. Cubbage (1997). Organized by state, the book gives telephone numbers for city, county, state, and federal government offices; hospitals and other health services; school systems; universities; insurance carriers; military bases; banks; and corporations. Two other books, *Government Job Finder* (1997) and *Non-Profits' Job Finder* (1994), by Daniel Lauder, list hotlines by subject area and geographic location. Job hunters do complain that hotline numbers are frequently busy, so try calling these 24-hour services at various times.

Mailing Campaign

Sending unsolicited letters with résumés can be effective in locating a job, if done selectively. Health and social services organizations often keep résumés on file and review these applications before advertising a job opening. Writing to employers who do not appear to have an opening can be productive for both local and long-distance job hunters, as part of an overall plan for direct practice positions, particularly at the entry level.

A warning: Quality is more important than quantity. Do not send standardized letters with résumés to 100 employers. You will be wasting time, money, and paper. Review the list of employers you created (see chapter 2). Group them into three categories: your first, second, and third choices. Then select three to five organizations and write specific letters to each (see appendix 5, sample 2). Often letters of inquiry go unanswered simply because employers do not have the time to respond. However, if you follow up with a telephone call and contact the employer periodically, you may be remembered when a job that matches your qualifications opens up.

Newsletters

Several professional societies, publishers, colleges, and nonprofit groups list job openings in newsletters and journals. *NASW News*, *Community Jobs*, and *Opportunity Nocs* are examples (see appendix 8 for a list of subscription newsletters). Before spending your hard-earned job-search funds on subscriptions, check your library and school of social work for the publications. You may even find that one of your contacts will share recent issues with you.

There are three concerns with taking out subscriptions or joining a professional society simply to receive a newsletter listing jobs. First, some newsletters, particularly those produced by professional societies, list fewer than 10 jobs an issue. For professional societies, the classified section of the newsletter is a courtesy, yet a minor function of the publication. Second, jobs are sometimes filled before the announcements come out, but keep in mind that it can take agencies two months to fill a job and, if the job is filled from within, another position may be opened. Third, in publications targeted for professionals in settings such as health, criminal justice, and public administration, where social workers are in the minority, many job listings will be irrelevant for social workers looking for direct practice positions. Review publications before you purchase them.

Newspapers

Obviously you will want to read the classified ads. Despite what you hear about the "hidden job market"—the view that only a small percentage of the available jobs are advertised—social services organizations are frequent users of classified advertising. BSW and MSW graduates, including those looking for director-level positions, can find jobs through the local newspaper. Besides scanning the job announcements, read feature articles, news articles, announcements of grants, and the society column for information on changes taking place in the community and for names for your contact network.

For distant locations, first check the Internet for newspaper home pages (see "Online Job Sources" in this chapter.) Remember that out-of-town newspaper subscriptions will arrive several days later in the mail. Your alternative is to visit the library or look for a newsstand in your local community that has papers shipped to them overnight so you can purchase the Sunday editions on Mondays.

Social workers will find possible jobs under many classified headings or keyword searches, such as those below; see also the job titles in appendix 4.

administration	fund-raising
alcoholism	health care
analyst	international
association	job development
BSW	management
case management	medical social work
case manager	mental health
clinical social worker	mental retardation
community development	MSW
community organizing	nonprofit
coordinator	planning
counselor	projects
development	research
director	social services
economic development	social work
education	social worker
employment	substance abuse
executive director	training

Online Job Sources

Services include job listings, résumé databases, career information, and organization information. Although services that are appropriate for social workers, particularly those in direct practice, are now limited, computerized social work information will very likely become more accessible in the future.

If you are associated with a university or a large employer, you probably have access to the Internet, through which you can reach various online services; some of these are free. If you do not have an organizational affiliation, you can pay to access online services through Prodigy, America OnLine, and CompuServe, among other servers. Or visit your public library or a "cyber cafe." It takes time to explore online sources; a friend with Internet experience or a reference librarian can speed up the process.

If you are considering using online services, look carefully at the potential before stretching your job-search budget. Some services are free, particularly those listing government information; others are fee-for-service businesses. If you surf the Internet, you may also find some job-listing services that are restricted to students and alumni of particular institutions. Even though the Internet may seem expedient, do not expect the hiring process to be so. One person identified a job in a distant city in February, but it took until May to receive an offer.

If you think you might want to subscribe to a job-listing service or a résumé databank, ask specific questions about openings and employer demand for résumés in your field. Most computerized services cater to technical and business clients; rarely do they have relevant information or sufficient volume to make it worth the expense for social workers. To get a sense of these resources, take a look at *The Guide to Internet Job Searching*, by Margaret Riley, Frances Roehm, and Steve Osennan (1996), *Electronic Job Search Revolution*, by Joyce Lain Kennedy and Thomas J. Morrow (1994), or *The Riley Guide* at http://www.dbm.com/jobguide/. Also see appendix 8.

Position-Wanted Ads

Many newsletters that list jobs also take classified ads from individuals looking for jobs (see the section on newsletters and publications listing jobs in appendix 8). Expect to pay a fee for this service. Again, carefully tailor your ad to the audience for that publication.

Résumé Databanks or Registries

Some nonprofit associations and for-profit companies offer résumé databanks or registries, which they make available to employers seeking candidates for jobs. You can submit your résumé, which goes into a computerized database or on a registration list. You may or may not be charged a fee for participating.

A few such services are relevant for social work. Among them are the National Association of Child Advocates, the Council of Jewish Federations, Family Service America, and CWSE. See appendix 1 for their addresses.

Like computerized job listings, most online résumé databases emphasize high-volume technical and business fields. If you are looking for opportunities in business, you might explore these services. Ask how many requests come in for your interest area and talk with your network to find out whether anyone has heard of the service. Like all other aspects of your communications, you will want to carefully tailor your résumé to the audience using that particular database. Remember that employers will use key words to search résumés, which means that you will want to use their language. Also note that you will need to prepare your résumé differently, depending on whether it will be scanned or entered online. Read *Electronic Resume Revolution* (Kennedy & Morrow, 1995) and *Electronic Resumes* (Gonyea & Gonyea, 1996) or visit the online *Riley Guide*.

Telephone Calls

Although many people are uncomfortable making cold calls to agencies to inquire about openings, such calls do generate job leads. Ask for a program director, clinical director, medical social work director, or other title pertinent to the kind of organization you are calling. When talking with people at agencies, focus on networking. Find out whether they have openings and ask whether they know of openings at other agencies. When you need a job quickly, there is nothing faster than making calls to agencies and to people on your contact list.

Remember that, as in any phase of your search, you are making an impression. Be prepared for a brief, to-the-point conversation, and at the same time be ready to discuss your interests, experience, and abilities (see chapter 1). If there is an opening, this call could serve as a screening interview. See chapter 5.

Temporary or Volunteer Work

Working on temporary, contract, *pro re nata* (PRN, or whenever necessary), postdegree internship, and volunteer jobs is a good way to get a foot in the door. If an organization that really interests you does not have a permanent opening and your situation is flexible, inquire about these short-term options. It is not uncommon for people seeking work with national advocacy groups; legislators in Washington, DC; or international organizations to use this method. For instance, a BSW graduate, while working on a postdegree internship at a nonprofit organization in DC, met a volunteer who worked in the federal government. His contact told him about an opportunity for a case worker handling correspondence at the White House. He got the position, and though it was not exactly what he wanted to do, it was a great position for learning about the executive branch, policy, and politics.

One of the great advantages social workers have is the ability to demonstrate their skills while volunteering. When you are between jobs, volunteer if you have the time and can make the commitment. Besides making a contribution, you will feel connected to the community, have a chance to exercise your skills, vary your daily routine of job hunting, and possibly learn about potential employers simply by being in that environment. When volunteering, take on extra responsibility, exercise good judgment, and get to know as much about the agency and the community as you can.

Pursuing Leads

When you hear about a potential job that you want to pursue; quickly gather some basic information; research the organization; and, if required, submit an application.

Screen Jobs

Because salaries and responsibilities vary greatly among social work employers, social workers often screen positions by first calling employers. Not everyone is comfortable using this technique, but for many it saves time. Talking with the person who will make the hiring decision is best; however, keep in mind that administrative assistants can also be helpful. When you call for information, be prepared to describe your qualifications briefly. Although you initiate the call, treat the conversation as a screening interview (see chapter 5). Make the best possible impression on anyone you speak with at the agency. Through this conversation you will want to

- determine whether you are interested in the position
- determine whether there is a possible match between you and the job
- request an interview if you are interested
- ask for a job description
- explore other potential options if the position is not of interest
- make a positive impression, regardless of the situation.

Gather basic information. If you want to pursue this job, find out the

- application deadline
- job description
- qualifications for the position
- contact's name, title, and telephone and fax numbers
- hiring timetable and whether there is an internal candidate.

The hiring timetable will tell you when they plan to interview candidates, if and when they will have second interviews, and when they will make their final decision.

Skip the Cover Letter and Go Directly to the Interview
Sometimes, if you are able to speak with the person doing the interviewing, you can set up an interview when you make that exploratory screening call. It will depend on how well your qualifications fit the employer's expectations, how effectively you present your qualifications over the telephone, and how soon the employer wants to fill the position. Although you may be able to bypass sending a letter with the résumé, take a résumé with you.

Explore options if the job does not fit your interests. If you discover the position is not what you are looking for, you can

- find out whether the position's responsibilities can be expanded
- ask to be considered for future possibilities related to your interests, and follow up with a letter and résumé
- ask for advice on seeking a more appropriate position in the field or community.

Should you apply even if you do not meet all of the qualifications? Yes, when the agency and type of work is of great interest to you and you meet most of the qualifications, go ahead and apply. In your letter, state your interest in the organization and indicate that you would like to be considered in the future for positions appropriate for your background. It is possible that the current opening will be filled by a present employee, which might leave another position open that is appropriate for you.

Should you apply even if you are not available now? Yes. It can take an employer two months to fill a position, particularly during the summer and around the holidays, when many staff take vacations. Indicate in your letter when you will be available, and state that if your availability and their timetable do not coincide, you would like to be considered for future openings. If you can start earlier on a part-time basis, say so in your letter. However, if it will be six months before you are available, file the information and contact the employer at a later date.

Research the Organization

Research the organization before applying by looking at the community service directory, requesting a brochure or annual report, picking up brochures at the site, and talking with your contacts. When possible, speak with clients, constituents, and colleagues associated with the organization. This information will enable you to tailor your letter and telephone conversations.

Also, try locating newspaper and magazine articles on the organization at the public library or look for home pages and other background information on the Internet. This is especially important if you are applying for a position with a large or well-known employer (for example, United Way, American Red Cross, or a state child welfare department). If your local or campus library has Nexus, an online information service, use it to locate articles. Even though you may not find articles written about the specific organization unit, chapter, or site you want to research, you will get some ideas about the accomplishments and issues facing similar units; the organization as a whole; or a parent company, in the case of a for-profit organization.

Unfortunately, ideal circumstances that allow plenty of time to research the organization are often out of reach. You could meet someone today who tells you about an opening with an application deadline of tomorrow. You will be lucky if he or she knows the correct spelling of the contact person's name and the address. If possible, call the organization, confirm the fact that there is an opening, and ask for details.

When time is short, deliver a letter and résumé in person. Or ask if you can fax a résumé to the employer or send a letter and résumé through e-mail. Include a letter with the fax unless time is short. Call the organization to make sure the fax or e-mail was received. Also send a hard copy by mail.

Cover Letters

Sometimes an exploratory call to an employer will result in an immediate job interview. In most cases, however, you will send a letter and résumé as a formal application. Each cover letter must be written specifically to the employer, using a person's name and addressing the organization's interests.

As a social worker, you have three advantages in writing cover letters. First, you can express and demonstrate a commitment to your work that sets you apart from applicants educated in other disciplines. Second, your social work education encompasses both micro-level and macro-level knowledge, giving you a broad understanding of systems and the issues facing organizations. You can bring knowledge of service delivery to a macro-level organization or macro-level function and you can bring knowledge of policy and funding to direct services. Third, if you are a BSW or MSW student, you are likely to have more hours of specific, well-monitored training in the field than students with other backgrounds.

Plan a Strategy for Your Letter

A résumé is a summary of what you have to offer; a cover letter is a very selective statement interpreting your experience for a specific employer. You can prepare a few stock paragraphs for a cover letter, which can be adapted to various situations. However, the letter should always have a single, unique reader in mind. It should go beyond the surface facts of when you graduate (if you are a student), what experience you've had, and how you heard about the job.

To produce a letter that will interest employers, you need to know their needs. Your research on organizations may not reveal specific details, but you can work from your knowledge of common issues facing the field. Consider the following:

- What issues have an impact on this organization or service?
- What are the unique characteristics of this kind of service?
- What are the primary functions and skills of the position?
- How can your knowledge, skills, experience, and interests solve problems and improve services or operations?

Prioritize your qualifications according to the position's requirements and then select your best playing cards for your letter. Tying your background to the employer's needs is the initial step in persuading an employer to identify with you. See sample letters 2, 3, and 4 in appendix 5.

Follow a Format

A traditional cover letter addresses four subjects: (1) why you are writing and how you heard about the position, (2) your related qualifications, (3) your interest in the organization, and (4) what you expect to happen next in the hiring process. In most cases each subject will have its own paragraph. Limit your letter to one page.

In the first paragraph, state why you are writing and how you heard about the position. If you had a conversation with the employer or an assistant, indicate that you are following up the discussion. For example, "Following up our phone conversation on January 20, I am submitting a résumé for the clinical social work opening." If someone suggested you contact the agency, put that person's name in the first sentence (for example, "James Hill, professor at Krane University's School of Social Work, suggested I contact you").

Summarize your related qualifications in the second paragraph. Emphasize your skills, knowledge, accomplishments, and what you can bring to the organization. Lead with your strongest qualification for the situation. That might be a range of experience, in which case you would open with a summary statement that sets the stage—for example, "My twelve years of experience include work with an inpatient hospital psychiatric unit, community mental health clinic, and family service agency." Or your strength might be experience with an organization known to the employer or a job performing the same function in a related area (see sample letter 4 in appendix 5). Follow your opening statement with other highlights related to the opening. You might say that "at Baron Medical Center, I served as interim supervisor for six months." If your salary history or salary expectation is requested in an advertisement, many people in the field of career development recommend that you not give specifics. You can say that your salaries have been commensurate with the position and that you are seeking a salary consistent with the market and your qualifications.

In paragraph 3 briefly express your interest in the organization. Take what you know about the organization or the field if you cannot locate specifics, and briefly indicate why you are interested or committed to that work. Keep your statements positive and realistic (see the sample letters in appendix 5). You may know from your research that the last director left under adverse circumstances. You certainly will not mention that in the letter, but you will talk about your interest in the organization's work.

Paragraph 4 is an action statement. The action statement is often a request for an interview, but many candidates take the initiative themselves, saying that they will call the employer in a few days (with the intent to arrange an interview). If you are not certain that you will be able to follow up with a call, do not say you will in the letter. You can refer to the résumé you enclose in this last paragraph or in paragraph one or two. If someone with a good connection to the organization is willing to put in a good word for you, mention the person's name in the final paragraph.

Other Important Points for Your Cover Letter

Use Column Format for a Specific Opening

You can replace the second paragraph with a list of requirements for the opening in a column on the left side of the page and your corresponding qualifications briefly stated on the right side. Each requirement should have a matching qualification. A social worker who has worked for several managed care companies found that this style worked well in her latest search. Note, however, that this format does not scan well.

Address a Specific Person

When you do not have the name of the person you need to address, call the organization's switchboard and request the appropriate name and title. Occasionally, telephone calls and networking fail to produce a name. When all else fails, address the letter to the executive director, clinical director, director of medical social work, and so on. However, don't make this a practice: This should be a rare exception, not a rule, for your correspondence.

Edit Your Letters Carefully

- Use "I" in a limited number of sentences.
- Using a highlighter, mark the most important words on your draft, and then try to eliminate as many extra words as possible.
- It is very easy to overuse words. Check to ensure that you don't.
- Be sure that your letter demonstrates enthusiasm.
- Look for any negative statements and rephrase them in positive terms or delete them.
- Use a natural, conversational tone and vocabulary.

Follow up your letter. If you are comfortable calling an employer, follow up your letter with a brief call. This call will be similar to the type of call that you would make to screen a job. Express your interest in the job and request an interview.

References

Boldt, L. G. (1993). *Zen and the art of making a living: A practical guide to creative career design.* New York: Arkana.

Bolles, R. N. (1997). *What color is your parachute? A practical manual for job-hunters and career-changers.* Berkeley, CA: Ten Speed Press.

Boston University, School of Social Work. (1996). *Survey of career development services within graduate schools of social work.* Boston: Author.

Boyd, K. (1996). There is a job market for BSW graduates! *New Social Worker, 3,* 18–19.

Burke, K. K. (Ed.). (1997). *The directory of executive recruiters* (26th ed.). Fitzwilliam, NH: Kennedy Publications.

Gonyea, J. C., & Gonyea, W. M. (1996). *Electronic resumes: A complete guide to putting your resume on-line.* New York: McGraw-Hill.

Grobman, G. (1997). *The nonprofit handbook* (national ed.). Harrisburg, PA: White Hat Communications.

Hakim, C. (1995). *We are all self-employed: The new social contract for working in a changed world.* San Francisco: Berrett-Koehler.

Helfand, D. P. (1995). *Career change: Everything you need to know to meet new challenges and take control of your career.* Chicago: VGM Career Horizons.

Hull, G. H., Jr., Ray, J., Rogers, J., & Smith, M. (1992, Fall). Revised BPD outcomes instrument findings initial report. *BPD Forum,* 28–41.

Kennedy, J. L., & Morrow, T. J. (1994). *Electronic job search revolution: How to win with the new technology that's reshaping today's job market.* New York: John Wiley & Sons.

Kennedy, J. L., & Morrow, T. J. (1995). *Electronic resume revolution: Creating a resume for the new world of job seeking* (2nd ed.). New York: John Wiley & Sons.

Larson, J., & Comstock, C. (1994). *The new rules of the job search game: Why today's mangers hire . . . and why they don't.* Newton, MA: Adams.

Lauder, D. (1994). *Non-profits' job finder, 1994–1995* (3rd ed.). River Forest, IL: Planning/Communications.

Lauder, D. (1997). *Government job finder: 1997–2000* (3rd ed.). River Forest, IL: Planning/Communications.

Riley, M., Roehm, F., & Osennan, S. (1996). *The guide to Internet job searching.* Chicago: VGM Career Horizons.

The Riley guide. Available online at http://www.dbm.com/jobguide/.

The United States government manual. (1996). Washington, DC: Office of the Federal Register.

Wendleton, K. (1993). *Through the brick wall: How to job hunt in a tight market.* New York: Random House.

Williams, M. P., & Cubbage, S. A. (1997). *The 1997 national job hotline directory.* New York: McGraw-Hill.

CHAPTER 4 QUICK TIPS: Identifying Jobs and Pursuing Leads

Here are some suggestions if you must find a position quickly.

- Get on the PRN lists for hospitals and social work temporary agencies.

- Start the application process for the social services organizations that have the highest turnover rates.

- Update your contact network list and call everyone. Besides telling them that you are looking for full-time work, ask them about contract work. Ask yourself whom you know or have met that does not know you are looking; contact them.

- Start calling every organization doing something related to your qualifications and every organization related to your interests.

- Find a job-hunters club. If you cannot find one through professional groups or your university, religious organization, or chamber of commerce, consider forming one.

- Put yourself on a strict schedule. When you are not calling contacts and organizations or replying to openings, research organizations, update your knowledge of developments in the field, and polish your message. Call search firms if you have management experience.

- Draft a letter, which you can tailor as needed, following the outline of those in appendix 5.

Interviewing Effectively

Ideally, the interview is a two-way street: It is a comfortable conversation between two individuals with similar interests. Your social work training in interviewing skills will be a great advantage in achieving this effect. Just as being an effective client interviewer took preparation and practice, so will being an effective job interviewee.

Planning Your Agenda

Go into your interviews with a plan. Think about five things you want the interviewers to know about you and five things you want to know about them. Five is just a guideline; it could be four or eight—that is up to you. This outline will help you concentrate on your agenda and approach the interviewer as an equal.

What You Want the Employer to Know about You

Think carefully about the message you want to convey to the employer—make it a theme that you continually present and support throughout the interview. Job hunters often focus on a theme that presents how they work or their work style, which of course is important. For example, an upper-level manager presented himself as a loyal, stable, straight shooter who kept management informed, thought in terms of the big picture, and liked to work on the cutting edge and face challenges, seeing tough problems as opportunities.

Reprinted with permission. Doelling, C. N. (1996, Fall). Strategies for the job interview. *The New Social Worker*, 3(2), 19–21. ©1996, White Hat Communications.

This style was manifested in the numerous accomplishments he wove into the interview and outlined in his résumé. Many social workers, however, simply focus on presenting a work style, making the false assumption that content—knowledge, skills, and accomplishments—

Day Treatment

culturally sensitive practice expertise

individual and family therapy experience

knowledge of development issues

work with emotionally disturbed youths

Medical Social Work

experience on neonatal and pediatric units

emergency department experience

discharge planning

work with an interdisciplinary team

like a fast-paced environment

work with families in crisis

Policy Analyst

concise, quick, clear writing

experience writing fact sheets, option papers, and sound bites

understand the big picture

broad knowledge of social issues and policies

high threshold for frustration; have a long-term outlook

astute learner; enjoy studying the opposition

Clinical Social Work Supervisor

licensed clinical social worker

member of the Academy of Certified Social Workers

[number] years of experience providing brief strategic and longer-
   term therapy

provided in-service training

supervised practicum students for [number] years

Gerontological Social Worker

knowledge of Medicare and Medicaid

experience with clients who have Alzheimer's disease

strong assessment skills

understanding of the dual role of working with elders and families

experience with many ethical dilemmas

will be evident on the résumé. Here are some examples of types of jobs individuals considered and the key content points they stressed during interviews.

One new graduate interviewed for a fellowship with an adolescent mental health program. The program entailed clinical work in an outpatient setting and a diagnostic clinic for developmental disabilities, as well as work at a Job Corps program. The applicant stressed the assessment and treatment planning skills she had developed in a community mental health practicum, experience with interventions used during a practicum at an adolescent shelter, knowledge of developmental disabilities gained as a part-time respite worker for families of children with autism, knowledge of adolescent issues, and leadership experience in student government.

Tailor your qualifications list to the specific employer. For example, if you are looking at entry-level positions as a policy analyst in a nonprofit advocacy organization and in government, your list will be slightly different for each setting. In a nonprofit policy office, you may be asked to quickly write several possible sound bites about a piece of legislation for a news conference. In the federal government, you will not write sound bites, but you will need to be adept at teamwork. Again, your network of advisers and contacts can help you tailor your list.

The more you can anticipate the needs of particular employers, the better you can tailor your list. Listen to what those in the field say about their needs. For example, a director of social work services at a large university medical center looks for the following when selecting supervisors.

> *I look primarily at two criteria. The first is technical competence. Often this person will have patient responsibilities concurrent with supervisory responsibilities, so I look at the scope, complexity, and depth of past responsibilities. Has the person dealt with broad and diverse circumstances? Is he or she agile—does he or she respond well to spontaneous situations? If the person has not had direct patient responsibilities, I consider the complexity of the work history—experiences that required adaptability. I want to determine how quickly and effectively this person can become acclimated to a new setting and apply existing skills. This person must be less prone to making mistakes, for he or she will set the example. A sound thought process is a necessity—I must be able to depend on this person's ability to make accurate decisions. If the person has good clinical experience, the more likely he or she will be able to understand situations and make appropriate decisions.*

The second criterion is the ability to lead—to organize work and shepherd, encourage, and monitor staff. How much experience has the person had in leading people? What were the contexts and results? Was this experience in the same type of setting, with similar levels of staff, a similar number of subordinates, the same mix of part-time and full-time staff with similar shifts? All of these details tell me about the person's knowledge of the issues inherent in this position. What are this person's expectations—will he or she be able to meet those expectations here or be amenable to change? Is this person unflappable? Does he or she have the stamina to handle negative reactions to his or her own ideas? This person must be able to buy into a culture of excellence. Will he or she be part of the team pursuing that goal? Can he or she lead a mix of personalities in pursuit of that goal? Can the person accomplish this in a complex organization, a fluid environment of perpetual change, providing services that have significant consequences for clients and providers? Will this person be able to maneuver staff who have their own agendas to participate in a consensus process, deal with change, and as a team advance patient care?

What You Want to Know about the Employer and the Position

The second item on your agenda is determining whether the position and organization are a good match for you. What are you looking for in a position and organization? Think about a model organization in your field of interest, then come up with a list of questions (see chapter 2 and appendix 4). For more ideas, talk with people in your network who know your field and possibly the organization you are interviewing with. Request a brochure on the program. If it is an organization that publishes reports, review them. See appendix 7 for a sample list of information you might gather.

In addition to reviewing materials and asking some questions during interviews, use your observational skills; look at facilities, personalities, energy levels, interactions, office arrangements, and location. How sensitive are the staff to the clients? Does the agency staff or social work department appear to be a cohesive group?

Preparation

You can expect a variety of questions during interviews—hypothetical questions; questions about work habits; questions about specific knowledge of issues, populations, policies, methods, and evaluation;

and questions about likes and dislikes, future goals, strengths and weaknesses, and so on. The following sections give suggestions on responding to questions. See appendix 7 for additional questions social workers have encountered in interviews.

Goals for an Interview

Employers of social workers are similar to most other employers. They seek candidates with related experience, honesty and stability, maturity, commitment, skills and knowledge, direction, a high energy level, and familiarity with their organization's work. Specific advice from employers follows.

Interpret Your Experience

"You need to convey a view of the world, in other words, go beyond describing the who, what, and where of your qualifications," recommends a clinical director of a youth service. Anyone can read your résumé for the what and when of your experience. Employers, however, are looking for you to interpret your experience, requiring you to think, summarize, and analyze your qualifications. Explain what you think, what you learned, and what you believe works and why.

"Take the pieces of what you have done and find the common thread that demonstrates you are analytical, can assimilate information, and so on," advises a vice president of a large funding agency.

A vice president of a community mental health agency suggests "Think about what you have done that applies. If you have worked at the agency before, stress the fact that you know the agency and the population it serves. Many interviewers will describe the agency and the position early in the interview. Throughout the rest of the interview, relate your experience directly back to the information you were given."

Do not take for granted that the interviewers have thought carefully about how your background fits their needs, that they remember anything from your résumé, or that they have even read your cover letter and résumé.

Present a Clear Direction

As best you can, be clear with yourself about what you do and do not want in a job. One interviewer stresses that you "be honest about client populations with whom you do not want to work." This should be done in a professional way. If you learn in the interview that some clients in your caseload are known sex offenders and you do not want to work with this population, state that you do not think you could work effectively with that population. Your research on organizations should help you screen out those jobs that are not a good fit for you.

Demonstrate Your Motivation and Commitment
Explain what motivates you to pursue this work and how you have
demonstrated your commitment. If you changed your career path,
articulate your motivations for your new direction. How have you
backed up your commitment to this work through jobs, professional activities, practica, and volunteer work?

Convey Maturity and Sound Judgment Skills
At all times demonstrate that you can fill the role required of the
position. This is especially important when you are attempting to
move across functions, for example, from direct practice to supervision, or fields. Make it clear that you understand the ethical dilemmas, the impact of funding sources and shifting policies on services,
differences in philosophies, complexities of evaluation methods, and
specific issues facing this particular field of social services.

In describing decisions you made in seeking funding, designing
a treatment plan, dealing with a crisis situation, building an effective board, or whatever efforts your work demanded, you can present
the employer with a picture of how you approach your work and
the depth of your understanding of the employer's concerns.

"Appreciate what you do not know about practice, and at the
same time show that you are confident. An unbeatable combination is someone who conveys confidence but knows that he or she
has a lot to learn," counsels a clinical director.

Practice Interviews

Without careful forethought, it is difficult to be spontaneous, confident, and organized in your discussion. Here are some suggestions for practice.

- Prepare a two- or three-sentence statement about each item on
  your résumé.
- For each category of jobs you are considering, outline your
  related work or practica experience, knowledge and skills gained,

One job candidate who was interviewing for a position working with families in crisis did not have family therapy experience, which was important to the job. However, she had worked
with children whose parents were going through separation and
divorce. She stressed her skills in helping families stabilize and
make transitions. She successfully convinced the interviewers
of her ability to handle crises and achieve resolution.

relevant coursework taken, and any leadership experience. This will help you organize your thoughts and enable you to highlight specific qualifications. Review this outline often. If you did the exercises in chapter 1, refer to them.

- Daydream your interviews. It's fun and great practice. If you were the employer, what would you ask?
- Practice interviews with friends. Ask them to play different roles: unorganized interviewer, friendly interviewer, aloof interviewer, abrupt interviewer, unexpected caller. One social worker recommends taping your answers to questions.
- Think about what excites you about the area of social work you have chosen. Convey this enthusiasm through your attitude and responses to interview questions.
- Review notes from your previous interviews.
- Visualize a scene in which you smile, introduce yourself, give a firm handshake, and when asked to take a seat, select an upright chair that puts you on the same level as the interviewer. View the end of the interview, as you remind the employer why you are the best candidate, inquire about the next step in the selection process, shake hands, and leave.

In the current job market you should look widely for opportunities, but do not interview just for practice. Interview only if you have a sincere interest in the job—do not waste your colleagues' time by interviewing for positions you know you do not want. Instead, thank that employer for the invitation and ask whether he or she has any suggestions for identifying an appropriate opportunity.

Difficult Questions

Common Questions

Several interview questions that are frequently asked often stump candidates. Most are dealt with in the following paragraphs. How much you say in response to the questions is up to you—the suggestions below are designed simply to get you in the habit of making well-thought-out, concise, targeted statements. Practicing responses and varying them to fit a variety of employers will help you develop a conversational interview style and avoid "canned" answers. None of the questions is as general as it may sound. All of them should be answered in terms of the position in question.

"What is your career goal?" Prepare a concise statement describing what type of work you would like to do. "My goal is to work with an employee assistance program where I can use my experience in mental health and chemical dependency treatment and have an

opportunity to do some training and marketing. In the future I hope to manage an EAP."

"Tell me about yourself." Prepare a four- or five-sentence statement on your professional development to date. "As you know, I will complete the MSW program in December; my interest is domestic violence. I started the program with work experience in developmental disabilities and volunteer experience with a women's shelter. My practica entailed crisis intervention and counseling with women and program planning and administration for a shelter. I also assisted a faculty member who was studying policy issues and domestic violence. And at this point I am looking for an opportunity to do direct practice, possibly combined with program planning."

"What are your skills?" Prepare a concise statement of your best skills that relate to the job. This should focus on social work skills, but you may include a sentence describing pertinent transferable skills and work habits. "I had wonderful practicum experiences that developed my confidence in my assessment skills, my ability to intervene in a crisis situation, my knowledge of discharge planning, and my ability to work effectively with the medical staff. I feel I am really ready to work in medical social work."

"What are your strengths?" Prepare two or three sentences on your strengths in terms of the job: experience, knowledge, and skills. Although you want to focus on your social work strengths, you can also weave life experience, previous career experience, and work habits into your statement. "I would say my strengths are in the management of mental health facilities, particularly in fiscal management and fund-raising. I have considerable experience in clinical program and staff development. And people have complimented me on my ability to rebuild programs and staff morale."

"What are your weaknesses?" This is asked to ascertain your level of self-awareness, not to undermine you. Prepare two or three sentences on your weaknesses. The director of a community mental health center recommends focusing on a professional area of knowledge that you have not been able to concentrate on and wish to develop. Use positive language. Be sure that you follow through on your efforts to improve. If an employer hires you, they are likely to watch for results. "My work has been primarily in child welfare case management. Though I use my family therapy knowledge, I know I still have skills to develop in that area. I have attended several workshops and read books, and I hope to enroll in a certificate program next fall."

Hypothetical Questions

Expect employers to present hypothetical situations; your responses can reveal not only specific problem-solving skills but approaches to making decisions. In your answer, don't try to offer the solution; just describe your approach.

- *Context: Supervisory position for an elder residential center.* "What if one of the people you supervise lied, mistreated a client, or breached confidentiality? What would you do? What if you saw a person who was supervised by someone else do the same thing? What would you do?"
- *Context: Women's shelter.* "A woman comes in. What would you first say to her?" The response will reveal to the interviewer the candidate's philosophy. Does the candidate start by describing the rules of the shelter or by telling the woman that what brought her here was not her fault?
- *Context: Youth outreach program.* "A youth, whom you do not know, approaches you in a park and says that his parents locked him out of the house. What would you say? What issues would you be thinking about?"
- *Context: Outreach program for families in crisis* (this question was posed to an African American candidate). "Someone with whom you have been working, a white woman, says, 'I don't think you can understand what I am going through.' How would you respond?"
- *Context: In-home therapy services.* "You are visiting a client family in their home when one person becomes very agitated. You are concerned about violence. What would you do?"

Improper Interview Questions*

"The aide prepared me. He said the senator really wants to get to know people before he hires them and that he might ask me personal questions. I knew that I would not get the job if I did not answer the questions."

---

*This section attempts to give you some general information and explore the subject of potentially illegal questions in social work–related settings, but it is not written as legal advice. Employment law is complex, dependent on federal court interpretation and varying from state to state. For more specific or updated information, contact the federal Equal Employment Opportunity Commission (EEOC) office, local state human relations offices, or a legal expert.

Like this social worker seeking a legislative assistant position, you will want to be prepared for potentially illegal or inappropriate interview questions or both. Social workers have encountered them in large and small agencies when interviewing for direct practice positions, as well as in interviews with elected representatives for policy-related positions. It is important to educate yourself on these issues and have some ideas about how you will handle questions comfortably. At the same time, try not to let concerns over anticipated questions prevent you from focusing on the purpose of your interview.

What Subjects Are Prohibited

Title VII of the Civil Rights Act of 1964 established that employers could not discriminate on the basis of race, color, religion, national origin, or sex in hiring or use discriminatory practices in hiring. The Age Discrimination in Employment Act of 1967 prohibited discrimination on the basis of age (over 40), and the Americans with Disabilities Act of 1990 further delineated physical and mental disabilities as issues of discrimination in hiring. The EEOC issued statements of "enforcement guidance" regarding discriminatory hiring practices including what questions it considered evidence of discrimination in the hiring process. EEOC regulations stated that questions employers use in the selection process should pertain to the requirements of the position and must be asked of all candidates. Case law has further defined legal issues around the hiring process. For further information on the subject, take a look at the EEOC Web site at http://www.eeoc.gov (see "Press Releases" and "Laws Enforced by the EEOC").

This section on improper interview questions attempts to give you some general information and explore the subject of improper questions in social work–related settings.

Age
An employer may ask whether a candidate is over the age of 18 but should not ask other questions to identify a candidate's age, nor can the employer indicate a preference for an age group. Once an individual is hired, the employer can ask for age or date of birth when the employee is signing up for benefits.

Arrests
Generally, and for most positions, questions may not focus on an arrest record, but interviewers may inquire about convictions.

Citizenship
An employer should not ask whether you are a U.S. citizen. Once a position is offered, the employer must verify your personal identifi-

cation and your right to work in the United States. You can be asked whether your visa status prevents you from being lawfully employed.

Convictions

Questions about circumstances surrounding a conviction may be asked if they are asked of all candidates and if the information has a bearing on job performance.

Disabilities

Questions regarding ability to perform essential functions of the job may be asked.

Education and Credentials

Questions on training and experience related to the position's requirements are fine. An employer may ask whether you have the certification or licensure necessary for the position or whether you intend to obtain certification or licensure.

Family

Employers may not ask questions regarding family planning, family size, children's ages, child care plans, or spouse's employment or salary. You can be asked about your ability to travel and to work the schedule required for the job; however, these questions must be asked of all candidates.

Health, Including Mental Health

Pre-employment questions regarding health status cannot be asked. Nor can employers ask whether you have received psychiatric care. However, you can be given a drug test.

Height and Weight

An employer cannot ask specifically about height or weight. There may be exceptions to this outside most social work positions.

Marital Status

Nothing can be asked about marital status, including whether you are engaged.

Name

An employer should not ask what your maiden name was.

National Origin

You can be asked questions regarding your facility with English or another language if required for the job. Questions regarding ancestry, birthplace, parents, or spouse are generally inappropriate. For instance, during an interview for a faculty position, a doctoral student whose résumé indicated that she had studied abroad was asked where her family was from. This was a potentially problematic question.

Organizations
Nothing can be asked about organizational affiliations that might indicate race, color, creed, sex, marital status, religion (see "Religion" below), or national origin. You can be asked about memberships with professional organizations, but questions about political leanings or your political-party affiliations are improper for most jobs. However, positions that involve national security are exempt.

Pregnancy
You can be asked how long you expect to stay in a position and whether you anticipate any absences. However, these questions must be asked of all candidates and may pose problems regarding motive.

Religion
Questions regarding religion cannot be asked, but an employer can ask whether you anticipate absences from work or about your ability to meet the work schedule. However, religiously based social services and other religious institutions are exempt from these restrictions under Title VII. They may ask you questions related to religion and make a decision to hire based on your religious beliefs.

When Questions May Be a Problem

When you are networking, you may encounter questions about where you are from, your family, and your personal plans. You may or may not feel comfortable with these topics, but because they are not being raised during a job selection process, they are probably not subject to challenge in this context.

Questions about the subjects listed in the previous section pose a problem if they are used during the selection process. This applies to screening interviews in person or over the telephone, job applications, formal job interviews, and informal conversations while visiting employers for the purpose of being considered for a position (including conversations during meals and trips to the airport, for example). Exceptions are affirmative action forms or equal employment opportunity questionnaires, which collect data on particular groups and enable employers to keep track of their progress in affirmative action recruiting. The forms might ask date of birth, marital status, number of dependent children, ethnicity, whether you have a disability, and whether you need accommodation if you have a disability.

These forms should be handled by the personnel staff; they should not be distributed to those making the hiring decision. Sometimes the affirmative action form accompanies the application, in which case you may want to mail the form separately from the application.

Difficult Choices: Handling Questions

First, decide ahead of time how you want to respond to questionable or inappropriate inquiries. Some social workers decide that they are not interested in working for an organization that inquires into personal background. Others decide that the job opportunity is more important to them than the inappropriateness of the questions and choose to answer the questions. Still others try to appreciate the concerns of employers and assure them that the requirements of the job will be met.

Second, be an attentive listener. It is easy to be caught off guard. A doctoral student who was applying for academic positions received a call at 7:30 AM. The person calling, the dean of a school of social work, asked the student whether she had any children. The student, who was barely thinking at this hour, found herself answering the question before she was fully aware of what was happening.

Third, keep the tone of the interview positive. Although you may be irritated by a question, want to ignore a question, or tell the interviewer what you really think about a question, consider the consequences carefully. You do not want to put the interviewer on the defensive or create a hostile atmosphere. Even if you decide that you have no interest in working for this organization, your work in the professional community or field may include interactions with the staff. Also, remember that many social services agencies do not have the benefit of a human resources specialist or training in interviewing techniques for its staff. As a result you may encounter an inexperienced interviewer who asks inappropriate or awkward questions.

Ask for clarification. "Can you tell me how this is important or related to the job?" or "May I ask how this might be helpful in selecting a candidate?" Here is an example of an inappropriate question and response: "Let's do a genogram of your family." "You mean do I know how to use a genogram?"

Fourth, respond to the concern. You can identify the concern of the employer and respond by reframing the question. "I understand that I would be consulting with nursing homes throughout the state. The travel is not a concern for me; in fact, I think I would enjoy it." "I am familiar with the ethical issues surrounding religion and the medical model such as . . . ."

Fifth, redirect the interview. Your training in interviewing should aid you in facilitating the interview process. Use a transition in your response. End with a question for the interviewer, an illustration of your work, or comment on an accomplishment that refocuses him or her on the position and your qualifications; for instance, "I know how to use a genogram; let me tell you about a particular case for which I used a genogram."

Sixth, remember that you have the right not to respond to a question if you choose. If you have attempted to clarify the question and addressed the concern but the interviewer persists with an inappropriate question, you can certainly choose not to respond. Just remember to keep your response professional, polite: "I would prefer not to respond to that particular question" or "That is not something I feel comfortable sharing." Then move on by redirecting the interview.

Responding to Particular Questions

The following paragraphs discuss some particular questions that social workers encounter during the hiring process. This discussion is meant to increase awareness but not to provide legal advice. If you have questions, consult the EEOC, state human relations office, or a legal expert.

"Have You Been through Your Own Therapy?"
This question is commonly used in clinical social work settings. However, such questions may violate federal or state laws. Think carefully about how you respond to this question. If you choose to respond, keep your response simple; do not state why you sought therapy. If you choose not to respond directly, you might indicate that you recognize your professional responsibility for your own issues and their possible impact on clients.

"Tell Me about Your Family."
When a group of family therapists was asked for their recommendations on handling this inquiry, they suggested the following. Consider treating it lightly and as well-intentioned. Respond with "all is well," and redirect the discussion by focusing on your knowledge of families.

"Are You Pro-Choice or Pro-Life?"
If these questions are work related or the organization has a religious affiliation, interviewers may ask these questions and consider the response in the hiring decision process. In addition, you can be asked whether you are willing to follow the agency's stand on this subject.

"Do You Belong to a (Church)?"
Sectarian agencies can ask questions on religious affiliation and take this information into consideration when selecting candidates.

What You Can Do to Minimize Unwanted Questions

- Do not put personal information such as marital status, number of children, height, weight, or health status on your résumé or vita.

- Develop a rapport with the interviewer. If he or she trusts you and has a positive feeling about you, the need for personal information may not seem necessary. Leave no doubts that you are trustworthy, use good judgment, make an effort to engage others, know when to listen, have experience with ethical dilemmas, appreciate team efforts, and can take the lead when necessary.

- Anticipate issues. Before an interview, think about any items in the job description, your background, or on your résumé that might prompt an illegal, inappropriate, or awkward question. For example, your name may be hyphenated, possibly indicating that you are married. Incorporate information throughout the interview that stresses your professionalism and addresses any concerns before the interviewer brings them up. This does not mean that you should reveal information or bring up unnecessary information, although you have the right to volunteer information that an employer cannot ask questions about. If the job requires you to be on call, for example, you might say, "I understand this position would require me to carry a beeper. That is not a concern for me; however, I would like to know more about how that works." If the job requires travel, you could say, "One of the reasons I am interested in this position is the travel" or "In my previous position I traveled; I am looking forward to doing that again." If the position is in clinical social work, you could say that "I know that as a professional it is very important to be aware of one's own issues and how they can affect work with clients. I feel this is an ongoing process and work hard to be aware of my own situation and its possible impact on my work."

Pitfalls

Be sure that the language you choose to describe your experience, accomplishments, and philosophy conveys the exact meaning and attitude you intend. In the interview situation, it is easy to use trite or vague phrases, overexplain a situation, or try to impress the interviewer with a poorly thought-out response.

Keep Your Comments Positive, Serious, and Honest

Do not generalize about individuals, groups of people, or institutions. For example, phrases such as "men are just horrible" and "corporations are the problem" do not indicate that you can be counted on to interact effectively with board members, elected representatives, funders, members of the public, or clients.

As a general rule, do not joke with interviewers. Respond to questions seriously and sincerely. Although you may have a great sense of humor, be careful how you show it during interviews. If you are asked, "Why are you interested in our organization?" responding with "Your location is only an hour away from the ski slopes" probably will not make the impression you desire.

Be honest. If you do not have an answer, do not bluff. You can say: "I don't know." "I don't think I have encountered that." "I have heard of that, but I am not familiar enough with the issues to respond at this time." "I have some familiarity with that. My understanding is [briefly outline a couple of issues or points]." "I have not worked with that issue directly, but this is how I would approach it."

Avoid Problematic Phrases

"I want to bring humanity to the field." "Mainstreaming is the way to go for all kids." "[Whatever approaches] are the only approaches." Be careful about speaking in generalities or making absolute statements. They can come across as naive or narrow minded, and they do not reflect well on your education, analytical thinking, and judgment. Here are some examples.

- "Our children are our future." OK, but what do you want to do about it?
- "I am fluent in [whatever approach] treatment method." What does that mean? Does it mean that you have used the method with clients for many years and now train others in the approach? It is better to specify your degree of direction.
- "I want to help people" or "I like people." These are vague phrases often used by people with limited experience or by those who don't know how to articulate their direction.
- "At first I was gullible." Inexperienced social workers commonly have difficulty judging situations and a clients' actions and verbal responses. Rather than using the term "gullible," which might leave a lasting impression, put your experience in context. "Like many new social workers, it took me a while to recognize when a client was being manipulative. I feel confident in my ability to recognize when this is happening now."

- "I don't know whether you know about this, but . . . ." Assume that your interviewer is up-to-date on policy controversies, current community issues, new programs, and treatment developments.
- "I plan to enter a doctoral program in a couple of years." This statement indicates your limited interest in the job at hand. Focus your discussion on the present. If your long-term goals do not serve the employer's interests, it is better not to mention them. You may unintentionally hit a raw nerve. One employer at a community mental health center said, "If [one more] person says, 'I want to start a private practice in a few years,' I'll throw up."

Focus on Professional, Not Personal, Information

Do you reveal personal characteristics or experiences that explain your motivation for entering the field, your commitment to your work, or knowledge of a particular issue? It is best to separate your professional self from your personal self, particularly in job interviews.

Do not express your feelings about negative personal issues or professional experiences during an interview. These are red flags to employers, indicating that you are not ready to move forward, that your attitude will affect staff cohesion, or that you may not be approachable. If you need to describe a negative incident, do so objectively and indicate that you have looked back on the experience and have learned from it.

As one clinical director says, "I do not want to know what your personal issues are, but I do want to know your philosophy on how personal issues impact work as a clinician."

What Not to Ask

An employer occasionally gets the question "What does this agency do?" or "What is this job again?" Think carefully about what you want to ask and how, or it could be a very brief interview.

Never ask interviewers personal questions such as these: "How long have you been in your position?" "How did you get your job?" "Are you married?" or "Is that a picture of your family?"

Packaging

"Your appearance is a sign of respect for me, my agency, and the field," says one executive director of a shelter who has been surprised by interviewees in shorts, jeans, and sandals. Although social work staff at many agencies may dress casually on the job, do not take that as a sign that you can present yourself casually at an interview. If you interview at a site where staff are dressed casually, you might ask about the dress code and comment that you like the relaxed dress policy. Keep your appearance simple and appropriate for the job.

- Women social workers in some settings wear slacks on the job, particularly in settings working with children. However, if you are a woman interviewing for a position as a play therapist, wear a skirt outfit, suit, or dress to interviews even though pants with matching jackets are in style.
- Tailor your appearance for the job. More than one employer of a program for adolescent boys has expressed concerns over female interviewees wearing short skirts, colorful makeup, and trendy hairstyles.
- If the job involves contact with corporate clients and board members, demonstrate that you understand business culture, including attire.
- Your clothing and accessories should project professionalism and not detract from the content of your presentation. Save the latest fashion items and artistic jewelry for social and casual occasions.
- Dress for an interview the way the executive director of an agency dresses for meetings with key funders.

The Interview Process

Organizations have their own interview processes. Some are simple, involving a single-hour interview; others might request a second or third interview or another interview with a group or a different individual. Role-playing, presentations, and writing exercises also may be used. The process will vary depending on the type and level of the opening and the employer's time frame for hiring.

Scheduling Interviews

Be prepared for an employer to call to schedule an interview. Keep a copy of your résumé, a list of the names and organizations you have contacted, a pad of paper, and several pens by your phone. This way you are always ready to identify a caller, take notes, and give a quick summary of your background.

Check the greeting on your message machine. A director of a women's shelter said the interview process began and ended with one candidate's message. When the director called to schedule an interview, she was greeted by a husky, sexy recorded message.

When you receive a call to schedule an interview, request details that will help you prepare. Get specifics on the interview process. Will this be a single interview, or a screening interview followed by a second interview? How long should you plan to be there? Will you be interviewing with several individuals or a group? Who will be the interviewers? If you do not already have information on the organization, request an annual report and a program brochure.

Interview Formats

First, Second, and Series Interviews

Most hiring processes for line positions involve a single interview or a screening interview with a second interview. In most cases, the interviewer follows a specific format. The organization and position will be described, you will be asked questions related to the position, and you will have an opportunity to ask questions.

Screening interview. This is a brief interview to determine whether your background is in the ballpark for this position and how interested you are. The interviewer will spend time describing the job and asking basic questions about your experience. Limit your questions to determining whether you want to explore the opportunity further. Some screening interviews are done by telephone.

Second interview. If you are invited to a second interview, it means that what you offer generally fits the profile for the position and you made a reasonably good first impression. The second interview may be with the person making the decision or with a group; it will focus on how well you could perform the job and whether you would fit the organization. You should have an opportunity to see where you would be working, tour the facility, and meet coworkers.

Series interviews. You may have several interviews as part of the process. They could be with the director, other managers, the direct supervisor for the position, coworkers, board members, and volunteers. This is particularly true if you are interviewing for an administrative position.

All-Day Interviews

If you are traveling a long distance for an interview, you are likely to go through a series of interviews over a day or two. Likewise, the higher the position, the more involved the interview process will be. You will meet with all the major constituents—the search committee, board members, colleagues in other divisions, administrative staff, supervisors and line staff, clients, and volunteers. Even if you are applying for a line position, you can expect a series of interviews with the director, supervisors, and potential coworkers and with the human resources staff, if that is a separate entity in the organization. Interviews for fellowships often take the better part of a day. Interviews for tenure-track faculty and administrative positions often last more than one day.

Itinerary. If a schedule is not provided ahead of time, ask for one with the names and titles of the people you will be seeing. Although you will find yourself repeating your story, have a strategy for addressing the individual interests of each party.

Pacing. All-day interviews are tiring. You are "on" all day. The schedule may or may not allow you time to be alone. One doctoral student said her only time alone was in the restroom. Pace yourself. Chances are that your last interview will be with the executive director or dean or whoever makes the final decision.

Travel plans and reimbursement. Do not make assumptions. Be clear from the beginning about what the employer will and will not pay for and who makes the travel arrangements. Except for high-level positions, social services organizations seldom cover travel expenses. Universities typically cover expenses for faculty and administration candidates. Keep a record of your expenses and get a receipt for everything.

Telephone Interviews

This is a screening interview that may be scheduled or come under the guise of an introduction and friendly chat. It is a quick, inexpensive way for an employer to shrink the pool of applicants. A director of a family preservation program uses telephone interviews to identify those applicants who are really serious about providing intensive services in clients' homes. Because you cannot know which employers will use this technique, you need to be prepared at all times. If an employer calls you at an inopportune time, request an alternative time.

Regardless of whether the telephone interview is scheduled or a surprise, it presents a unique challenge to the interviewee: One cannot get visual cues from the interviewer. This is frustrating, especially if it is a conference call involving several staff members. A telephone interview requires intense listening. If there is more than one interviewer, write down each person's name and title, asking each to repeat that information if necessary, before you begin the interview. When someone asks a question, ask him or her to identify himself or herself. This technique will help you begin to form a picture of each person and his or her particular interests. Pace yourself; you will probably find yourself responding to questions at a slower rate than you do in person. Take notes and ask for clarification when necessary. Try standing during this interview—it will give you a greater sense of command. To prepare for this type of interview, ask friends to play the role of the employer and practice interviews over the telephone. This is especially important for long-distance job hunters.

Panel Interviews

Although they are expedient for a staff, interviews with a group of staff members, board members, or other key people can be particularly demanding for the candidate. At least initially, you will not know whether the panel format was selected as a time saver or a test to see how well you can work with a group, among other reasons.

As people are introduced, write down their names and titles. If their roles in the agency are not clear to you, ask for clarification. This will help you tailor your responses. To help you keep names and functions straight and personalize the situation, address people by name at the beginning of a response. Obviously, you do not want to overuse this technique.

Some interviewers will play different roles, some friendly ("good cops" that put you at ease), some quiet and observant, and some challenging ("bad cops" who ask harder questions). As in individual interviews, you will want to use eye contact and develop a rapport with the panel.

Group Exercises

You might encounter a group exercise, involving several candidates, as part of the interview process. Its purpose is to observe how you and the other candidates work in a group: Do you take an active part, do you work toward consensus, do you work well in a team, do you take a leadership role? Usually the group is given a topic to discuss or a problem to solve within a set time limit.

For example, the selection process for a leadership training program incorporated a group exercise. A group of five candidates were seated around a table and given the following scenario: "You are a group of local leaders in a city where a riot has erupted. Your task is to prepare a statement for a news conference that will take place in five minutes." Two members of the interview team observed the discussion.

Role-playing

It is common for direct services agencies to use role-playing as part of the selection process. Staff members take the roles of clients and you take the role of the social worker for about 10 minutes. After the role play, there is a debriefing in which staff members ask you what you thought, why you chose to proceed as you did, and other questions specific to the situation. Sometimes they will give you feedback on your performance, but do not expect this. Role-playing scenarios follow.

Context: Youth outreach service. The employer has instructed you to de-escalate a situation, resolve the crisis, formulate a treatment plan, and come to a contract in the following scene enacted by staff. A mother and daughter come to the office to meet with you. Both start screaming at the top of their lungs without intermission.

Context: Family preservation services. Staff play members of a family whom you, the social worker from the family preservation program, are visiting for the first time. You learn that the son has been involved in a burglary and is hanging around with a bad crowd, the father is gone most of the time working, and the mother is depressed and abusing alcohol. After 15 minutes of role-playing, the staff ask you the following question: What is your assessment of the situation? How would you handle each family member? What are the strengths of the family? What would you do during the next 45 minutes of the visit?

Presentations

Sometimes you are asked to give a presentation as part of the interview process. This is more likely to occur in interviews for positions involving training, teaching, educational programming, public speaking, or leadership. For example, people interviewing for tenure-track academic positions always give a colloquium, usually based on dissertation research. Presentations may be requested in settings other than higher education, however. A candidate for a position with an extension service in a rural area was asked to prepare a 10-minute presentation on how she would involve the community in developing a new program.

In most cases, you will prepare a presentation in advance. If possible, find out who will be your audience so that you can tailor your remarks, arrange to use visual aids such as transparencies or handouts, and practice your presentation with colleagues who can ask pertinent questions.

Sometimes the presentation will be in the form of an extemporaneous speech. In past years, semifinalists for the Federal Presidential Management Intern Program gave a 10-minute speech. They were presented with three topics, instructed to choose one, and given 20 minutes to prepare. The topics could be on any national issue—trade, environment, welfare, defense, health care, energy, or transportation, for example. To compete effectively in this situation, candidates must be well read. They certainly cannot be an expert on every issue, but they should have some awareness of national issues. Of course, candidates also need to practice quickly outlining ideas and speaking for 10 minutes on a range of subjects.

Writing Exercises

In addition to asking candidates to furnish writing samples, an increasing number of employers are giving interviewees writing exercises during the interview process. This enables the employer to see how well candidates write without the benefit of time to polish or get a critique. Sometimes the exercises are timed to see how well candidates think under pressure. You might, for example, be given three cases and instructed to write treatment goals for each.

Interviewers You May Encounter

Friendly

It is common in direct social services to find an interviewer who is very friendly, gives you encouraging feedback throughout the interview, and seems enthusiastic about you. Take this with a grain of salt; no matter how positive you feel during the interview, assume that all candidates are treated exactly the same. You want to be pleasant and build rapport, but do not step out of your professional role of candidate even if you know the interviewer.

Reserved

You may find yourself interviewing with a poker-faced, aloof, or abrupt interviewer. Do not expect someone to be a good listener, to reflect, or to encourage you in any way. Some interviewers collect information without showing the slightest reaction to it. They may appear objective or even disinterested. Do not let their affect rattle your confidence.

Unorganized

You may encounter an unorganized or uncomfortable interviewer. In this case, take the lead in bringing up topics you think are important.

Distracted

If the interviewer seems to be distracted or allows others to interrupt your appointment, take this opportunity to observe the work environment.

Example of an Interview Experience at a Conference

This story describes the job interview and offer experience of a
new MSW graduate, referred to as "the social worker," seeking a
position in employment, training, and microenterprise development. She had two years of social services experience before graduate school and was searching for positions back in that general location. This interview, for a training position with a large
multiservice organization, was arranged by phone in March and
took place in late April at a conference that both parties happened
to be attending. The position was with a self-employment program teaching skills, including marketing, pricing, advertising,
operations, and finance.

The story, as interpreted by the candidate, illustrates both the
advantages of meeting with agency staff at conferences and the hec-
tic and unpredictable circumstances that candidates and employers
encounter at conferences; it also shows that candidates must always
be in the interviewee role or mindset, ready to respond at all times.

> *The interview was tentatively set for lunchtime on Thurs-
> day during the conference; the social worker would meet with
> the training coordinator, another supervisor, and the direc-
> tor. She was told that the interview would take place after
> the lunch and that the intense questioning during lunch re-
> ally wasn't part of the interview, but the social worker knew
> that the interview really did start during lunch. She quickly
> discovered that she was meeting with three very different
> personalities: the director was quiet; the second supervisor
> was a strong, tough interviewer; and the training coordina-
> tor was pleasant and encouraging without being overprom-
> ising. As it turned out, the planned formal interview after
> lunch did not take place, because the director had to leave for
> another meeting. Before parting they simply exchanged busi-
> ness cards, and the social worker met four or five more staff
> members who stopped by. The training coordinator said she
> would be in touch. At this point, the social worker thought
> she was home free.*
>
> *The next day the social worker went to a conference session;
> unexpectedly, the director was on the panel. The social worker
> had learned the day before that the agency was starting a pilot
> project in a neighboring city, where she had worked before go-
> ing to graduate school. During the conference session she real-
> ized that the agency's project could be more effective by working
> with the leadership in that community. At the session break, she*

went up to speak with the director, and as luck would have it, they were joined by the pilot project director, whom the social worker had met the day before. The social worker told them that she had a connection in [city] and thought she could help. The directors said "Great."

The director suggested that they meet after the session in the hotel lounge; the meeting turned out to be an impromptu interview, attended by the three people she had met with Thursday. "What was the most frustrating thing about your last position?" she was asked. She responded that the grassroots agency she worked with had a patchwork funding strategy, which was frustrating for her. The interviewer with the strong personality, who was the only one asking questions, said "Can you handle another position like that? In this job you will not have an opportunity to do top-level administrative functions." To which the social worker replied, "Learning the training position will be my top priority. In three years, I want to be doing administration." The social worker had not seen a job description or an annual report, so she requested them. She got the sense that an annual report was something that was not usually shared beyond the administrative level. The interview was followed by lunch, during which the social worker gave the staff advice on their project. She spent the rest of the afternoon with them. Although everyone had been friendly and the director had requested her reference list during the impromptu interview, the social worker was not sure at the end of day whether she had the job.

On Saturday morning the social worker went to the conference's final session, which the agency staff had encouraged her to attend. The staff were presenting a session for supervisors of employment training programs. They included a list of eight criteria they used for selecting staff: independence, public speaking, good rapport with clients, understanding where clients are coming from, innovative thinking, knowledge of business skills, experience as an entrepreneur, and willingness to go the extra mile, such as when clients need an advocate in dealing with social services.

The training coordinator said she would call the social worker a week after the conference. In the meantime, the training coordinator would be checking references. The social worker hadn't expected this—in fact, she had not yet asked everyone on her list to be a reference, so she immediately called each person. Fortunately, all of her references thought well of her and responded positively to the surprise calls.

During the week after the conference, the social worker thought about the minimum salary she would accept if she got an offer and how she would negotiate on the basis of her experience and education. The training coordinator called two days later than planned and offered the job at a salary higher than the worker had expected. The social worker took detailed notes because she still did not have the job description (she got the description in the mail soon thereafter; requirements were a bachelor's degree in business plus five years of experience). She said she was interested and asked whether she could call with her answer the next day. After thinking about the offer and discussing it with a family member, she called to accept the offer as it stood.

The social worker thought that the key to landing the job was her understanding of clients' situations, realistic expectations of what clients can accomplish, and patience to work with clients. After accepting the position, she learned that the agency staff had not planned on hiring until June.

Following Up after the Interview

Write down everything you can remember from each interview as soon as possible.

After a job interview, always send a typed thank-you letter as soon as possible. This letter summarizes your interest in the position and your qualifications. If you would like to emphasize or clarify any point from the interview, now is the time. In addition to thanking the interviewer, indicate your enthusiasm for the job and organization. It is also important to name any other interviewers or key individuals you met and express appreciation for their time.

If you would like to clarify any information about the position, call the employer after sending the thank-you letter. This type of call is appropriate and certainly indicates seriousness on your part.

If, after the interview, you are no longer interested in the position, state this in the thank-you letter. For additional information on interviews, read *The Smart Woman's Guide to Interviewing and Salary Negotiation* (King, 1995), *Every Employee's Guide to the Law* (Joel, 1996), *Sweaty Palms* (Medley, 1993), and *Can They Do That?* (Zigarelli, 1994).

References

Joel, L. G. (1996). *Every employee's guide to the law*. New York: Pantheon Books.

King, J. A. (1995). *The smart woman's guide to interviewing and salary negotiation*. Franklin, NJ: Career Press.

Medley, J. A. (1993). *Sweaty palms: The neglected art of being interviewed*. Berkeley, CA: Ten Speed Press.

U.S. Equal Employment Opportunity Commission. http://www.eeoc.gov.

Zigarelli, M. A. (1994). *Can they do that? A guide to your rights on the job*. New York: Lexington Books.

Chapter 5 Quick Tips: Interviews

- List five points you want an employer to know about you.

- List five or more questions you have about the organization and the job.

- Practice giving answers to common questions: What is your career goal? Tell me about yourself. What are your skills? What are your strengths? What are your weaknesses? Why should we hire you?

- Think about how you want to respond to inappropriate questions should they come up: Choose to respond to the concern, choose not to respond, or choose to respond to the question.

- Recap your qualifications in a typed thank-you letter.

Chapter 6

Evaluating Job Offers

Getting an Official Offer

This is the moment you have been waiting for—they want you on their staff. You are excited and relieved, but there are many things to think about before making a commitment. For example, does the person offering you the position have the authority to do so? Is this opportunity consistent with what you know is available in the market? Do you need to negotiate the salary or starting date? Does this job fit your plans for the future? This chapter is designed to help you think through this process.

Congratulations, You Have an Offer (or at Least You Think You Do)

It is important to know whether you have an official offer. An official offer is made after the person with the authority to make a final hiring decision approves the selection. The offer includes the job title, salary, and starting date. If applicable, it should include the department and location.

Sometimes it is not entirely clear whether you have an offer. You may have a conditional or an unofficial offer. The employer might say you are a finalist for the position, or the interviewer might say simply, "We really want you." Although these are good signs, neither is an official offer requiring a decision to accept.

Conditional Offer
Were you told "This is a conditional offer"? Is the offer contingent on positive outcomes of references, a police record check, information from the child abuse registry, and a basic physical examination? Is it also contingent on a favorable review of your writing samples?

Unofficial Offer
Were you told "This is an offer; the board just needs to approve it"? If yes, this gives you some extra time to weigh your options, but be aware that the person you talked to does not have the power at this point to make the offer; it could evaporate.

Finalist
In one hiring process two individuals were each told "You are the finalist; now all you have to do is meet with the division director at the umbrella agency." Each had the understanding that she was being offered the job; that was not the case. Know who has the power to make the hiring decision and to extend the job offer.

We Want You
Were you told "You are the person we want"? If this was followed by "We are offering you the position of [job title] at a starting salary of [amount]," then congratulations—you have an offer. If not, then ask whether they are offering you the position.

> *Marie and I responded to an advertisement just after Thanksgiving for family support specialist positions; we applied as a husband-and-wife team. Marie had been working for the state's family services department for 15 months and I with a supported-parenting program at an agency that works with individuals with developmental disabilities. We thought we had nothing to lose by applying and so we did. Within the first week of applying we were called for an interview; at that point even if we did not get job offers we knew we could apply elsewhere. It was confidence building and allowed us to see just how marketable we could be with enough creativity. The first interview went well, and we were called in for a second interview. All had seemingly been going in our favor by Christmas, when we received a phone call from the program coordinator, who said, "I would like to talk to you [both] about placement in our agency." We interpreted this to mean that they were offering us jobs; however, we found that by the middle of January a decision had not been made. We learned to be careful about interpretations, but we remained hopeful because she [the program coordinator] still was interested in us. After three interviews, for which the agency paid our flight and lodging expenses, we were finally offered positions with the agency. In fact, although I was not hired for a stated position to work with a middle school, the agency felt so strongly about both of us that they created a position for me to work not with one area school but with each of the four area schools.*

Interestingly, we had met with the executive director, program coordinator, program director of the adolescent treatment unit, the assistant principal, and the counselor of the middle school, on separate occasions, all before a decision was finally made. We never could say for sure whether we had the jobs, even with all the interviews and three expenses-paid trips. In fact, following the third meeting, I was told that I had a 90 percent chance of having a job. The position had to be created and money for a salary had to be agreed on before the program coordinator could give a definite yes. Quite an experience for us, one that, fortunately, worked out.

The Offer

When you receive an offer, it is likely to be made over the telephone. The call should be followed by a letter or contract specifying the job title, unit or department, starting date, starting salary, location (if there is more than one), and moving or travel reimbursement terms, if relevant. If you negotiate any items successfully, you ought to receive a new letter or contract. Items you will want to see before accepting the offer include a job description and material detailing benefits.

Compensation and Benefits

Your compensation or salary may be stated in yearly, monthly, hourly, or in the case of a project, lump-sum terms. Be sure you understand the terms. Travel reimbursement, bonuses, and profit sharing (for-profit organizations only) also may be part of the compensation.

Benefits typically average between 25 percent and 30 percent of the total compensation package. Your benefits will consist of many, if not most, of the following:

- continuing education
- dental insurance
- disability insurance
- family leave
- flexible ("cafeteria") benefits
- health insurance
- holidays
- liability/malpractice insurance
- life insurance

- retirement
- sick leave
- social work professional liability insurance
- stock options
- supplemental benefits
- tax benefits (social security, Medicare, unemployment)
- vacation leave
- worker's compensation
- COBRA.

Notes on Particular Benefits

The following are items to look for in the information given to you at the time of the offer. Ask questions if that written material is not clear. This information is an overview; particulars will vary across organizations.

Disability Insurance

Is there a waiting period for eligibility? Long-term disability insurance is more important than life insurance. If disability insurance is offered, buy it; the premium is very reasonable. The bills continue to come in when you are disabled, even though you are not receiving your full salary.

Pretax Benefits

You may be able to designate some of your salary for either out-of-pocket health care or child care and pay those expenses with before-tax dollars. The money goes directly into an account for that specified purpose. If you choose to use this option, estimate conservatively—by law, any funds left in the account at the end of the year are forfeited.

Health Insurance

What are the premiums, deductibles, and copayments? If there is an employee premium, is it pretax or posttax? What is the out-of-pocket maximum? The maximum, plus the deductible, would be what major surgery would cost you. Are prescriptions, chiropractic services, and vision needs covered? To help you make comparisons, find out the community rates for health insurance. New federal law states that insurance companies may not consider and exclude you from coverage because of pre-existing conditions. It is not advised that you ask about mental health services.

Liability/Malpractice Insurance

Most employers purchase a blanket liability/malpractice insurance policy for the organization, which covers the organization if it is named in a lawsuit and for its employees, in which case an individual social worker is covered under the employer's malpractice/liability insurance policy. See also the section "Social Work Professional Liability Insurance."

Life Insurance
Your employer may provide basic life insurance as part of your benefits. You may also be able to purchase conditional term insurance through the employer, which would cover burial costs and pay debts, such as home, automobile, and student loans, upon your death. Some people recommend that you not buy whole life insurance because it is too expensive. Review this option with your personal financial adviser.

Social Work Professional Liability Insurance
Although not common, some employers pay the premium or reimburse employees who purchase a professional liability insurance policy from an independent firm such as NASW Insurance Trust. The current director of the NASW Insurance Trust, which has insured the largest pool of social workers for three decades, advises that individuals should be encouraged to obtain a personal policy even if they have some coverage elsewhere. Although this may result in duplication of some coverage, the person who owns and pays for the policy has far better long-term control and coverage against a lawsuit. A personal policy is especially indicated if the social worker conducts any social work outside the employed environment (for example, volunteer or private practice or teaching) (personal communication with Loretta S. Robinson, director, NASW Insurance Trust, Washington, DC, May 17, 1997).

COBRA
This benefit, stipulated by federal law for organizations of 20 or more employees, enables you to continue your health care insurance at your own expense for a limited time after you or your dependents are no longer eligible for health care coverage under your employer's plan. COBRA is important for bridging health insurance between jobs.

Retirement
The most common retirement benefits are defined-benefit plans and 401(k) and 403(b) defined-contribution plans. If the employer offers a retirement benefit, find out when you can become eligible for the plan and whether it is a defined-benefit plan or a defined-contribution plan. Under the defined-benefit plan, the employee is paid a set amount by the employer upon retirement. There are five major types of defined-contribution plans:

1. *Money purchase plan:* The employer makes a contribution, based on a percentage of your salary, to an account in your name.
2. *401(k) and 403(b):* Both you and the employer make contributions to an account. If you choose not to sign up for this benefit at the outset of employment, ask whether you can do so in the future (this option may come up once or twice a year).
3. *Profit sharing:* At the end of the year, the employer makes a contribution, based on a percentage of the company's profits, to an account in your name.
4. *Employee stock purchase plan:* For-profit companies may offer a stock purchase plan as their retirement benefit. This means that you have the opportunity to buy stock in the company. The cost is deducted from your paycheck, and the company covers any brokerage fees.
5. *Employee stock option plan:* The employer purchases shares of its own stock and puts them in an account in your name. This is sometimes considered a defined-benefit pension plan.

Tax Benefits
The employer pays federal and state unemployment taxes and worker's compensation. These costs are not deducted from your paycheck. However, 7.65 percent of your salary is deducted from your paycheck under Federal Insurance Contribution Act (FICA) regulations for social security (6.2 percent) and Medicare (1.45 percent). Note that the salary cap on social security is indexed annually, which affects the amount deducted.

Supplemental Plans
The employer may offer supplemental plans such as life insurance or home health care through payroll deductions.

Making a Decision

To make a wise choice, you'll need to look carefully at your original goals and the information you have on the market. Ask yourself a few more questions.

Questions Related to Job Fit
- Is this job directly related to what you want to do now?
- Is this opportunity in line with what you learned in researching the market?

- What are the positive and negative aspects of this job?
- Will you be giving up anything by taking this position? (This is an especially important question when you are comparing two offers.)
- Can you work with the supervisor, coworkers, subordinates, volunteers, and board members?
- Can you support the mission of the organization?
- How well do the philosophy and values of the organization match yours?
- Does this job offer enough challenge? In other words, can you do this job without thinking, will it challenge you, or is it out of the range of your current skills? Is there a good balance between the two extremes?
- What can you learn from your superiors in this job?
- How well does this job fit the dream job you originally outlined?
- Is there an orientation? Is it "Here are the policy manuals and go to it," or is there a detailed orientation?

Questions Related to Career Goals

- Is this a good stepping-stone for future jobs?
- Will you be using the skills that you want to develop?
- What type of supervision will you receive?
- Will the job meet your needs for licensure or certification?
- Will future employers regard the experience you gain on the job as valuable to their organizations?
- How well does this job prepare you for what you want to do next?

Questions about the Compensation Package

- Is this a salaried, hourly, contractual, or per diem position?
- Is the pay in the appropriate range?
- Does the employer require that you bring in a percentage of your salary? How do you do this? What is the penalty for not meeting that target? How often does the percentage goal change and at what rate?
- Do you pay for the supervision required for licensure?
- Will you be traveling for the job? What is the reimbursement rate?
- What opportunities are there for continuing education? Does the employer pay for enough continuing education hours to meet licensure requirements? Do you get time off to attend seminars?
- How flexible do you need to be with your time? Many, if not most, social work jobs require hours beyond a 37- to 40-hour workweek. Is there a policy on compensatory time?

- Must you meet a required number of billable hours each week? How many? What happens if you do not meet that minimum?
- Does the agency prohibit staff from doing outside contract work or consulting or holding a second job?

Questions about the Hiring Process

- Were you given a tour of the facility? Did you see where you would be working?
- Did you meet your direct supervisor, coworkers, and other pertinent people?
- Did you see a job description? (Sometimes organizations do not have job descriptions.)
- Did the staff take time to consider whether you were the right candidate? Did they interview other candidates? If your answers are no and it seems that the decision to hire you was made too quickly, consider whether you are looking at a red flag. Why are they so enthusiastic and hasty?
- Is the job too good to be true? Is the salary unusually high for your experience and this type of position, organization, and geographical area? Why? What can your network advisers tell you?
- Is there a probation period, and how long is it?

An Early Offer

Like the person described in the chapter on researching the market, you may get an offer early in the job-search process. If so, you may have some anxiety about your decision to accept or decline the offer. Often, an early offer is an unusual opportunity; it may be extremely attractive monetarily, a chance to do something out of the ordinary, or a chance to get you into a field you hadn't considered before. In any case, you will need to weigh your options carefully.

If the offer is a solid stepping-stone to your future and you feel positive about the job and organization, take advantage of the opportunity. This is a particularly important decision if you are geographically restricted.

For alumni or new graduates with previous experience who are seeking a promotion, changing functions or even fields, knowledge of the market and a clear sense of direction are critical to decision making.

Waiting for a Second Offer

A challenge in the job-search process is timing a decision on your offers. When the offer is made, ask when the employer needs a decision.

If you have another interview scheduled or are waiting to hear about another offer, see if you can negotiate a decision date for the offer you have. Respect the needs of the employer as well as your own; he or she may not be able to extend the deadline. Be certain to explain to the employer that you want to make the best decision for you and the organization. Being able to consider the other option will help you do that.

Of course, you may have to make a decision on the offer without a second offer to consider. This is when your knowledge of the job market is particularly critical. Is the market so tight that you ought to secure this opportunity? Or does your research and overall feedback from contacts and employers indicate that the market is good, and you have a chance at other opportunities? And how long can you wait for another opportunity to come along?

Sometimes employers want a decision the same day they extend an offer. It may be that their first-choice candidate accepted the job two weeks ago and changed his or her mind just a few days before the training program began. On the other hand, it could be a red flag indicating that the organization does not plan ahead. Regardless, ask for an extension, if only for 24 hours.

> *In December, a social worker interviewed with two hospitals for comparable jobs. She would have enjoyed either position. The first hospital director called to say that she would be away for a few weeks and would make a decision when she returned. She also requested that the candidate call her if she got a second offer. The second hospital director did not indicate when she would make a decision. After the holidays, the social worker, who had not heard from either employer, decided to send a copy of a paper she had written to the first hospital director—they had discussed the project during the interview, and the social worker thought it would demonstrate her continued interest in the job. A couple of days later, she received a temporary job offer from a third hospital. The social worker called the first hospital director to say that she had a second offer but was still interested in the job.*
>
> *Perhaps because she was pressed for time, the director was not very talkative on the telephone. The social worker, who wanted to give the third hospital a decision soon but remained more interested in the pending opportunities, sought advice from a contact. Consequently, she took the following steps: She called the third hospital and asked whether they could wait until Friday for an answer; they understood the circumstances and said yes. Next, she called the second hospital director, told her of the offer and deadline, and asked when the director*

might make a decision. The director said that she would call back with an answer but could not be more specific. The social worker then sent a fax to the first hospital director, indicating her continued interest and the deadline for the decision on the temporary job. The first hospital director called the social worker that evening to invite her in for a second interview. They met. The director said that the social worker was her first-choice candidate if a current staff member did not accept the position. Late Friday morning, the director of the first hospital called to offer the job. The social worker accepted, called the third hospital to decline the temporary job, and later that day received an offer from the second hospital.

Unfortunately, the timing of job offers does not always work so well.

In another instance, a social worker received an offer for a job she would be satisfied with. The agency wanted a decision the next day. The social worker made a request for more time to decide, but it was not granted. In the time that she had, she called a second organization with which she had interviewed and whose job was more interesting to her. The person she spoke with told her that the person who would be making the decision was out of town and that he did not know how likely it was that an offer would be extended. Although the person she talked to in the office tried to be of assistance, nothing could be done before the social worker had to make a decision on the first agency's offer. She decided to take the position—she knew from her research and job-search experience that the market was tight. Later she learned that the second agency had planned on offering her a job.

Negotiation

If you decide that you want the job but you want to negotiate on the terms, this is the time to do it—before you accept the job. You may want to discuss salary, benefits, time off for your wedding or the family reunion that was planned a year ago, or a starting date. For example, you may be able to negotiate a starting date, so that you can take a break between jobs or begin on a part-time basis before graduation. Although it is best to negotiate before accepting the job, it is not unheard of for social workers to successfully increase their salaries after beginning work, as did the graduate with the bachelor's degree discussed in chapter 4, a home health social work director who made a point of raising the issue every six months, and a master's degree holder who after a week on the job with supervisory responsibilities decided that she was underpaid.

Salary Negotiation

Before you discuss salary or the compensation package of salary and benefits, you need to answer several questions and consider special cases.

- How much do you want the position?
- What salary do you want and think is appropriate for the position and title?
- What salary would you accept?
- What salary are you worth, and what do you need? If you were able to get a salary range from the employer during the last interview, is there room to negotiate upward within the range?
- What specific assets do you bring that would justify a high figure?
- What is the going salary or salary range for this type of position at your level of experience in this community or field?
- Review the salary data you gathered earlier (see chapter 2). Factor in the local demand for your background, the economic sector, field of service, level of responsibility, and size of the organization.
- Is this a permanent position, a consulting position, or a temporary grant position?
- Is there a bonus plan (primarily offered by for-profit but occasionally seen in nonprofit organizations) or profit sharing (for-profit organizations)?
- When are raises given and on what basis? Are they based on performance and contributions? What has been the average annual salary increase in the past two years? How does that compare with national and local trends?
- Does the package include benefits? If yes, how do they compare to benefits for your present position or for other positions you considered? How much will be taken out of your paycheck for benefits? If the compensation package does not include benefits, you will want a salary that is at least 25 percent higher than a comparable position that includes benefits.

Other Considerations

Contract Positions

If you take a contract job and you do not make enough to pay taxes, you must prepay social security quarterly in a lump sum. Also check

---

Factors to Consider When Negotiating

- level of responsibility (new program, supervision, fund-raising, client development)
- viability of the organization (start-up, rebuilding)
- salary data from your alma mater
- salary data and recommendations from NASW
- other offers you received
- unusual skills (second language, computer skills, ability to work with a particular community)
- your experience (work, practicum, and community experience; leadership)
- your degree (quality and particular features, especially compared with other degrees or programs)
- your connections
- cost of travel (if required)
- cost of living
- your student loans
- cost of social work professional liability insurance
- cost of supervision for licensure (if it is not paid by the employer)
- safety on the job.

---

on social work professional liability coverage, because you probably are not covered as a contract worker.

PRN (Pro re Nata, or Whenever Necessary) Positions
If you are a PRN employee, you work on an as-needed basis. You are not likely to have benefits, but your social security and other taxes are withheld. Be certain that you do not take all of this for granted—check it out.

Handling Negotiations for Salaries and Benefits

Once you have done your homework, there are several ways to handle negotiations. Each of these approaches has been used by social workers.

- Tell the employer what you are looking for, such as a specific salary figure, and state your reasons.
- When negotiating a salary, give the employer a figure that is higher than you are willing to accept.

- If you have another formal offer that you will accept if this negotiation is not successful, tell the employer with whom you are negotiating that you have another offer and what the salary is. The employer may match or exceed that offer. Do not bluff.

For example, a new MSW graduate decided to negotiate a salary for a position she had been offered in fund-raising for a large development organization. She had completed a practicum in this organization and had at least one additional opportunity with a similar organization.

> *In preparation for this meeting, I put all my thoughts down on paper. Before I started negotiating, I told him that I appreciated the offer. I added that I would take the job, but I wanted to know that I had made all the efforts I could to negotiate a higher salary. He seemed to appreciate my honesty and initiative. I negotiated for an increase by referring him to my experience in the office and community and pointed out that he did not have to spend money to "bring me out" for an interview, a cost which this organization, which recruited nationally, would normally incur. He agreed with my negotiating points and asked me how much additional salary I would like. Now, here is where I was a little taken aback, because I had not predetermined an amount. My offer from the similar organization was $1,500 more for a higher-level position, but it was for a job I did not want as much. I asked for $1,000. He increased the base salary by $500.*

Many in the field lament that social workers undersell themselves, taking their skills and experience for granted and settling for less than they are worth. Even if you do not intend to negotiate an offer, read about negotiation. Your understanding will increase your confidence, particularly in making decisions about offers. If you plan to negotiate, be sure that you adapt what you read to your circumstances and the market. One social worker found that reading about negotiation gave her a framework to consider, but that elements of it did not fit her field of social work. For more details on negotiation, read the books listed at the end of appendix 3.

Deciding among Offers: Some Examples

> *I turned down the program director position for one agency—low pay, no benefits, and an executive director with whom I would have had great difficulty working. I also turned down the position of executive director of the assistance program, a homeless shelter under the umbrella of another agency.*

This job probably would have been extremely stressful, partly because of the nature of the agency's work but also because its board, although supportive of the agency's work, is not suffi- ciently involved to provide a good working relationship with the executive director. It also needs a lot of work on diversify- ing its funding base—it has solid revenue from government, but cash-flow challenges. It would have been a very lonely job— lots of responsibilities and stress, but with no built-in support for the executive director.

The job I accepted is in the family division at an agency. It has the decidedly unglamorous title of project coordinator, but is designed to serve as a leadership position to help expand the division. I have several major assignments: (1) provide lead- ership in getting the division's center accredited, (2) develop and implement a marketing plan for the center, and (3) help in development of management systems to integrate an early childhood program grant with the existing regular research project. Other possible smaller projects include diversity work for the division and help in the area of job placement and re- tention for division clients.

The plus side of this job is that I know and like this agency, they know and like me, and the job content is work that will be important to them and fulfilling to me. The minus side is that the project work will be completed in about 18 months, so I will have to find another position afterward. But the agency really wanted me—including the executive director and the human resources director—so I'm willing to deal with that situation.

A new MSW graduate had two interviews. One was for a youth development position in a small community for a university exten- sion service; she received an offer after the interview. The second was for a position as an entry-level public policy specialist with a multiservice agency for people with disabilities. The second agency said it would try to let her know the outcome before the next week, when she had to make a decision on the first offer. This is how she compared the positions, anticipating a second offer:

The job description for the extension position sounds inter- esting, the benefits and salary are good, there's a lot of flex- ibility and autonomy in the position; the drawback is location. My fear is that I may not be in an ideal part of the state to network and eventually to move into policy, which is what I ultimately want to do.

> *The job description for the second job also sounds like I'd have a lot of the tasks and responsibilities that interest me. I could obviously gain the public policy skills in this job. The drawback is that it is not directly related to children and families. It came out in the interview that I would not be doing any child-specific policy work. The issues they deal with are accessibility, telecommunications, transportation, appropriations for independent-living centers, and so on. The salary would not be as high as that for the first offer.*
>
> *A third possibility is to not take either job and keep looking, but this may be based on the false notion that there is a "perfect" job.*

She did receive the second offer and took it. Although the population of the first job met her interests, she concluded that she had a better chance of working in child and family policy by getting policy experience, even though it was on behalf of a different population. Furthermore, during discussions with the employer about her acceptance of the position, she was able to negotiate for the opportunity to develop some policy initiatives for children with disabilities.

Accepting or Declining the Offer

Give yourself at least 24 hours to think about a job offer. If you are having difficulty making a decision, consider calling one of your advisers. Then accept an offer as soon as you make your decision. A telephone call followed by a letter is appropriate. Confirm the following in your letter and keep a copy of it:

- position title
- specific department in which this position is located (if applicable)
- one sentence stating the responsibilities
- salary
- starting date
- special items (moving expenses, for example).

After you accept an offer, you should receive a letter or contract from the employer that states the title, salary, and starting date for the position. Read it carefully; make sure it is what you agreed to orally. Keep the formal letter of offer or a copy of the contract. It is not recommended that you start a position without a formal written offer and job description. Both you and the employer could encounter a surprise in this process, as the following example shows:

> *A school district made an offer over the phone to a social worker who was looking for her second career position. She*

accepted it and requested it in writing. A week and a half later, she received a contract showing a lower salary than what was stated over the phone. The social worker called the employer, who said that he lowered the salary after reviewing her transcripts. The employer assumed that the 60 credits for the master's degree was in addition to credits at the bachelor's level. However, the social worker had received advanced-standing credit in her master's program for some of her BSW coursework. According to the district's salary schedule, which sets salary steps by credits and not by degrees, the credits could not be applied to both degrees.

The change in salary was a disappointment, but the social worker accepted the position because it met her goal to work for the district.

If you decide to decline the offer, then let the employer know as soon as possible by telephone and follow-up with a letter of thanks. These courtesies leave the door open for future communication.

After Accepting the Offer

Stay in touch with the supervisor between the time you accept the offer and your starting date. This is particularly important if you are relocating. Keep the employer informed about how to reach you, particularly during your move.

You may be asked to take care of personnel paperwork, get a physical, meet with the staff, attend a particular function, or participate in a training session before your starting date, without pay. This is not uncommon.

Many people are excited about new jobs and want to start right away and demonstrate their interest in the job. However, if you have prior commitments, explain the situation and work out a mutually beneficial solution with your supervisor.

Changes in the Job

For most people, the process of starting a new position goes smoothly. They find their perceptions and sources of information were accurate, the job descriptions they were given match what they are doing, and the organizations anticipated their arrival.

However, unforeseen events not under the control of the employer sometimes occur: a new grant comes through or is unexpectedly not renewed, a staff member leaves suddenly or becomes seriously ill, upper-level management decides to cut all department budgets and eliminate positions, or a natural disaster hits. Such events can quickly affect positions at all levels. You might discover that your new job will be at a different location or that, instead of working with adults, you will work primarily with children. You may look at such a change as an opportunity. Alternatively, you could decide to leave, if you feel the change takes you too far afield from your goals or you do not like the way the organization handled the situation.

Chapter 6 Quick Tips: Evaluating Offers

- Make sure that you have an official offer that does not need to be approved by anyone else.

- If the organization has not given you information on benefits in addition to the salary figure, request it and ask for clarification if you need it.

- Spend at least 24 hours considering whether the offer fits your career, salary, and benefit needs. If you need more time, request it—especially if you are waiting to hear about a second offer—but be reasonable.

- Contact other organizations with which you have interviewed or applied to inform them that you have an offer; inquire about their timetables for making a decision. Try to determine whether you are among their top candidates, and remind them of your interest in and qualifications for the job.

- If you choose to negotiate for salary or benefits, carefully outline the reasons the organization should compensate you differently for your services. In the case of salary, state a figure above the salary you will accept and expect to negotiate downward, if the employer will negotiate at all.

- As soon as you have made a decision, either yes or no, tell the employer orally and follow up with a letter.

Chapter 7

Career Management and Professional Development

"People do not plan careers—they happen." This is the observation of one social worker whose career has consisted of many positions, including a transition into the managed care industry. You might agree with this statement, but if you ask people how they heard about each job they had and what enabled them to make each move, you will hear about actions each person took that triggered changes or created circumstances that eventually made that strand of career opportunities happen.

That focus on personal actions that galvanize careers has never been more important than today. The volatile employment patterns of the for-profit sector are now affecting social work, even more powerfully than did the political changes of the early 1980s. There are no guarantees of permanent employment in any economic sector today (Bridges, 1994; Hakim, 1994; Rifkin, 1995). However, there are actions you can take and habits you can develop that will increase your confidence and options.

"Career resilience" (Waterman, Waterman, & Collard, 1994) and "career self-reliance" (Collard, Epperheimer, & Saign, 1996) are becoming slogans in the current business environment, where employers can no longer guarantee jobs, much less manage careers for employees, as some corporations once did. Although social workers typically have not received career management assistance from organizations, they have until recently enjoyed relative stability in employment in social services. Now, however, the cost-cutting, outcomes-driven business environment is being adapted to traditional social work employment settings. Social workers, even in the most stable of settings, are not protected by niches or profession-specific work carved out over the past 60 years. Social workers now have to define what they do and demonstrate their cost-effectiveness.

"Social workers must be able to demonstrate competencies rather than advocate only for discipline protection. The fact that one is a *social worker* does not guarantee that one can achieve the outcomes that a given employer is seeking," says Vivian Jackson, former director of the NASW Office of Policy and Practice (personal communication, October 8, 1996). Discussion in social work education about competencies—what graduates should know and be able to perform—has been extensive. Like social workers at all levels and in all types of work, you must be able to define what you can do, verify how effective your work is, and articulate your contributions to the organization, regardless of whether you are in or are competing for a job titled "social worker." Assume that you will be competing with people from other disciplines for every opportunity you seek and that management, with rare exceptions, will not fully understand what social work has to offer.

Career Management

To manage a career today, you need to think proactively, experiment, and pursue specific interests. This is not a clear-cut strategic planning process but a journey, as Stumpf (1989) and others describe career management. The following approaches will help you address your social work career management needs:

- Stay current on trends.
- Improve your performance.
- Increase your visibility.
- Build and use your contact network.
- Advocate for political and professional change.
- Research your options.
- Experiment with ideas and expand goals.
- Update your self-assessment and résumé or vita.
- Increase your qualifications through professional development.

In each section that follows you will find questions and suggestions to consider as you think about strengthening and managing your career. Interviews with social workers in various fields and functions generated several of these ideas.

Trends

Your career opportunities and daily work activities will continue to be influenced by several of the following trends.

- *Economics:* Reductions in public and private funding have increased expectations for managing health and mental health care costs and documenting all service outcomes, spurred competition for funding resources, and pushed the need for entrepreneurship in social services and health care. Limited funding also has prompted collaboration, reorganization, teamwork, merging, downsizing, and declassification among public and private entities, and it has created a trend toward temporary employment.
- *Technology:* Your work will depend more and more on your ability to manage information through technology, whether you are following cases, manipulating budgets, analyzing records, researching program options, or evaluating policies.
- *Demographics:* The increasing average age and cultural diversity of the U.S. population will change policies, service delivery, and funding not only for elders but also for other populations.
- *Policy:* Recent changes in social policies and continued efforts to balance the federal budget, among other national and state issues, also are affecting services, practice, and funding.
- *Regulation:* The increases in licensure, certification, vendorship, and declassification of jobs in the public sector are giving more options to some social workers and limiting them for others. New state-regulated credentials are emerging in several fields of practice, such as marriage and family therapy, and thereby increasing the competition for jobs and, in some cases, restricting the scope of work previously done by social workers.
- *Globalization:* As in all industries and professions, communication, cooperation, and competition across cultures are growing. Although the U.S. nonprofit sector has not felt the impact of globalization to the same degree as the for-profit sector, exchanges around intervention technologies and, ultimately, competition for funding resources are increasing.

Keeping up with internal organizational changes; shifts at the local, regional, and national levels; developments in credentials; and advances in technology can be overwhelming. Professional associations (NASW, Council on Social Work Education [CSWE], International Federation of Social Workers) and advocacy or trade associations (Child Welfare League of America, Family Service America) with strong advocacy, legislative, or credentialing committees can help you keep track of the progress on various issues through action alerts, news summaries, and reports. Reading key publications can help you stay abreast of situations. For example, for people following the field of domestic relations, LaDeana Gamble (manager, Family Mediation and Assessment Center, Las Vegas) recommends the *Journal of Family Issues* and reviews done by the Association of Family and Conciliation Courts on research in the child custody arena (personal communication, November 4, 1996). Fr. Matthew Kawiak, who has a private practice, recommends *Practice Strategies*, a newsletter of the American Association of Marriage and Family Therapy, for private practitioners trying to maintain a practice (personal communication, February 3, 1997). If you have access to the Internet, listservs, which are discussion groups, are excellent sources for clarifying and expanding your knowledge of issues (some Internet sites are listed in appendix 8).

Ask yourself these questions and follow this advice:

> *How are you keeping up with changes in funding, policies, and services? How are public and private funding patterns changing? What will be the focus tomorrow in social and economic policy and social services? What opportunities do these changes present? Try to anticipate the outcomes of new or anticipated legislation. Make it your business to know how the objectives of your organization are being adapted to the current environment. Legal credentials, state licenses and certificates, and employer or third-party preferred professional credentials could restrict mobility among fields of practice and work settings. Who is your source for information on these issues?*

Performance

Peak performance adds leverage to any career move you make. If you are performing well in your current professional work, chances are that your accomplishments and contributions are being noted by others. In addition, your confidence is probably high and your messages crisp. This is when special projects and invitations to participate in particular groups are likely to be offered to you, or you begin to see a solution to a problem or a new way to approach your work, for example. Think about past opportunities you discovered or received unsolicited.

> *Were you at peak performance? What is your performance level now? If you are at peak performance, are you thinking about how your reputation might enable you to make a change?*

Or is your performance preventing you from making a career move? Do others see you as an effective problem solver, a team player with a positive attitude, a strong advocate, an independent staff member, a leader, a staff member with good judgment, or as someone who looks for opportunities tied to change? What would references say about your performance? Do you need to improve your performance before you apply for new positions?

For example, on the basis of her performance, a social worker with an MSW who was employed by a county foster care unit was offered the position of supervisor of a newly created miniunit designed to improve the supervisor-to-staff ratio. She had excelled in managing a caseload of foster care, adoption, independent living, and adolescent foster care services. Her work had included supervising one social worker with a BSW.

Visibility

Although a contact network is important to your day-to-day work and job-search efforts, the visibility of your work is even more powerful. A contact may be able to introduce you to someone, but a colleague who has seen your performance or products can recommend you highly. It is the person whose work is seen by audiences outside his or her organization who receives unsolicited opportunities.

Ask yourself these questions:

Who sees your work? Are your job tasks, community efforts, or professional activities visible to other social workers, community leaders, politicians, and people from other disciplines? Have you sought out opportunities for projects, writing, presenting, and leadership, which let others see you perform? If you are looking for a job, consider positions that give you opportunities to work with professionals and volunteers from outside your organization, positions that give you visibility.

For example, one social worker who was a labor representative and lobbyist for a union used his community-organizing skills to tackle social issues at the state and national levels; he ran for the state legislature and narrowly lost. In his campaign, he brought new social issues of pay equity, family leave, and health care access to the political debate. After the election he continued his work on these key issues. His visibility enabled him to win a legislative seat in the next state election.

Contact Network

"Who you know"—whomever that is—cannot guarantee you a job, but your network of contacts can provide a critical communication conduit. A well-developed contact network increases the chances that you will find out not only about jobs but also about changes in organizations, trends, policies, funding, and leadership. Contacts, especially distant contacts, can be particularly useful in identifying jobs and other professional opportunities that those in your more immediate network are not likely to have heard about (Granovetter, 1973). The reach of your network and the care you give it (currency) will influence the types of information you receive. A social worker whose job required participation in the local chamber of commerce had a broader understanding of the community and its opportunities. Another social worker with a part-time private practice was a member of 40 different panels for managed care companies; he found that he had to call companies every three months to maintain contact and generate referrals. He estimated that 20 percent of the referral department staff turned over every quarter year, which meant that he had to constantly rebuild relationships.

Ask yourself how well you have maintained your contact network. For example,

> *Do you know the local leaders in your field of practice? Do you know those at a state, regional, national, or international level? Are you involved in a professional, advocacy, or community organization that enables you to be part of the discussions on issues and puts you in contact with others in your field? Do you have contact with political leaders or professionals in other disciplines who are working on issues critical in your field of practice? If you use a referral network on the job, is it as up to date as you would like it to be? Do you need to get involved to reconnect? What steps can you take to establish your presence?*

> *For example, a social worker had networked to find work at the federal level. Her work as a child protective services supervisor entailed contact with a coworker who had recently moved from the county child welfare system to the federal government. The social worker heard about an opening for a child welfare policy specialist from the coworker. She applied and received an offer.*

Advocacy

You have seen how public policies and regulations affect every aspect of social work. They affect the policies of private, nonprofit organizations and corporations such as insurance companies, health corporations, and banks, as well as the regulations of credentialing bodies that concern your clients, your work, and even your future. If you are not already involved in advocacy, look into the efforts of professional societies, such as NASW, the Federation of Societies for Clinical Social Work chapters, and the American Society on Aging; advocacy and trade associations, such as the American Public Welfare Association and Child Welfare League of America; advocacy or consumer groups specific to your local community, such as units or committees associated with United Way, Junior League, or Urban League; and state licensing boards.

How can you advocate for clients and legislation and policies that affect practice, credentials, and vendorship? John Morris, MSW, professor in the Department of Neuropsychiatry and Behavioral Science at the University of South Carolina and former director of mental health for that state, cautions, "Your career is at high risk if you are simply doing your assigned duties every day; in an increasingly competitive work environment, professionals need to be active in professional organizations that further the broad goals of the field" (personal communication, April 21, 1997).

Options

Options for your next career move and later moves can be grouped into actions that enhance your current position, opportunities in your organization, social work opportunities in other organizations, and opportunities to make contributions in other fields. These categories can give you a starting point for exploring alternatives.

Enhancing Your Current Position
Are there aspects of your job that you can do differently? Could you delegate more work? Could you rotate responsibilities with another staff member? Could you take on a special project? Is there a program for cross-training at your organization, or can you create one?

Opportunities in Your Organization
For what other positions in your agency do you qualify or could you qualify in the future? What changes are anticipated in your organization, and what needs or opportunities might those changes create (Bridges, 1994)? Does your organization need expertise on a new issue, or computerization, evaluation, or fund-raising skills that you could develop? How have others with or formerly with the organization enhanced their jobs, received promotions, or moved to new agencies? Perhaps others on staff also are ready for a change. Listen to the needs expressed by staff, and consider their

skills and the expanding needs of your employer. Could you propose a new staffing configuration to management? Use the skills listed in appendix 10 to help you detail job tasks in a proposal. If you work in a large bureaucracy, consider moving into central administration. Sally Hein, executive director of Southern Human Resources Department Consortium for Mental Health, recommends jobs in central administration for a good overview of the field in general and state mental health policy and services in particular (personal communication, June 11, 1996).

Social Work Opportunities in Other Organizations
If your position and organization do not offer attractive career growth options, what else is available in the community? Do you want to make a lateral move, look for a promotion, or find temporary work? Refer to the following resources, especially to sort out your options for moves across social work fields.

- Use appendix 4 and *What Social Workers Do*, by Margaret Gibelman (1995), for additional ideas on your options in social work.
- Read appendix 10 if you need help deciding on a new functional area.
- Use chapter 2 as a guide for researching options in your market.
- Use the exercises in chapter 1 and the lists in appendix 10 to assess your background.
- If you are a member of NASW or of other associations, ask the staff, leaders, and members whether they know of others who have switched fields. Ask for information interviews with those who have made transitions.
- Ask your undergraduate or graduate school for names of alumni working in the fields that interest you; contact them and seek their advice on transferring your present social work skills to their specific fields.

For example:

> *A social worker who had several years of experience in services for people with mental retardation, foster care, and family preservation wanted to make a move to macrolevel social work at the national level after adjunct teaching and part-time consultation for a couple of years while raising children. The move was proving difficult, so she took a lateral position and continued to teach part-time. A colleague who was working for a national association encouraged her to continue applying for national arena jobs—the social worker had been the number-two candidate for nine national-arena jobs over the*

years she had been looking. Then another part-time instructor told her about a part-time temporary job at a national organization. She got the temporary job, proved herself, and when her supervisor left, the organization promoted her to that full-time slot. Her later projects and publications established her reputation and resulted in invitations from outside organizations to sit on commissions.

Opportunities to Make Contributions in Other Fields
If you went through the exercises in chapter 1, you may have found that you would like to try switching fields in social services or moving outside the traditional realm of social work. Here are some resources for exploring options.

- Use the sections in chapter 1 on educating yourself on new areas and moving across fields and functions to look at the process of making a move.
- If you are having difficulty identifying options, start with an issue area that you now address and brainstorm all the roles, disciplines, types of organizations (nonprofit, for-profit, public), fields, and services that research or study, organize, problem solve, serve, finance, regulate, coordinate with, and in any other way interact with or affect that issue. Think beyond the settings and roles in appendixes 4 and 10, which focus on more traditional social work. Who else has to deal with this issue, use this skill, and so on? Who else works on these issues? How are they funded? Who does something related? How much do you know about the other field or industry?
- You could do the same exercise with a population, a field of practice, a skill, a technology, a job function, a subject matter, or any other knowledge or skill asset you have. As described in chapter 1, using part of a present knowledge or skill base increases your chances of finding a realistic option. Perhaps you have years of experience managing social services agencies and see yourself as a manager who could lead other types of nonprofit organizations, using those broad knowledge and multiple skills sets that all nonprofit organizations need. Or perhaps you have identified new settings where you could use your knowledge and experience with diversity issues or with older adults.
- Make a list of needs associated with that same issue, population, or whatever category you are using; make another list of trends that are affecting or may affect that category. Study the lists. What questions do these lists suggest about how problems are being tackled and by whom? Use networking and information

interviewing to find answers to these questions. From this process you may be able to identify some problems that your knowledge and skills can help solve.

Consider these questions if you are just beginning to think about options for work:

> *Are you ready to leave a social work focus, a social services focus, a nonprofit or public setting culture, a functional role? Would you or could you work a contract or temporary job or a constellation of part-time, contract, and temporary jobs? One social work administrator recommends that you stay open to new opportunities and develop a training or consulting business on the side. Can you see yourself working in other settings described in appendix 4? Have you developed a new interest that you would like to explore? Are you happy with your current work but need to design a backup plan for your peace of mind? As you think about recent changes in social policy, trends in service delivery, and alternatives for future legislation and funding, think also about what opportunities those changes might bring about. What do you have to offer in those arenas? Perhaps there is someone in your organization, community, or specialty with whom you would like to work or study.*

Consider this example:

> *A project manager for an association outgrew his position. From time to time in his work he had assisted staff members of a computer consulting firm by giving them contact names in various states, and he had talked to them about automation of systems and seen them give demonstrations at conferences. When the firm began to expand its business with state governments, he received a call. The firm expressed interest in hiring him specifically for the contacts he had in state governments and his understanding of their information management needs.*

Experiments and Goals

Stumpf (1989) found that for successful, experienced managers, the career management process is largely one of repeated discovery and diagnostics around three questions: (1) What do I want to do? (2) What do they (significant others) want? and (3) What (skills) can I do?

You may want to work toward a long-range goal, or others may be encouraging you to seek advanced positions. If this is the case, consider how much you know about reaching the goal you might have. For example, Elizabeth Cole explains that there are two routes that you can take to move from direct practice to the central office in public child welfare: (1) Either you become noticed for your management skills, or (2) you are recognized for substantive expertise in a program or service, such as adoption. These routes represent a career split. The first is based on strong management problem-solving skills. You must be mobile to pursue this path, and at higher levels your job tenure will be subject to political changes. The second is based on consultative skills and expertise in particular topics and, perhaps, recognition at the national level (personal communication with E. S. Cole, president, Elizabeth S. Cole and Associates, New Hope, PA, September 22, 1993).

Have you sought advice on the basic and intermediate achievements that can prepare you for those additional steps? Have you identified opportunities for working with leaders and management staff from whom you want to learn? In the course of seeking advice and working with and for experienced leaders, is there potential for a mentor relationship?

To discover career opportunities and assess their fit, you can also experiment. This approach is cleverly illustrated in Dale Dauten's (1996) book *The Max Strategy:* "Achievers don't know where they are headed—they just figure they'll play around and see what happens" (p. 24). Such experimentation not only rejuvenates careers by expanding personal interests and confidence, but also encourages thinking outside the professional box, which experienced social workers strongly recommend, and enables you to adapt to the changing environment.

Many books on career management stress the importance of setting goals. Crafting plans and timetables results in valuable strategy maps for some people, but not for all—some people feel overwhelmed and boxed in by goals and action plans. Some social workers find it helpful to identify particular interests or a general direction and use short-term goals to build the skills, knowledge, and experience they will need to take a next step. Others like structure and the process of thinking something through before initiating change, but they may be unable to move beyond this point. Use such approaches to outline and support your experiments in your career management journey rather than to detail elaborate schemes for final aspirations. For example, you might

> *Try out a leadership or advocacy role through professional activities. Get experience in a new area through volunteer work, a special project on the job, a part-time job, coursework or a training program, or self-directed study; this will broaden*

your base and perhaps become a stepping-stone in a new direction. Work with your boss to take on additional responsibilities, such as project management. Brainstorm a list of all the things, personal and professional, that you might like to do some day, find intriguing, or just think are interesting. Is there a way of incorporating some of these experiences into your present activities? Would any of these items serve as a diversion while you try to renew your interest in your job or make a transition? What would you like to state on your résumé in six months?

Ask yourself what work settings value the knowledge and skills developed in another environment. For example, people who work for the federal government often move to consulting firms that contract with federal agencies, and social workers with state and local experience "outside the beltway" are recruited by advocacy organizations that want to bring those perspectives to the national level. Could you experiment with an opportunity in another sector and pick up a different knowledge or skill set, with the goal of taking those assets back to your core field? Note that such transitions, although they may be only temporary, often require that you step outside the boundaries of traditional social work values or put commitments to causes and populations aside until you develop new skills to take back.

On the other hand, social workers have always experimented with service delivery options that meet their values. J. Robin Robb, PhD, vice president for professional development and research chair, National Federation of Societies for Clinical Social Work, Arlington, VA, reported that some private practitioners are not pursuing third-party reimbursement: "They are keeping overhead low in order to offer low fees. Some are forming networks with others committed to social work values, marketing services together, offering confidential services to low- and middle-income clients" (personal communication, June 13, 1996). Other social workers are developing products for managed care companies, taking the lead in creating public–private partnerships and community-based collaborative services, training people with low incomes to start businesses, and setting up services in physician practices.

Self-Assessment

At least once a year, go through the exercises in chapter 1. You will have new accomplishments, skills, knowledge, and possibly new interests. Record them and update your résumé or vita. You may also have a new perspective on your values and needs.

Through this process you may find yourself renewing your commitment to social work values. You may find yourself questioning your direction, however, which may motivate you to explore other options. One person working in mental health at the state level recommends that you routinely do a self-assessment, thoroughly know your own values, and carefully think about your overall goal or mission. As a result, you may re-evaluate your personal criteria for work—for example, autonomy may have become more important to you than money, or just the opposite. One social worker suggests that you ask whether you are satisfied with the limits of your work or position—its impact, service limitations, salary, and influence. Perhaps you have decided that moving up the management ladder is no longer important or that the new philosophy of your organization is unworkable. For example, consider this scenario:

> *A social worker who had been working in the chemical dependency unit of a multiservice children's center decided to leave her position, in part because she questioned the center's treatment philosophy of sending some kids to psychiatric facilities for institutionalization when she felt it was not necessary. She began seeking a new position, which she found in the newspaper. On the basis of her experience with adolescents and chemical dependency, she was hired as a psychiatric reviewer for an insurance company.*

Qualifications and Retooling through Professional Development

"The question is, do you have the competencies, knowledge, and attitude to accomplish the objective?" says Steve Fishbein, chair, Human Resources Division, National Association of State Mental Health Program Directors, Alexandria, VA (personal communication, May 22, 1996). This question is at the heart of any potential employer's inquiry or that of colleagues who might consider you for leadership positions in professional or community groups. It also is a query for yourself as you test new career directions. Your qualifications for work opportunities typically include an academic degree, specialized training, licensure and certifications, work and community experience, and skills and knowledge acquired through self-directed study. What will it take for you to upgrade your qualifications and pursue your interests or meet market needs in the environments to come?

If you have not analyzed what you need to compete for the opportunities you desire, see the sections on options in this chapter and on outlining your qualifications in chapter 1. Answer these questions as well:

- Do you need another certificate to qualify for work in a new interest area?
- Have your professional interests expanded to include research and perhaps a doctoral degree?
- Will you need specific training or education for your new role in, for example, supervision, budgeting, or management?
- Would a specialized training program give you a stepping-stone into a new field of practice?
- Would taking a leadership role in an advocacy or professional association enable you to make a move from, say, program management to policy analysis?

You might also look at the trends discussed earlier in this chapter. How are these affecting your field? What others would you add to the list? Consider selecting one or more areas as the center of your professional development activities this year. Here are some ideas to think about.

> Could you take courses on advanced or basic computer packages, including spreadsheets, databases, and word processing; the Internet and home page design; fund-raising; languages; cultural differences; or small business development or entrepreneurship? Do you have a friend who enjoys surfing the Internet and who would be willing to share his or her knowledge? Is there a continuing education program available on documenting outcomes, evaluating services, or using technology to manage information? Can you join a committee of a professional society or advocacy or trade association that concentrates on technology in human services, issues in aging, practice and cultural diversity, policy development, or managed care and vendorship? Request membership information, a publications list, and a sample newsletter from an association in a field that is new for you; consider joining. Use your contact network to identify newsletters, journals, magazines, books, listservs and newsgroups on the Internet, and possibly video and CD-ROM material. You probably already participate in one work team or collaborative group. Can you develop expertise in making such groups succeed? If work abroad interests you and you have the resources, consider a long-term volunteer commitment overseas.

J. Robin Robb offers this advice for clinicians: "One will constantly need to retool through continuing education, structured peer supervision groups, informal mentors, mentor programs offered through professional associations, group mentoring, consultation, and purchased supervision" (personal communication, June 13, 1996).

Marie Sanchez, senior staff associate, Office of Workforce Development at the Western Interstate Commission for Higher Education Mental Health Program, Boulder, CO, recommends that social workers going out into the field "Look at demographic trends, special populations, and cultural backgrounds of potential clients in areas you are considering for employment. What are your skills? Your knowledge of these cultures? Is there a match? Work at developing culturally competent practice skills. Acquire a second language and the ability to provide bilingual services" (personal communication, July 26, 1996).

Reed Henderson, senior vice president for programs and services, Family Service America, Milwaukee, WI, observes this about qualifications for nonprofit managers: "Boards are looking for executives who have the rare ability to couple traditional social service values with an entrepreneurial approach and leadership style. If you can demonstrate this hybrid combination of traditional values and entrepreneurial leadership, you can compete against business and other disciplines for executive positions. Focus on developing entrepreneurial thinking and experience (risk taking, strategic planning, fee-for-service revenue generation) that positions not-for-profit organizations for long-term growth" (personal communication, June 18, 1996).

In health care, William Spitzer and Kermit Nash (1996) define this expectation: "Social workers must anticipate a focus on documentable performance and goal or outcome measurement, particularly through total quality management and continuous quality improvement methodologies, or in re-engineered environments employing techniques such as critical pathways and/or 'care-mapping'" (p. 26).

No matter what field-specific qualifications you develop, the following skills, common to all fields, are worth enhancing throughout your career:

- Your writing skills—quick, concise, and in the appropriate format—are your core skill set. They reveal your subject knowledge and your ability to think critically and to organize your thoughts. Improving your writing skills will positively affect all other aspects of your qualifications, regardless of your social work field or function.
- Your ability to articulate your competencies, and in many instances what the discipline of social work is, will directly affect

your career path. Believe in yourself as the product, and practice marketing yourself.

- Your ability to assert your argument professionally—particularly with the use of documented outcomes, including data—is critical to your ability to compete in all arenas.

Four Social Workers' Career Development

The career paths described below show how people found new opportunities—or new opportunities found them—and explain the keys to the progression of their careers. None of these people mapped a series of moves in advance. All performed their roles well and made decisions on options, experiments, and interim jobs as they came along.

Example 1

A social worker with a bachelor of science degree and an MSW earned part-time while working has held seven positions. Upon graduation from college, he found a position as a juvenile probation officer through the newspaper. Next, he was promoted to domestic relations counselor after hearing about the job from other staff members and seeing the internal posting; he got the job on the basis of his performance in the first job. Through his work at the court, staff of a private agency became familiar with his work and approached him about a position running a group home, which he took. His contact network expanded, and staff of a residential center approached him about a job as a house manager. It was while he held this position that he began work on his master's degree. Performance on the job resulted in one promotion and then a second, to program director. The agency had created the program director position as a result of ideas he suggested to the executive director. His most recent position as an independent contractor is associated with a group practice, which provided services for his previous employer. He had a conversation to discuss mutual interests with the practice group; they liked his work and his values.

Example 2

A social worker who has a bachelor of arts, an MSW, and a DSW has held 13 positions over a 22-year career. Fresh out of college and with a suggestion from a faculty member, she landed a foundation fellowship that placed her in a mayor's office working on aging issues. She decided to go to graduate school and researched agencies to determine whether any paid for graduate school; she found one and successfully applied.

After graduate school, on a tip from a friend, she moved on to a department of education as an adult education and family life teacher. A professor from graduate school told her about the next position she held, associate project director for research and education in geriatrics. While serving on the board of a hospital's women's auxiliary, she identified a project that interested the auxiliary; the auxiliary gave initial funding for the project, and the social worker wrote grants for outside funding. This three-quarters-time position enabled her to work on her doctorate.

Through a contact made at the hospital project, she learned of a position as director of a geriatric adult health education center. She had developed an acquaintanceship with the former director of the center, who told her about a special assistant position in a state health department; this position provided her with a dissertation topic. Someone who knew her work in an earlier position had become the chief executive officer (CEO) of a hospital; that CEO asked her to take a position as vice president of human resources and program development, a job that gave her high visibility and allowed her to participate in the chamber of commerce. That exposure expanded her contact network.

When colleagues learned that she was interested in career moves, they passed on information about a geriatrics project and program directorships, which she filled in succession. By this time she had developed a reputation in the long-term care field through her positions, board work, publications, and awards. One day, while waiting to have a manicure, she entered into a conversation with someone who turned out to be the manager of health care services for a consulting group. They discovered that, although they had not previously met, they knew of each other. The manager said that he had considered offering her a position before but had assumed that she would not make a move into the private sector. They spoke further. The head of the company also knew her work; he was on the board of a hospital she had worked with earlier. After this initial move into the for-profit sector, she continued as a health care consultant when the initial company merged with another consulting group. Later, when a client company began growing and decided to hire its own health care staff, she was offered the position of vice president of state accounts. The CEO of the company was someone whom she had known for several years; she liked his values and signed on with the company.

Example 3

A social worker with a bachelor of arts degree and an MSW degree has held nine positions since completing his undergraduate work. Upon graduation from college, he went to stay with a friend in a Pacific Rim metropolis where English is widely spoken; he landed a job with a large group-work organization. After a year, he returned to the West Coast and located a job with a similar organization through a newspaper ad. A year or so later, he enrolled in an MSW program. Between his two years of graduate school, he took a summer job as program director for an employment program in an Asian community; he had seen a notice posted for the position at his practicum site. His final MSW field practicum turned into a full-time job in the same Asian neighborhood after graduation.

In less than a year, he was ready to move to another city. He found the next two jobs he held through notices posted at his agency (in one instance, friends had brought the job to his attention). While waiting to hear about an offer in his target city, he took a temporary training and supervision job with youths. The offer to work on a federal grant in the new location did come through, thanks to his community experience abroad, his summer experience supervising youth programs, and his voluntary leadership role in the Asian community. Part of his job entailed anticipating the needs and interests—specifically, the issues of resettlement, adjustment, and welfare for refugees—of the federal officials that he would host on their routine visits to the community mental health care project. Two years later, when he was interested in a new challenge, he sent one official a letter indicating his interests. The official, who happened to have a job opening, encouraged him to apply and eventually hired him. The key to this transition was his knowledge of federal government needs for information and his analytical skills.

After moving to Washington, DC, and spending about five years examining budgets for several programs, including Medicaid, he wanted to further develop his career. He again looked to the private sector. One day he happened to see a former colleague, who was now working for a consulting firm. He sent her a letter and then called to get her advice on making a transition from the public to the private sector. She not only gave him advice, she arranged an interview with the firm. He was particularly interested in this firm when he learned that it had an office in his home state, where he eventually wanted to return. For its part, the firm was anticipating a change in health care policy and was thus quite interested in the knowledge the applicant could bring with him. The personal connection with someone who knew the applicant's work, coupled with his federal experience and a successful interview, resulted in an offer for the position of senior associate.

Although it was exciting to work for a company that was continually developing business ahead of trends, the heavy travel schedule was hard on his family. Eventually, he transferred to the office in his home state to consult with health and insurance providers, and he began to look for a position that would be a better lifestyle fit. That search took him back to the local government through an ad in a government job bulletin. Earlier, when he had run the federal grant program, he had become familiar with the inner workings of the local government. When he interviewed for this new position, he therefore focused on how he would address the critical issues of concern to the administration—funding, political sentiments, and privatization. He believes this was the key to securing a position as a staff officer managing several projects and services in a system that usually promoted from within.

Example 4

With assistance from a friend who was a hospital administrator, this social worker participated in a management training program in the business office of a hospital before going to college. When he completed his bachelor's degree, he left the hospital to attend an MSW program full-time. After he had finished his graduate education, he returned to the hospital to complete the process for state licensure. While working as a medical social worker, he began moonlighting with a home health agency to which he sent business (patients). He had good relationships with the social work and nursing staffs at the agency. His interest in management prompted the social work manager of the agency to recommend him for her position when she was preparing to leave. Based on the relationship he had built with the agency over time and the interview, management hired him.

About two years later, he was ready for a new challenge and applied for a job listed in the newspaper as hospital social work director. The chief operating officer (COO) liked him—there seemed to be a personality match—and the hospital was looking for someone who respected and could be respected by the nursing staff. He got the job, won the respect of the nurses, strengthened social work's role in a new organizational matrix, and began talking with the COO about new ideas. After a year he was given more departments, including utilization review—he knew the big picture and the utilization review process and its part in the mission of the hospital, and he could entrust the operation to the nurse supervisor. The key to his increasing responsibilities was his cost-conscious approach—others respected him as a health care manager. He continued to pursue his entrepreneurial interests by setting up a continuum-of-care program that included outpatient case management to reduce recidivism, obtaining grants for projects, and recruiting physicians for programs he designed. When the hospital went through a major reorganization, he acquired additional departments and now focuses on business development, contracting, marketing, and fund development.

Professional Development

Professional development can occur through unstructured self-directed study or work with a mentor, or it can take place through structured mechanisms, such as professional certifications, professional affiliations, training programs, fellowships, and academic programs. State regulations, although not created for professional development, do entail meeting standards and increasing one's qualifications, so they are included in this section.

State Regulations: Licensure and Certifications

All states regulate the practice of some types of social work or positions social workers might hold through licensing, registration, or certification (Biggerstaff, 1995). State legislatures pass laws to regulate practice. The resulting regulations or rules are designed to protect the state's citizens by ensuring a minimum standard of clinical or direct service. State statutes affect requirements for social work practice in several fields:

- state licensure or certification for social workers
- certification for school social workers
- licensure for marriage and family therapists
- certification and licensure for substance abuse counselors.

Some states are also beginning to regulate domestic violence workers, and there is some discussion of licensing for the fields of employee assistance and managed care as well. Stay informed about anticipated or potential changes in state licensure and certifications through the professional societies in your state, which follow licensure and certification issues. NASW state chapters, which usually follow legislation affecting a range of practice areas, can help you locate a contact.

Various state departments and regulatory boards administer state regulations for licensure and certification for fields of social work practice. They are not housed in a central office in each state. The descriptions below will give you some direction.

Because most states license social workers rather than certify them, the term "license" is used throughout the remainder of this section. Acronyms such as LCSW are used to describe the type or level of licensure a social worker has earned. LCSW refers to "licensed clinical social worker," LBSW refers to "licensed baccalaureate social worker," CSW refers to "certified social worker," and LSW refers to "licensed social worker." Other titles, which vary from state to state, are used as well.

Who Needs to Be a Licensed Social Worker?
Social work licensure has long been associated with mental health services, particularly those offered by private practitioners, and many states have passed legislation in recent years regulating three or four levels of social workers, covering a much broader array of service areas. Now, however, social services agencies usually must have licensed staff to be reimbursed by funders or contractors of social services agencies—insurance and managed care companies and government. As Medicaid and managed care increasingly join together, so social workers providing services outside mental health increasingly need to be licensed. Licensure has replaced the academic degree as a measure of minimum competence.

Licensure rules and their effect vary across states. Social workers must therefore understand the specific requirements of their states. Some general guidelines on who should be licensed follow:

- Social workers intending a career as a solo or group private practitioner must be licensed.
- In general, social workers in or planning a career in clinical or direct services in organizational settings must be licensed.
- Social workers pursuing a career in program planning or management of social services should be licensed. North Carolina, although an exception, has a license termed "certified social work manager" (American Association of State Social Work Boards [AASSWB], 1996).

If you are pursuing a career in such areas as policy, community organizing, social development, and fund-raising, you probably do not need to be licensed. States do not regulate practice in these fields, nor do funders require particular credentials. However, read the section on long-term considerations before you decide not to pursue a license. In some states and in the District of Columbia, anyone calling himself or herself a social worker or practicing as a social worker must be licensed.

Long-Term Considerations

If you anticipate moving to another state, you will want to look at licensing requirements in that state, or at least be aware of how regulations differ among states. According to AASSWB, some contiguous states have reciprocal agreements, but most states do not have reciprocity—that is, a second state will not automatically recognize your license and grant you an equivalent license. You may need to take a different exam, do additional coursework, earn approved continuing education credits, or complete additional supervised hours (personal communication with D. DeAngelis, executive director, AASSWB, Culpeper, Virginia, October 16, 1996). All states use the same set of exams, however, so the new state will accept your score on an examination taken in another state.

If you are considering "stepping out" of social work to pursue other interests, seriously consider getting and maintaining your license. People do return to the field. A license could mean the difference between a position comparable to the one you left and an entry-level job when you re-enter the field.

If you are working in a macrolevel area of practice but think that you may relocate at some point to a community where macrolevel opportunities are rare, you might consider working on a license. For example, one person who had both direct practice and policy experience worked for several years as a legislative aide. When it seemed that she and her spouse might move overseas, she thought about working in employee assistance services for an American corporation with overseas operations, but licensure was required. In this case, the license could have been from any state, however.

Like other aspects of the profession, licensure continues to evolve. AASSWB recommends that you be prepared to meet new criteria not only if you are moving across jurisdictions but also if you stay in the same location. The trend is to verify continued competence by requiring documentation of continuing education for recertification (personal communication with D. DeAngelis, October 16, 1996).

Obtaining Information

Each state has a governing board that determines and reviews licensure regulations, reviews applications, and issues licenses. You should have your own copy of the licensure regulations in your state. Telephone numbers for the licensing boards are available from AASSWB; call 1-800-225-6880 or visit their home page at http://www.aasswb.org.

AASSWB offers the following publications (see appendix 1 for the address and telephone number):

- *Not Just Another Piece of Paper: Why Getting Your Social Work License Matters*, a free pamphlet, answers basic questions and lists telephone numbers for each state board.
- *Social Work Laws and Board Regulations: A State Comparison Study* briefly notes state licensure requirements in a chart format and also outlines continuing education requirements for each state.
- The AASSWB *Candidate Handbook* (1995–96) outlines the content of each exam and details how and where to take the exams. Each state gives this free publication to social workers who inquire about licensure.
- AASSWB study guides are available for each of the four exam levels. In addition to sample questions, they offer references for further reading and advice on taking the exams.

Requirements

Although requirements for licensure vary among states, most include a social work degree from a school accredited by CSWE, often a set number of hours of supervised experience, and a written examination. In California, an oral exam is required as well. Many states have several levels of licensure.

All state licensing boards except Michigan, which does not use an exam, contract with AASSWB to administer examinations. AASSWB offers four types of examinations: basic, intermediate, advanced, and clinical. The type of exam taken depends on the regulations of a particular state and the level of licensure a social worker is pursuing. The AASSWB *Candidate Handbook* (1995–96) is usually included in the packet you receive from the state. AASSWB exams are computerized tests, and results are prompt.

Note that the AASSWB *Candidate Handbook* usually includes an insert with details on taking the exam. It does not tell you what exam you need to take or whether you need to take one, however— you must read your state's licensing rules to determine whether the exam is applicable.

Exam Study Guides

You can order a study guide from AASSWB by completing the form in the *Candidate Handbook* or by calling the telephone number in appendix 1. Private groups offer study courses, which are often advertised in *NASW News*. Be advised that courses vary in quality and may not be necessary because the tests are practice based.

Structure of the Exams

Each state, depending on the type of licensure it requires, determines which of the AASSWB exams match its level of licensure.

The exams are based on a job analysis and a lengthy testing procedure. The *Candidate Handbook* (AASSWB, 1995–96) and study guides (AASSWB, 1996) detail topics and percentage weights for each exam. The major topics are

- *Basic examination:* human development and behavior; effects of culture, race, ethnicity, sexual orientation, and gender; assessment in social work practice; social work practice with individuals, couples, families, groups, and communities; interpersonal communication; professional social worker and client relationship; professional values and ethics; supervision in social work; practice evaluation and the utilization of research; policies and procedures governing service delivery; and social work administration.
- *Intermediate examination:* This second-level exam addresses similar major topical areas, but the subtopics vary and some areas are weighted differently from others.
- *Advanced examination:* Although the advanced examination includes similar areas and weights as the intermediate exam, its degree of difficulty is matched to the MSW degree and a minimum of two years' postdegree experience.
- *Clinical examination:* human development and behavior; effects of culture, race, ethnicity, sexual orientation, and gender; assessment and diagnosis in social work practice; models of psychotherapy and clinical practice; elements of therapeutic communication; the therapeutic relationship; professional values and ethics; clinical supervision and consultation; practice evaluation and the utilization of research; policies and procedures governing service delivery; and clinical practice in the organizational setting.

Certification for School Social Workers
More than half of the states require certification of school social workers through the state department of education. If you intend to be a school social worker, you must obtain your target state's certification requirements from the department of education. Like social work licensure and other certifications, specific coursework and an exam may be necessary. Reciprocity across states for school social work certification is an issue—do not expect it. In many states you must study education law, and in some states you must take a teachers' exam (personal communication with S. San Miguel, lead school social worker, Seminole County Public Schools, FL, July 26, 1996). Both the School Social Work Association of America and NASW (see appendix 1) can provide you with contacts in school social work (in states with school social workers) and in state departments of education. Another source of information is the

Manual on Certification and Preparation of Educational Personnel in the US from the National Association of State Directors of Teacher Education and Certification, which summarizes requirements for certification in each state.

Marriage and Family Therapy Licensure

You can obtain an address list for the state boards regulating marriage and family therapy from the American Association for Marriage and Family Therapy (see appendix 1 for the address and telephone number). The association also publishes a comparison of state laws.

Substance Abuse Certification and Licensure

All states offer certification for substance abuse counselors, but certification is not mandatory in all states. The credential is often referred to as "certified alcohol and drug counselor," "certified alcohol counselor," or "certified drug counselor." According to the National Association of Alcoholism and Drug Abuse Counselors (NAADAC), the trend is toward licensure, a more demanding level of competency. The small number of states that offer licensure have a wide range of requirements—for example, not all require degrees, but most require an exam. NAADAC also sees a trend toward higher standards for education and expects master's degrees to be required in the future. Unlike social work, some states have multiple credentialing boards for substance abuse counselors. For the address of your state contact, check with your local library or NAADAC (see appendix 1 for mail and e-mail addresses and telephone number).

Domestic Violence Worker Certification

According to the National Coalition Against Domestic Violence (NCADV), there is a trend in some states to certify domestic violence workers. This trend puts the focus on service delivery rather than on social change, a concern for NCADV. For current information on this trend, contact NCADV (see appendix 1 for address and telephone number).

Licensure for Long-Term Care Administrators

Long-term care or nursing home administrators are licensed in all states. Regulations vary. All states require the National Association of Boards of Examiners for Nursing Home Administration (NAB) exam. The education requirements range from a high school education to a master's degree in long-term care administration. Some states require completion of an administrator-in-training or intern program specified by the state, which can range from two months to two years. Some states also require a state-specific examination.

The NAB publishes *Directory of U.S. Colleges and Universities Offering Programs in Long-Term Care Administration and State Board Licensure Requirements for Long-Term Care Administrators* (Courtney & Allen, 1997). You can contact NAB at 808 17th Street, NW, Suite 200, Washington, DC 20006; 202-223-9750.

Qualified Mental Retardation Professional
The Health Care Financing Administration (HCFA) regulations require that Medicaid intermediate-care facilities for people with mental retardation have qualified mental retardation professionals on staff; these may include social workers. To qualify, you must have a bachelor's degree and one year of experience working with people with mental retardation or other developmental disabilities (personal communication with M. Reinke, survey and certification program review specialist, HCFA Region 7, Kansas City, KS, November 6, 1996). For details, contact the nearest regional HFCA office; check with your public library for a telephone number.

Professional Certifications

State laws set minimum competence levels, whereas professional credentials set standards for practice (personal communication with D. DeAngelis, executive director, AASSWB, Washington, DC, October 16, 1996). Professional credentials are not the same as licensure. States pass laws regulating social work practice through licensing (although the term "certification" is used in some state regulations). Other credentials are professional certifications. These are not required by law, yet "private practitioners who lack professional certification find it more difficult to get third-party reimbursement and referrals from other professionals" (Barker, 1995, p. 1907). If you are thinking about adding a professional credential, look carefully at the vendorship law in your state, if it has one. Reimbursement for services may depend on your professional credentials, not just on your state license (personal communication with J. Robin Robb, PhD, research chair and vice president for professional development, National Federation of Societies for Clinical Social Work, Chester Springs, PA, June 13, 1996).

Professional credentials are usually offered by professional associations. Some common credentials are described briefly in the sections that follow.

Academy of Certified Social Workers (ACSW) Certification
This certification is often referred to as simply "ACSW." To become a member of the academy, you must have a graduate degree

from a CSWE-accredited school, be a member of NASW, pass an exam, complete two years or 3,000 hours of supervised and paid postmaster's or postdoctoral social work experience in an agency or organized setting, and provide three professional references as well as a written application. NASW offers *A Study Guide for ACSW Certification* (4th ed.), by Ruth R. Middleman (1996; see appendix 1 for address and telephone number).

Diplomate in Clinical Social Work (DCSW)

The DCSW is NASW's highest clinical credential. It requires an MSW from an accredited graduate school, five years or 7,500 hours of postgraduate direct clinical practice of which two years must be under the direct supervision of a clinical social worker, clinical state licensure or certification, documentation of the currency of clinical practice, and successful completion of an examination. Each candidate must affirm adherence to the *NASW's Code of Ethics, Standards for the Practice of Clinical Social Work*, and *Continuing Education Standards*. As a DCSW, you are listed in the *NASW Register of Clinical Social Workers*, which is available in print copy, CD-ROM, and online.

Qualified Clinical Social Worker (QCSW)

The QCSW is offered to clinical social workers with an MSW from an accredited graduate program; two years or 3,000 hours of postgraduate, supervised, and paid clinical experience in an agency or organized setting; and state licensure or certification and/or ACSW certification. As a QCSW, you are listed in the *NASW Register of Clinical Social Workers*.

School Social Work Specialist (SSWS)

NASW offers the SSWS credential. It requires two years of postgraduate, supervised school social work experience and documentation and completion of the School Social Work Specialty Area Test of the National Teachers Examination.

Board Certified Diplomate (BCD)

The American Board of Examiners in Clinical Social Work (ABE) offers the BCD. This is an advanced certification for clinical social workers. It requires a master's degree, five full-time years of clinical practice (including two years under supervision), the highest level of state licensure or certification, and yearly recertification, with requirements for currency of practice, maintenance of license, and continuing education. ABE publishes a directory and has an online database of those who hold the BCD, which it markets to the health care industry. For more information, contact ABE (see appendix 1 for mail and e-mail addresses and telephone number).

Certified Case Manager (CCM)
The Commission for Case Manager Certification offers the CCM. It requires a license or certification to practice in one's field independent of supervision, verified employment experience, an examination, and recertification every five years. For more information, contact Commission for Case Manager Certification, 1835 Rohlwing Road, Suite D, Rolling Meadows, IL 60008; 847-818-0292.

Certified Employee Assistance Professional (CEAP)
The Employee Assistance Professionals Association offers this certification for employee assistance professionals. It requires experience and an exam. Professional development hours beyond the certification are required for recertification (Professional Testing Corporation, 1994–95). Contact the association for details and information on review classes (see appendix 1 for mail and e-mail addresses and telephone number).

Certified Fund Raising Executive and Advanced Certified Fund Raising Executive
The National Society of Fund Raising Executives (NSFRE) offers a certification program for fund-raising professionals with a minimum of five years' experience (NSFRE, n.d.). Contact the association for more information (see appendix 1 for the mail and e-mail addresses and telephone number).

Substance Abuse Credentials
NAADAC and many small regional groups offer professional certifications, which in some states meet regulations for state certification (personal communication with E. Sargent, director of clinical issues, and B. McCall, director of government relations, NAADAC, Arlington, VA, October 17, 1996). For more information, contact NAADAC (see appendix 1).

Long-Term Care Credentials
The American College of Health Care Administrators offers professional certification for long-term care or nursing home administrators. Contact them at 325 South Patrick Street, Alexandria, VA 22314; 703-549-5822.

Health Care Management Credentials
The American College of Healthcare Administration offers several levels of membership and credentialing, including board certification in health care management. The address is One North Franklin Street, Suite 1700, Chicago, IL 60606-3421; 312-424-2800, fax: 312-424-0023.

Professional Affiliations

Membership at particular levels in some professional associations is itself often considered a credential. Requirements to qualify for such membership are extensive. The standards are similar to those for licensing and professional credentials. Membership in the American Association for Marriage and Family Therapy (AAMFT), for example, is often referred to as a credential.

Additional Credentials

You may come across other desired credentials that are not licenses, certificates, or memberships. For example, if you meet the requirements to become an AAMFT-approved supervisor, then you may find social workers and others seeking you out as they work on their supervised practice requirements toward AAMFT membership.

Special Opportunities: Fellowships, Internships, and Training Programs

Fellowships, internships, and training programs are sponsored by academic institutions, professional associations, public and private organizations, and foundations. These internships and postdegree training opportunities are excellent vehicles for enhancing your qualifications, expanding your professional network, and building a résumé or vita. Many of these programs serve as springboards for career growth, and competition for these opportunities is often stiff. If you are a student, ask your field education office whether a program could meet your practica requirements. A list of these opportunities is in appendix 9.

Before applying for these programs, ask for names of current program participants and consult with them on the quality of the experience and strategies for making a successful application. Always address the interest of the program in every aspect of your application, and ask several people with knowledge of the subject to critique your essays. Your writing should be concise, analytical, and focused on results. Sponsors are not looking for essays that merely describe well-known problems and offer nothing but rhetoric.

Academic Degrees

As you explore options, you may find that you want to pursue a graduate degree at the master's or doctoral level to bolster your qualifications for social work practice, to move into research and teaching, or to complement your social work education with training in another field. Graduate education is a serious time and dollar commitment that will have a great effect on the remainder of your career. Below are brief overviews of social work education at the master's and doctoral levels and a few thoughts on seeking degrees in other disciplines; appendix 11 offers suggestions for considering advanced education.

Master's Degree Programs in Social Work
The master's degree is considered the terminal practice degree in social work. Programs at the master's level are organized by methods or fields of practice. CSWE lists those methods as direct practice, community organization and planning, administration or management, and generic. Fields are categorized as aging or gerontological social work; alcohol, drug, and substance abuse; child welfare; community planning; corrections and criminal justice; family services; group services; health; mental health or community mental health; mental retardation; occupational or industrial social work; public assistance and public welfare; rehabilitation; and school social work. Many programs offer combinations of methods and fields of practice (Lennon, 1996). You can obtain a list of master's-degree programs from CSWE (see appendix 1).

Doctoral Degree Programs in Social Work
If you are interested in advancing the field of social work through research, education, leadership, and policy development, doctoral education may be your next step. All doctoral programs require coursework, a comprehensive or qualifying exam, and a dissertation. Most doctoral programs focus on research and teaching on social work practice. A few programs provide advanced training in practice skills; degrees from these programs are sometimes called "advanced practice doctorates." Regardless of the focus, all programs prepare students to do research on practice. Note that some universities offer the PhD (Doctor of Philosophy) and others the DSW (Doctor of Social Work). Neither title is associated with a particular type of program (personal communication with C. Garvin, chair, Group for the Advancement of Doctoral Education, University of Michigan, Ann Arbor, October 17, 1996). For a list of doctoral programs, visit the Group for the Advancement of Doctoral Education's Web site at http://www.rit.edu/~694www/PHD.htm/.

Considering Degrees in Other Disciplines
As work environments become increasingly interdisciplinary, social workers are often asked to fill multiple functions. Consequently, you may want to build on your social work education by earning a degree in another field. One social worker employed by a large fund-raising organization considered pursuing a master's degree in business administration to complement her work in financial planning with major donors. Another social worker with a concurrent degree in law is seeking a doctorate in geography;

she plans to advocate for people with low incomes who face environmental problems in their communities. Another social worker chose a law degree to complement her background in family therapy; she now works in estate planning. If you are considering an additional degree, research the job and academic program markets carefully.

The following passage is about a master's-prepared social worker who broadened her background with a second master's degree, always called herself a social worker, and pursued international interests.

> *A bilingual MSW graduate with several years of practice experience in pediatrics decided that she wanted to expand her knowledge of health care policy. While still working as a peri-natal social worker, she earned her master's degree in public health. At the completion of her program, someone she knew through earlier consulting work asked her to apply for a position as public health social work consultant with the state health department. She was offered the job in part because she also had the public health degree. In this position she provided consultation and technical assistance for child and maternal health programs, reviewed grant proposals, negotiated and monitored contracts and budgets, and analyzed proposed state legislation. She also had the opportunity to conduct a study and oversee a large statewide program.*
>
> *Several years later, she received a call from a social worker who led a federally funded program at a major teaching hospital and who was now retiring. The social worker encouraged her to apply for the position, which she did. Shortly afterward, she was hired. Reputation was the key. Through her work and professional activities, she was known to federal funders and had developed a network statewide and across the country in the field of maternal and child health.*
>
> *A couple of years later, through her leadership in a multidisciplinary professional society, she became a contact for a Central American country seeking funding in the United States. A private nonprofit agency included her name in a grant proposal, which led the U.S. government to arrange for her to provide training in the nonprofit agency's country. That work led to consultation and teaching opportunities throughout Central America and, later, to a temporary position with an organization in the original country.*
>
> *In the meantime, she had remained in contact with the dean of her master's program, who gave her name to the faculty of another school of social work that was creating an institute on children and families at risk. The director of the*

institute recruited her to head international projects and hired her for her knowledge of Latin America and program development. When the funding for the institute ended, she returned to consulting work in the United States and Latin America.

While visiting a chapter office of a national health care organization to gather information for a parent education group she was forming, she met the chapter president. Because she was then actively looking for employment, she always carried her résumé to give to people she met. In a conversation conducted in Spanish, she gave the résumé to the president and told him about her background. He invited her to an event, at which he introduced her to a vice president of a public relations firm. The firm had just established a Latin American office and, although there were no current job openings, the vice president asked that she stay in touch.

In the meantime, the public health social worker, as she called herself, had decided to move back to Latin America. She was so busy making plans that she did not return a couple of calls from the vice president at the public relations firm until shortly before moving. When they did talk, it was about a potential job opportunity; nothing was firm, however, and the social worker moved abroad as planned. Soon thereafter, she received a call informing her that the public relations firm had made a proposal to a client company and, if she was interested, the firm would book her on a flight to join the meeting. She followed through and in less than two weeks was hired. As before, she continued to call herself a social worker in her new capacity of program developer for health and social development projects in the United States and Latin America.

References

American Association of State Social Work Boards. (1995–96). *Candidate handbook.* Culpeper, VA: Author.

American Association of State Social Work Boards. (1996). *AASSWB study guide.* Culpeper, VA: Author.

American Association of State Social Work Boards (AASSWB). (1996). *Social work laws and board regulations: A state comparison study.* (Available from AASSWB, 400 South Ridge Parkway, Suite B, Culpeper, VA 22701)

Barker, R. M. (1995). Private practice. In R. L. Edwards (Ed.-in-Chief), *Encyclopedia of social work* (19th ed., Vol. 3, pp. 1905–1910). Washington, DC: NASW Press.

Biggerstaff, M. A. (1995). Licensing, regulation, and certification. In R. L. Edwards (Ed.-in-Chief), *Encyclopedia of social work* (19th ed., Vol. 2, pp. 1616–1617). Washington, DC: NASW Press.

Bridges, W. (1994). *Job shift*. Reading, MA: Addison-Wesley.

Collard, B., Epperheimer, J. W., & Saign, D. (1996). *Career resilience in a changing workplace*. Paper adapted from Information Series 366, ERIC Clearinghouse on Adult, Career and Vocational Education, Center on Education and Training for Employment, College of Education, Ohio State University, Columbus.

Courtney, S., & Allen, J. E. (1997). *Directory of U.S. colleges and universities offering a curriculum in long-term care administration and state board licensure requirements for long-term care administrators*. Chapel Hill, NC: National Association of Board of Examiners for Nursing Home Administration and the University of North Carolina at Chapel Hill Long Term Care Administration Teaching Resources Project.

Dauten, D. (1996). *The max strategy*. New York: William Morrow.

Gibelman, M. (1995). *What social workers do*. Washington, DC: NASW Press.

Granovetter, M. S. (1973). The strength of weak ties. *American Journal of Sociology, 78*, 1360–1380.

Group for the Advancement of Doctoral Education. http://www.rit.edu/~694www/PHD.htm/.

Hakim, C. (1994). *We are all self-employed: The new social contract for working in a changed world*. San Francisco: Berrett-Koehler.

Lennon, T. M. (1996). *Statistics on social work education in the United States: 1995*. Alexandria, VA: Council on Social Work Education.

Middleman, R. R. (1996). *A study guide for ACSW certification* (4th ed.). Washington, DC: NASW Press.

National Society of Fund Raising Executives. (n.d.). *NSFRE membership benefits*. Alexandria, VA: Author.

Professional Testing Corporation. (1994–95). *Certification examination for employee assistance professionals: Handbook for candidates*. New York: Author.

Rifkin, J. (1995). *The end of work: The decline of the global labor force and the dawn of the post-market era*. New York: G. P. Putnam's Sons.

Spitzer, W. J., & Nash, K. B. (1996). Education preparation for contemporary health care social work practice. *Social Work in Health Care, 24,* 9–34.

Stumpf, S. A. (1989). Towards a heuristic model of career management. *International Journal of Career Management, 1,* 11–20.

Waterman, R. H., Jr., Waterman, J. A., & Collard, B. A. (1994, July–August). Toward a career-resilient workforce. *Harvard Business Review,* pp. 87–95.

Professional and Advocacy Associations

This appendix includes credentialing bodies and associations of individuals, organizations, or state chapter affiliates. Some of them offer membership to individuals as well as to agencies or programs. The associations often lobby on behalf of their individual or institutional members. Other membership services may include training, consulting, research, program development, publications, and personnel services. Remember that their purpose is not to provide career and job-hunting services, although some of their services may be beneficial to those seeking positions and career development. Most important, associations offer the opportunity to network and work with others interested in the same issues.

American Association for Marriage and Family Therapy (AAMFT)

1133 15th Street, NW
Suite 300
Washington, DC 20005
202-452-0109
Fax: 202-223-2329
Internet: http://www.aamft.org

The association offers membership at individual and student levels. At its annual conference in October or November, it presents "Showcase of Accredited Programs" for students or new professionals, which includes information on planning a career, job listings, and a career center with résumé consultants and other services. There is an employment section in the AAMFT newsletter, *Family Therapy News;* AAMFT also publishes *Practice Strategies*, which advises professionals on practice and career issues.

American Association of State Social Work Boards (AASSWB)

400 South Ridge Parkway, Suite B
Culpeper, VA 22701
800-225-6880
E-mail: info@aasswb.org
Internet: http://www.aasswb.org

Members are state boards of social work; they meet each fall and spring. AASSWB develops and maintains the licensing exams used by all states. Career-related resources include several publications: licensure study guides, a comparison of state laws, and a summary of continuing educa-tion for state licensure, among others.

American Association on Mental Retardation (AAMR)

444 North Capitol Street, NW
Suite 846
Washington, DC 20001-1512
800-424-3688 or 202-387-1968
Fax: 202-387-2193
E-mail: aamr@access.digex.net
Internet: http://www.aamr.org

Membership is offered to individuals. The annual conference, held in May, features a job bank. The association has a social work division and announces job openings in its periodicals.

American Board of Examiners in Clinical Social Work (ABE)

21 Merchant's Row
Boston, MA 02109
800-694-5285
Fax: 800-694-7882
E-mail: abe@abecsw.org
Internet: http://www.abecsw.org

ABE offers an advanced certification—the board-certified diplomate (BCD)—for clinical social workers. Career-related resources include a directory and online database of those who hold the BCD.

American Planning Association

1776 Massachusetts Avenue, NW
Suite 400
Washington, DC 20036
202-872-0611
Fax: 202-872-0643
Internet: http://www.planning.org

Membership is at individual and student levels. Career-related resources include *JobMart* (a job newsletter) and *Planner's Salaries & Employment Trends*. It also offers the Planners Referral Service, a computerized résumé databank. The association sponsors a job market at its annual conference.

American Public Health Association (APHA)

1015 15th Street, NW
Washington, DC 20005
202-789-5600
Fax: 202-789-5661
E-mail: comments@msmail.apha.org
Internet: http://www.apha.org

Membership is at the individual, student, and organizational levels. The annual conference, held in October or November, features a job placement service; positions for social workers are included.

American Public Welfare Association (APWA)

810 First Street, NE
Suite 500
Washington, DC 20002-4267
202-682-0100
Fax: 202-289-6555
Internet: http://www.apwa.org

Membership is at the individual and organizational levels; specialized meetings are held throughout the year. The association publishes *Public Welfare Directory*, which is a nationwide list of public social services agencies at all levels.

American Society of Forensic Clinical Social Workers

135 East 50th Street
Suite 102
New York, NY 10022
212-753-1355

The 150 or so members of this organization hold the highest clinical social work credentials, either the board-certified diplomate or the NASW diplomate. The society provides evaluations for courts in those states that allow social workers to perform this function. The society does not hold a conference, nor does it publish a newsletter. It can provide information on the only training program for forensic social workers, which is sponsored by the Society for Clinical Social Workers in New York.

American Society on Aging

833 Market Street
Suite 511
San Francisco, CA 94103-1824
415-974-9600
Fax: 414-975-0300
Internet: http://www.housecall.com/oac/asa

Membership is at the individual and organizational levels; the annual conference is held in March. The association offers job and career resources on the Internet (including JOB ALERT for postings of résumés and job announcements and sections on continuing education and profiles of members).

The ARC (a national organization on mental retardation)

500 East Border
Suite 300
Arlington, TX 76010
817-261-6003
Fax: 817-277-3491
Internet: http://www.thearc.org/welcome.html

Membership is at the individual level; an annual conference is held in the fall, usually in November. The organization publishes *Making a Difference: Career Opportunities in Disability-Related Fields*, which includes a list of university-affiliated programs, salary information, and contact information for associations addressing specific disabilities.

Association for Advancement of Behavior Therapy

305 Seventh Avenue
New York, NY 10001-6008
212-647-1890
Fax: 212-647-1865

The association offers individual and student memberships; the annual conference is in November. Career-related resources include a job placement service for registrants and a free professional consultation service regarding education and career decisions; the association also lists job openings, position-wanted ads, and fellowships in its publication, *The Behavior Therapist*.

Association for the Advancement of Social Work with Groups (AASWG)

c/o University of Akron
Akron, OH 44325-8050
800-807-0793
Fax: 330-072-5739
Internet: http://www.barry.edu/ssw/aaswg/aaswg.html

Membership is at the individual level; conferences are held annually in October. AASWG offers opportunities for networking and continuing education. It has a group work discussion forum on the Internet; send an e-mail message to listproc@martin.barry.edu and in the body of the message type the following: subscribe groupwork-aaswg [your e-mail address, first name, last name]. It also responds to position-wanted ads on SOCWORK LISTSERV and the GROUPWORK LISTSERV on the Internet if the candidate appears qualified and is seeking a position in group work. It also responds to e-mail inquiries at jhramey@uakron.edu. Position-wanted classified ads are accepted for the *Social Work with Groups* newsletter.

Association for Experiential Education (AEE)

2305 Canyon Boulevard
Suite 100
Boulder, CO 80302
303-440-8844
Fax: 303-440-9581
Internet: http://www.princeton.edu/~rcurds/aee.html

Membership is at individual and organizational levels; the annual conference is held in September. The association publishes *AEE Membership Directory and Handbook*, *Directory of Experiential Therapy and Adventure-Based Counseling Programs*, *Experience-Based Training*, and *Development: Directory of Programs and Jobs Clearinghouse*.

Association for Women in Social Work (AWSW)

National Coordinator
Colorado State University
780 Grant Place
Boulder, CO 80302

Individual membership is at the national level. There are some state chapters. The annual conference, which is sponsored by the FemSchool Chapter and entitled "Summer Institute for Feminist Social Work," is held in the summer. The organization's newsletter, published periodically, lists job ads.

Association of Family and Conciliation Courts (AFCC)

329 West Wilson Street
Madison, WI 53703-3612
608-251-4001
Fax: 608-251-2231
E-mail: afcc@igc.apc.org
Internet: http://www.igc.org/afcc

Membership is at the individual and organizational levels; the annual conference is held in May. Members may purchase the AFCC annual directory of members, and AFCC maintains a résumé databank for all experience levels and publishes job openings in the quarterly newsletter.

Association of Jewish Family and Children's Agencies (AJFCA)

3086 State Highway 27
Suite 11
P.O. Box 248
Kendall Park, NJ 08824
800-634-7346
Fax: 908-821-0493
E-mail: ajfca@aol.com

Membership is at the organizational level; the annual meeting is held in late spring. The association publishes a membership directory, which is available only to members. It maintains a databank of available candidates at all experience levels, although the bank is used primarily for executive and upper-management positions. The *Professional Opportunities Bulletin*, a bimonthly national job newsletter, includes a section for "situations wanted," which may be used by people at any level of experience.

Association of Oncology Social Work (AOSW)

1910 East Jefferson Street
Baltimore, MD 21205
410-614-3990
Fax: 410-614-3991
Internet: http://www.biostat.wisc.edu/aosw/aoswhello.html

Membership is open to students and to individual professionals. At annual meetings in May, employers with exhibit booths sometimes interview job candidates. Some jobs are published in the association's quarterly newsletter, *AOSW News*.

Association of Pediatric Oncology Social Workers

The address varies depending on the location of officers; contact NASW for a telephone number. Membership is at the individual level, and meetings are held annually in May. The association lists job openings in its newsletter.

Association of State and Territorial Public Health Social Work

Mississippi State Department of Health
2423 North State Street
P.O. Box 1700
Jackson, MS 39215-1700
601-960-7464
Fax: 601-354-6104

State health departments appoint individuals to this organization; individual social workers also can join. Conferences are held annually in September. The association offers opportunities for networking and continuing education.

Child Welfare League of America (CWLA)

440 First Street, NW
Suite 310
Washington, DC 20001
202-638-2952
Fax: 202-638-4004
E-mail: hn3898@handsnet.org
Internet: http://www.cwla.org

Membership is offered only at the organizational level; the annual conference is held in February, March, or April. The CWLA directory of member agencies is available for purchase. Classifieds, most of them for executive positions, are listed in the journal *Child Welfare*; free samples are available. CWLA also conducts a salary survey.

Children's Defense Fund (CDF)

25 E Street, NW
Washington, DC 20001
202-628-8787
Fax: 202-662-3510
Internet: http://www.childrensdefense.org

CDF is an advocacy rather than a membership organization. It offers an internship hotline at 202-662-4579, an employment hotline at 202-662-3680, and an annual conference hotline at 202-662-3684.

Christian Community Development Association

1909 Robinson Street
Jackson, MS 39209
773-762-0994
E-mail: askccda@aol.com

The association offers organizational, individual, and student memberships; its annual conference is held in November. Career-related resources include a directory of member organizations and the quarterly *Job Referral Listing*, which describes administrative, community-outreach positions in Christian organizations located throughout the United States. It also lists position-wanted ads from individuals and posts news about internships.

Community Development Society

1123 North Water Street
Milwaukee, WI 53202
414-276-7106
Fax: 414-276-7704
Internet: http://www.infoanalytic.com/cds

Membership is at the individual level; the annual conference is held in July. The society publishes *Vanguard*, a quarterly newsletter; some job openings are listed therein.

Community Information Exchange

1029 Vermont Avenue, NW
Suite 710
Washington, DC 20005
202-628-2981

This is a network of organizations involved in community revitalization. It publishes *Exchange News*, a monthly newsletter that includes some job listings.

Council of Jewish Federations (CJF)

730 Broadway
New York, NY 10003-9596
212-475-5000
Fax: 212-529-5842

Membership is at the organizational level; the annual conference is held in November. The council publishes the *Directory of Federations*. The council also offers a personnel service for candidates interested in employment with Jewish federations and coordinates job interviews during conferences held several times a year. The quarterly job newsletter, *CJF Personnel Newsletter*, is free to registered candidates; 50–60 jobs are listed in each issue (contact the Personnel Services Department, 212-598-3585, for further information).

Council of Nephrology Social Work

National Kidney Foundation
30 East 33rd Street
New York, NY 10016

Council on Social Work Education (CSWE)

1600 Duke Street, 3rd floor
Alexandria, VA 22314
703-683-8080
Fax: 703-683-8099
E-mail: cswe@access.digex.net
Internet: http://www.cswe.org

Individual membership is at the national level; most members are faculty and administrators at schools of social work. An annual program meeting is held each year in March. Career-related resources include a teachers' registry and information service, which publishes *Vacancy Announcements* three times each year. If you are looking for a faculty position, you can register with the service, which sends candidate profiles to schools of social work. Both vacancies and candidate information are posted at the annual conference. A message service facilitates communication between interviewers and candidates, who need not be registered for the conference to participate.

Employee Assistance Professionals Association (EAPA)

2101 Wilson Boulevard
Suite 500
Arlington, VA 22201-3062
703-522-6272
Fax: 703-522-4585
E-mail: eapamain@aol.com

Membership is at individual, student, and organizational levels; the annual conference is held in October or November. Organizations can place ads on the Employment Bulletin Board at the annual conference. The association offers employment services to members through Job Bank USA, a job posting site and a résumé databank. Individuals interested in the field of employee assistance are encouraged to network at local chapter meetings. A certification program is available through the association.

Evangelical Lutheran Church of America

8765 West Higgins
Chicago, IL 60631-4101
312-380-2689
Fax: 312-380-2707

The association holds its annual meeting in April. It publishes a directory of member institutions, which is available to members, and maintains a résumé databank for chief executive officer, nursing home administration, and upper-management positions. It also publishes *Personnel Information and Referral Bulletin*, which can be purchased. See appendix 8.

Family Service America (FSA)

11700 West Lake Park Drive
Milwaukee, WI 53224
414-359-1040
Fax: 414-359-1074
Internet: http://www.fsanet.org

Membership is at the organizational level; the annual conference is held in October. The association publishes a directory of member agencies, which is available for purchase, and *Management Opportunities Bulletin*. It also maintains a résumé databank that member agencies can access.

Gerontological Society of America

1275 K Street, NW
Suite 350
Washington, DC 20005-4006
202-842-1275
Fax: 202-842-1150
E-mail: geron@geron.org
Internet: http://www.geron.org

Membership is at the individual level; the annual conference is held in November, at which the society sometimes sponsors a job fair. *Gerontology News*, the society's newsletter, lists jobs, fellowships, and grants. A mentor program for students is available.

Institute for the Advancement of Social Work Research (IASWR)

750 First Street, NE
Suite 700
Washington, DC 20002
202-336-8393
Fax: 202-336-8351
E-mail: iaswr@capcon.net

This is not an association; it does not hold an annual meeting, nor does it have a membership structure. It does facilitate careers in social work research by providing technical assistance to researchers and opportunities to network with other researchers.

International Federation of Social Workers (IFSW)

Office of the Secretary General
P.O. Box 4649, Soflenberg
N-0506 Oslo, Norway

Membership is available to individuals and organizations. Global and regional meetings are held in alternate years. The IFSW roster of 63 member associations worldwide is available for $5.00 from NASW's Peace and International Affairs office.

Jewish Community Centers Association (JCCA)

15 East 26th Street
New York, NY 10010-1579
212-532-4949
Fax: 212-481-4174
E-mail: info@jcca.org

Jewish community centers nationwide are the members of the association. Conferences are held in alternate years for professional and volunteer leadership. JCCA offers personnel services to member centers and individuals seeking positions with Jewish community centers; it also refers registered candidates to positions and provides guidelines on seeking employment. It publishes *JCC Association Personnel Reporter*, which lists in each issue about 45–50 positions in Jewish community centers; the publication is available to registered candidates.

National Association for Family Based Services

1513 Stoney Point Road, NW
Cedar Rapids, IA 52405
319-396-4829

An annual conference is held in December.

National Association of Alcoholism and Drug Abuse Counselors (NAADAC)

1911 North Fort Myer Drive
Suite 900
Arlington, VA 22209
703-741-7686 or 1-800-548-0497
Fax: 703-741-7698
E-mail: naadac@internetmci.com
Internet: http://www.naadac.org

Individual and student membership is at the national and state chapter levels; annual conferences are held in July. Career-related resources include a certification program, a salary and compensation report, a national directory of certified addiction counselors, and state contacts for certification.

National Association of Black Social Workers (NABSW)

8436 West McNichols
Detroit, MI 48221

Individual membership, open to those of African descent, is at the national and state chapter levels. Contact the national office for the address of your state chapter. Annual meetings are held in April. Career-related resources include job listings in the association newsletter and job fairs at some conferences. You can also connect with agencies and graduate schools that have exhibits at the conferences.

National Association of Child Advocates

1522 K Street, NW
Suite 600
Washington, DC 20005
202-289-0777
Fax: 202-289-0776
E-mail: hn1315@handsnet.org
Internet: http://www.childadvocacy.org

ibership is at the individual and organizational levels; there is no
al conference. Two membership lists are available upon request. In-
uals who register for the résumé bank are notified when job an-
:ements are received.

National Association of Community Action Agencies (NACAA)

1100 17th Street, NW
Suite 500
Washington, DC 20036-4601
202-265-7546
E-mail: info@nacaa.org
Internet: http://www.nacaa.org

Membership is at the organizational level; the annual conference is held in
September. The association publishes *The Community Action Directory* of
its members. It occasionally prints job announcements in its newsletter.

National Association of Perinatal Social Workers

Address varies according to the addresses of officers; contact NASW for
a telephone number. Membership is open to students and other individuals. The association, which holds its annual meeting in May, offers opportunities for networking.

National Association of Regional Councils

1700 K Street, NW
Suite 1300
Washington, DC 20006
202-457-0710
Fax: 202-296-9352

Membership is at the organizational level; conferences are held in February and June. The association publishes a member directory, and job announcements are listed in its newsletter.

National Association of Social Workers (NASW)

750 First Street, NE
Suite 700
Washington, DC 20002-4241
1-800-638-8799
Fax: 202-336-8340
Internet: http://www.naswdc.org

Individual membership is at the national and state chapter levels; a student
membership rate is available. NASW holds annual meetings in the fall.
Career-related resources include JobLink, which lists job openings in social work (303-221-4970; TDD 202-336-8396); *NASW NEWS,* the
association's newspaper; and a job fair at the annual conference, with booths

set up by some employers and graduate schools in the conference exhibit hall. Many state chapters also offer career-related resources, including newsletters with job listings and position-wanted ads. Its Peace and International Affairs Program offers *Overseas Job Placement Tips*; send a self-addressed stamped envelope to NASW, Peace and International Affairs, at the address above.

National Coalition Against Domestic Violence (NCADV)

P.O. Box 18749
Denver, CO 80218
303-839-1852
Fax: 303-831-9251
E-mail: ncadv1@ix.netcom.com
Internet: http://www.webmerchants.com/ncadv

The coalition publishes the *National Directory of Domestic Violence Programs*.

National Coalition for the Homeless (NCH)

1612 K Street, NW
Suite 1004
Washington, DC 20006
202-775-1322
Fax: 202-775-1316
E-mail: nch@ari.net
Internet: http://www.nch.ari.net

Individual- and student-level memberships are available. The coalition publishes *A Directory of Statewide & National Homeless/Housing Advocacy Organizations*.

National Conference of State Legislatures (NCSL)

1560 Broadway
Suite 700
Denver, CO 80202
303-830-2200
Fax: 303-863-8003
Internet: http://www.ncsl.org

Memberships are available to state lawmakers and legislative staffers; the annual conference is held in July. NCSL publishes the *Legislative Staff Directory* and employs college interns each year.

National Congress for Community Economic Development (NCCED)

11 Dupont Circle, NW
Suite 325
Washington, DC 20036
202-234-5009
Fax: 202-234-4510

Membership is at the organizational level; two conferences are held each year. The NCCED membership directory is available to members.

National Council for Community Behavioral Healthcare (NCCBH)

12300 Twinbrook Parkway
Suite 320
Rockville, MD 20852
301-984-6200
Fax: 301-881-7159
Internet: http://www.nccbh.org

Membership is at agency and individual levels; annual conferences are held in spring. The council publishes a membership directory; it also lists job openings at various levels in its newsletter, *National Council News*, and in its *JOBank* newsletter—a recent issue listed nine announcements. Both publications can be purchased by nonmembers.

National Council on the Aging (NCOA)

409 Third Street, SW
Suite 200
Washington, DC 20024
202-479-1200
Fax: 202-479-0735
E-mail: info@ncoa.org
Internet: http://www.ncoa.org

Membership is at individual, student, and organizational levels; annual conferences are held in the spring. The council offers Job Bank, a networking service at the annual conference, and publishes jobs openings in the newsletter *Networks;* it also publishes its membership directory.

National Council on Alcoholism and Drug Dependence (NCADD)

12 West 21st Street
New York, NY 10010
212-206-6770
Fax: 212-645-1690
E-mail: national@ncadd.org; publicpolicy@ncadd.org
Internet: http://www.ncadd.org

Membership is at the organizational level; the annual conference is held in October or November. The council publishes its *Affiliate Directory* of about 200 state and local organizations. Call 1-800-475-HOPE for the telephone number of the affiliate in your local area.

National Court Appointed Special Advocates Association

100 West Harrison Street
Suite 500
Seattle, WA 98119-4123
1-800-628-3233
Internet: http://www.nationalcasa.org

Membership is at the program and individual levels; annual conferences are held in April or May. Directories are available to programs. Job openings are sometimes published in the newsletter that goes to program-level members.

National Federation of Societies for Clinical Social Work (NFSCSW)

P.O. Box 3740
Arlington, VA 22203
703-522-3866
Fax: 703-522-9441
Internet: http://www.webcom.com/~nfscsw

Membership in this organization, which offers opportunities for networking and continuing education, is through state chapters. National meetings are held, but not annually.

National Hospice Organization (NHO)

1901 North Moore Street
Suite 901
Arlington, VA 22209
703-243-5900
Fax: 703-525-5762
E-mail: drsnho@cais.com
Internet: http://www.nho.org

Individual and student memberships are available; the annual conference is held in November. The organization maintains a job bank hotline and publishes the directory *Guide to the Nation's Hospices*.

National Low Income Housing Coalition (NLIHC)

1012 14th Street, NW
Suite 1200
Washington, DC 20005
202-662-1530
Fax: 202-393-1973
Internet: http://www.handsnet.org//nlihc

Membership is at individual and organizational levels; the annual conference is held in February or March. The coalition announces job openings in its monthly newsletter, *Roundup*, and offers legislative internships.

...al Mental Health Association (NMHA)

...ince Street
...ia, VA 22314-2971
... ..~-684-7722
Fax: 703-684-5968
Internet: http://www.nmha.org

Individual membership is at the state level; the annual conference is held in May. The association occasionally lists job openings in a newsletter.

National Network for Social Work Managers (NNSWM)

1316 New Hampshire Avenue, NW
Suite 602
Washington, DC 20036-6353
202-785-2814
Fax: 202-785-2904
Internet: http://www.uncg.edu/swk/nnswm/htm

Membership is at the individual professional and student levels; annual meetings are held in February. This organization promotes networking among members, provides a membership directory to members, and lists some job openings in its newsletter.

National Society of Fund Raising Executives (NSFRE)

1101 King Street
Suite 700
Alexandria, VA 22314
703-684-0410
Fax: 703-684-0540
Internet: http://www.nsfre.org

Membership is offered at individual, student, and intern (new professional) levels; annual meetings are held in March. The society publishes *ESS Employment Opportunities*, a monthly job listing, and *Who's Who in Fund-Raising*, a directory of members. Training and certification programs are available.

North American Association of Christians in Social Work (NAACSW)

P.O. Box 7090
St. Davids, PA 19087-7090
610-687-5777

Membership is for individuals. Annual conferences are held, usually in September or November, at which some employers have booths in the exhibit area and list openings on the job board. Some jobs are posted in the association's newsletter *Catalyst*. Some employers mail job announcements directly to members.

Poverty & Race Research Action Council (PRRAC)

1711 Connecticut Avenue, NW
Suite 207
Washington, DC 20009
202-387-9887
Fax: 202-387-0764
E-mail: prrac@aol.com

This is a network of researchers and activists; it does not have a membership structure. There is no annual meeting, but local meetings are held occasionally. The council publishes *PRRAC Network Directory*, a membership directory available to members. It also prints job and fellowship opportunities in its newsletter *Poverty & Race*.

School Social Work Association of America (SSWAA)

P.O. Box 2072
Northlake, IL 60164
Fax: 630-355-1919
E-mail: sswaa@aol.com

Membership is at the individual level; the annual conference is held in the spring. The association connects people who are interested in school social work with information on contacts; it also provides telephone numbers for state departments of education.

Society for Social Work Administrators in Health Care (SSWAHC)

c/o American Hospital Association
One North Franklin Street, 31st Floor
Chicago, IL 60606
312-422-3774
Fax: 312-422-4580
Internet: http://www.sswahc.org

Membership is at the individual level; the annual conference is held in early spring.

Travelers Aid International (also known as National Organization of Travelers Aid Societies)

512 C Street, NE
Washington, DC 20002
202-546-3120
Fax: 202-546-1625

Membership is at the organizational level; the annual conference is held in June. Travelers Aid publishes *Travelers Aid International Guide to Inter-City Services*, a directory of its member agencies.

United Neighborhood Centers of America (UNCA)

3135 Euclid Avenue
Suite B-08
Cleveland, OH 44115
216-391-3028
Fax: 216-391-6206
E-mail: unca@en.com

Membership is at the organizational level; several regional meetings are held each year. The organization publishes its membership directory, which may be purchased. Upon request of member organizations, it mails job candidates' résumés.

United Way of America

701 North Fairfax Street
Alexandria, VA 22314-2045
703-836-7100
Fax: 703-683-7840
Internet: http://www.unitedway.org

The membership consists of United Way affiliates nationwide; the annual meeting of the national organization is held in May. Job openings and career advice are listed in the organization's monthly newsletter *Focus*.

Work Preferences

The following questions regard work preferences. For each question, think of specific examples from your recent experience that support each choice and underline your preference in each item or write a response to the side; then select the five most important items.

Think about these preferences in terms of how you would naturally operate in an ideal social work role, not in terms of current market opportunities. If you try to fit your choices to market trends or constraints alone, you will probably make poor work choices or inadequate work matches. Once you have thought about your preferences, then you can go back over your choices to see whether they also reflect your other needs.

Keep in mind that these questions are meant to provoke reactions, trigger ideas, and clarify preferences. The extremes depicted are not meant to assign negative views to any settings but are written to create exaggerated contrasts. There are no right, wrong, or clear answers to these questions. Students and social workers with limited experience may find it difficult to respond to these questions. However, the items may be helpful to keep in mind when exploring career options. In that case, answer those that you can and skip the others.

1. Do you prefer a quiet environment, or a bustling, lively work setting?
2. How important are the aesthetics of the work environment to you?
3. Do you prefer the challenges of a competitive or political work environment?
4. Do you prefer organizations with clear lines of authority, strict procedures and clearances, specific job descriptions, and defined career paths, or a less-structured, fluid, quick-response, experimental organization?
5. Do you prefer to work for well-known institutions or organizations?
6. Do you prefer or aspire to have authority, power, or influence, or are these unimportant?
7. Do you aspire or prefer to be a leader?
8. Do you want to advance to supervisory or management functions?
9. Do you want to found a social services or advocacy organization?
10. Do you want to influence the big picture?
11. Do you want to own an organization, consulting group, or private practice?
12. Do you prefer to work autonomously, or with a team?

13. Do you prefer close supervision?

14. Do you prefer designing and creating solutions, or implementing the plans and maintaining efforts?

15. Are you interested in or willing to work in communities that are not considered safe?

16. Are you interested in work that develops specific skill sets related to a long-term goal, or work that is interesting and meets your lifestyle needs at this time?

17. Do you prefer a regular menu of work activities, constant new challenges, or a mix of both?

18. Do you prefer an organization or field offering job security, or opportunities that might be temporary?

19. Do you prefer an adequate income and work that you enjoy, or an excellent income and a job that you can tolerate?

20. Do you prefer to take risks and experiment, or to follow well-established models, procedures, and operations?

21. Do you prefer to be involved in cutting-edge interventions, programs, or policy developments? Do you want to work on the leading edge or the cutting edge?

22. Do you prefer routine and regular hours or a flexible schedule?

23. Is there a theme or commitment that describes your life's work? Do you want to make a specific contribution to society?

24. Do you prefer work that uses your specialized knowledge or that focuses on your commitment to an issue?

25. Do you prefer to work in a relaxed, informal environment or in a structured, formal one?

26. Do you prefer full-time work, or the flexibility of a combination of contract, part-time, and temporary work?

27. How important is it to work with a staff that is as strongly committed to services and advocacy as you are?

28. Do you prefer a work culture that encourages staff interaction and socializing, or one that encourages independence or perhaps competition?

29. Do you prefer being near extended family or friends over moving for the best work opportunity in your field of social work?

30. Which takes priority, personal life or work life?

31. Do you prefer to work with organizations that follow a particular philosophy or model?

32. Are you looking for a steady pace in your work, or a fast pace in your work?

33. Do you like to be "on the go," switching from one activity or location to another throughout the day, or to be stationary, doing a consistent set of activities?

34. Do you prefer to work with established organizations, or with young, grassroots initiatives?

35. Would you like to work in a particular geographic environment?

36. Do you prefer an internal focus of creating, analyzing, and conveying ideas, information, knowledge, and problem solutions, or an external focus on activities that connect the organization to outside groups and institutions?
37. Do you prefer an environment with constant deadlines and short learning curves, or ongoing assignments requiring few radical changes in your knowledge base?
38. Do you prefer to be a provider, gatekeeper, or designer of services?
39. Do you want to work in a specific culture, or in a multicultural setting?

Appendix 3

Directories and Career Information Publications

Community Services Directories for Specific Cities

If you are looking for a job in a particular community, use the local community services directory. Publisher information for major cities is listed below. Libraries usually carry the local directory.

Atlanta: *The Help Book*
Publisher: United Way of Metropolitan Atlanta, 404-614-1026 (annual)

Baltimore: *Agency Services Directory and Contributor's Guide*
Publisher: United Way of Central Maryland, 1-800-228-8929 or 410-547-8000 (annual)

Boston: *1996-97 Human Service Yellow Pages of Massachusetts and Rhode Island*
Publisher: George D. Hall, 1-800-445-1215 (annual)

Chicago: *1997 Human Care Services Directory of Metropolitan Chicago*
Publisher: United Way/Crusade of Mercy, 312-906-2416 (biannual)

Cincinnati: *Directory of Community Services, 1996*
Publisher: United Way, Community Chest Information, Information and Referral Center, and United Way Helpline, 513-721-7900 (annual)

Columbus, Ohio: *First Link 1997*
Publisher: First Link, 614-221-6766 (annual)

Dallas: *1997 Directory of Health, Welfare, and Recreation Services*
Publisher: Community Council of Greater Dallas, 214-741-5851 (annual)

Denver: *Where to Turn: Guide to Community Services in Metropolitan Denver*
Publisher: Mile High United Way Helpline, 303-433-8900

Houston: *Community Resources & Services Directory*
Publisher: United Way of the Texas Gulf Coast, 713-685-2727 (biannual)

Indianapolis: *Family of Agencies Directory 1996–97*
Publisher: United Way of Central Indiana, 317-923-1466 (biannual)

Los Angeles: *United Way Directory of Community Core Services*
Publisher: United Way of Greater Los Angeles, 213-630-2100 (annual)

Miami: *Helpages: The Professional's Reference to Community Resources in Dade County*
Publisher: Switchboard of Miami, 305-358-1640 (annual)

Minneapolis: *United Way's First Call for Help Directory of Community Services 1995–96*
Publisher: United Way, 612-340-7400 (biannual)

New York: *The Source Book 1995–96: Social and Health Services in the Greater New York Area*
Publisher: Oryx Press, jointly published with City of New York and the United Way of New York City, 1-800-279-6799, fax: 1-800-279-4663

Phoenix: *1997 Directory of Human Resources for Maricopa County*
Publisher: Community Information and Referral, 602-263-8845 (annual)

Portland, Oregon: *Directory of Human Services Multnomah County*
Publisher: Information and Referral Services, United Way of Columbia-Willamette, 503-226-9360

San Diego: *Directions 1997*
Publisher: United Way Information and Referral Division, 619-531-4799 (annual)

Seattle: *Where To Turn Plus 1997*
Publisher: Where to Turn, Crisis Clinic, 206-461-3210 (annual)

St. Louis: *Community Service Directory*
Publisher: United Way of Greater St. Louis, 314-421-0700 (biannual)

St. Paul: *East Metro Resource Directory 1996–97*
Publisher: United Way First Call For Help, 612-291-8420 (biannual)

Washington, DC (includes Northern Virginia): *Agency Directory*
Publisher: United Way of the National Capital Area, 202-488-2000 (annual)

National Directories of Organizations, by Subject Category

Directories of organizations across the country and throughout the world can be found in print and, increasingly, online. Printed directories are published by associations, government departments, and publishing companies. Many are costly. When you are talking with your contacts, ask whether you can look at any pertinent directories in their offices. For directories or lists of local organizations in a particular field, check with state government offices and local association chapters, collaboration groups, or task forces.

Children and Youth Services

The Adoption Resource Guide
L. Posner & James Guilanelli. Washington, DC: Child Welfare League of America, 1990

Careers in Child and Family Policy: A Resource Guide to Policy Settings and Research Programs
R. A. Seidensticker. Chicago: University of Chicago, Chapin Hall Center for Children and the Harris Graduate School of Public Policy Studies, 1993

The Directory for Exceptional Children: A Listing of Educational and Training Facilities, 1994–95
J. Kathryn Sargent, ed. Boston: Porter Sargent.

Directory of Local Head Start Programs and Head Start Parent and Child Centers
Washington, DC: Department of Health and Human Services, Project Head Start, 1988

Directory of Member Agencies (annual)
Washington, DC: Child Welfare League of America.

Directory of Public Elementary and Secondary Education Agencies 1993–94 (public school districts)
Washington, DC: U.S. Department of Education, Office of Educational Research and Improvement, 1995 (annual)

Directory of Residential Facilities for Emotionally Handicapped Children and Youth
Barbara Smiley Sherman. Phoenix: Oryx Press, 1988

The Intensive Family Preservation Services National Network Directory, 1994
Intensive Family Preservation Services National Network, c/o Center for the Study of Family Policy, Hunter College, 695 Park Avenue, East Building, Room 1209C, New York, NY 10021; 212-772-4256, fax 212-650-3845

The National Directory of Children, Youth and Families Services, 1997–1998: The Professionals' Reference
Longmont, CO: Marion L. Peterson, 1997

The North American Directory of Programs for Runaways, Homeless Youth and Missing Children
Mary A. Wyman. Washington, DC: American Youth Work Center, 1993

Community Development, Government, and Public Policy

The Community Action Directory, 1997
Washington, DC: National Association of Community Action Agencies, 1997

The Complete Guide to Public Employment
R. L. Krannich. Manassas Park, VA: Impact Publications, 1995

Government Job Finder, 1997–2000
Daniel Lauber. River Forest, IL: Planning/Communications, 1997

InterAction Membership Profile, 1997–1998
Tracey Geoghegan & Kristen Allen, eds. Washington, DC: InterAction, 1997

PRRAC Network Directory
Washington, DC: Poverty and Race Research Action Council, 1994

Public Interest Profiles
Washington, DC: Congressional Quarterly, 1996

Public Welfare Directory
Washington, DC: American Public Welfare Association, 1996

United States Government Manual
Washington, DC: Office of the Federal Register and National Archives and Records Administration, 1996

United Way of America Membership Directory
Alexandria, VA: United Way of America.

Criminal Justice and Victim Services

Directory of Juvenile and Adult Correctional Departments, Institutions, Agencies, and Paroling Authorities
Lanham, MD: American Correctional Association, 1996

Membership Directory
Reno, NV: National Council of Juvenile and Family Court Judges (annual)

Disabilities

The Complete Directory for People with Disabilities
Leslie Mackenzie, ed. Lakesville, CT: Grey House, 1996

Domestic Relations and Domestic Violence

National Directory of Domestic Violence Programs: A Guide to Community Shelter, Safe Home and Service Programs, 1994 Edition
Denver: National Coalition Against Domestic Violence, 1994

Family and Multiple Services

Charitable Organizations of US: A Descriptive and Financial Information Guide 1992–1993 (2nd ed.)
Doris Morris Maxfield, ed. Detroit: Gale Research (annual)

Directory for Catholic Charities: 1989 Agencies and Institutions
Alexandria, VA: Catholic Charities, USA, 1989

Directory of Jewish Family and Children's Agencies (annual)
Kendall Park, NJ: Association of Jewish Family and Children's Agencies

Directory of Member Agencies
Milwaukee: Family Service America, 1995 (annual)

National Directory of Nonprofit Organizations
Rockville, MD: Taft Group, 1996

National Directory of Private Social Agencies
San Diego: Croner Publications, 1997

The Women's Information Exchange National Directory
Deborah Brecher & Jill Lippitt. New York: Phillip Lief Group, Avon Books, 1994

Gerontology and Health Care

Careers in Aging: Opportunities and Options
Washington, DC: Association for Gerontology in Higher Education, 1996

Directory of Investor-Owned Hospitals, Hospital Management Companies and Health Systems, Residential Treatment Facilities and Centers, Key Management Personnel
Little Rock, AK: FAHS Review, 1995 (annual)

Directory of Members
Washington, DC: American Association of Homes and Services for the Aging, 1997

The Directory of Nursing Homes, 1996
Baltimore: Health Care Investment Analysts, 1995

The Directory of Retirement Facilities, 1997
Baltimore: Health Care Investment Analysts, 1996

A Directory of State and Area Agencies on Aging
Washington, DC: National Association of Area Agencies on Aging, 1981

Encyclopedia of Medical Organizations and Agencies: A Subject Guide to Organizations, Foundations, Federal and State Government Agencies, Research Centers, and Medical and Allied Health Schools
Karen Boyden, ed. Detroit: Gale Research, 1996

The Guide to the Managed Care Industry
Baltimore: Health Care Investment Analysts, 1996

Guide to the Nation's Hospices
Arlington, VA: National Hospice Organization (annual)

Hospital Blue Book
Atlanta: Billian (annual)

The Hospital Phone Book
New Providence, NJ: U.S. Directory Service, 1996

Local AIDS Services: The National Directory
Washington, DC: U.S. Conference of Mayors, 1994

Managed Behavioral Health Market Share in the US
Monica Oss & Trev Stair, eds. Gettysburg, PA: Behavioral Health Industry News, 1996

Medical and Health Information Directory: A Guide to Organizations, Agencies, Institutions, Programs, Publications, Services, and Other Resources Concerned with Clinical Medicine, Basic Biomedical Sciences, and the Technological and Socioeconomic Aspects of Health Care
Karen Burden, ed. Detroit: Gale Research, 1996

Membership Directory
Washington, DC : National Institute of Senior Centers, National Council on Aging (annual)

Membership Directory
Washington, DC: National Institute on Adult Daycare, National Council on Aging, 1992

National Directory for Eldercare Information and Referral: Directory of State and Area Agencies on Aging, 1994
Washington, DC: National Association of Area Agencies on Aging (annual)

The National Directory of Adult Day Care Centers (2nd ed.)
Wall Township, NJ: Health Resources, 1993

National Directory of HMOs
Washington, DC: Group Health Association of America, 1995 (annual)

International Work

Alternatives to the Peace Corps: A Directory of Third World and US Volunteer Opportunities
A. Olson, ed. Oakland, CA: Food First Books, 1996

Careers in International Affairs
Maria Pinto Carland & Michael Trucano, eds. Washington, DC: Georgetown University, School of Foreign Service, 1997

Complete Guide to International Jobs & Careers
R. L. Krannich. Manassas Park, VA: Impact Publications, 1992

The Development Directory: A Guide to the International Development Community in the United States and Canada
Pamela Korsmeyer. Detroit: Omnigraphics, 1991

The Directory of Jobs and Careers Abroad
Princeton, NJ: Peterson's Guide, 1997

Encyclopedia of Associations and International Organizations: Pt. 1. Descriptive Listings, and *Pt. 2. Indexes*
Linda Thurn, ed. Detroit: Gale Research, 1995 (annual)

Guide to Careers in World Affairs
Manassas Park, VA: Foreign Impact Publications, 1993

International Jobs: Where They Are and How to Get Them
Eric Kocher. Reading, MA: Addison-Wesley, 1993

Internationalizing Social Work Education: A Guide to Resources for a New Century
Richard J. Estes. Philadelphia: University of Pennsylvania, School of Social Work, 1992

Mental Health, Employee Assistance, and Chemical Dependency

Directory of Residential Centers for Adults with Mental Illnesses
Phoenix: Oryx Press, 1990

Drug, Alcohol, and Other Addictions: A Directory of Treatment Centers and Prevention Programs Nationwide
Phoenix: Oryx Press, 1993

EAP Consultants Directory
Arlington, VA: Association of Labor-Management Administrators and Consultants on Alcoholism

Managed Behavioral Health Market Share Book
Creston, CA: Open Minds, 1996

Membership Directory
Rockville, MD: National Council for Community Behavioral Healthcare, 1995

Mental Health Directory, 1995
Rockville, MD: U.S. Department of Health and Human Services, Public Health Services, Substance Abuse and Mental Health Services Administration, 1995

National Directory of Drug Abuse and Alcoholism Treatment and Prevention Programs
Rockville, MD: U.S. Department of Health and Human Services, Public Health Services, Substance Abuse and Mental Health Services Administration, 1993 (annual)

National Registry of Community Mental Health Services
Thomas R. Willis, ed. Rockville, MD: National Council of Community Mental Health Centers, 1991

Substance Abuse Residential Treatment Centers for Teens
Phoenix: Oryx Press, 1990

Women's Recovery Programs: A Directory of Residential Addiction Treatment Centers
Phoenix: Oryx Press, 1990

Research Centers, Consulting Services, and Foundations

The Foundation Directory
Margaret Mary Feczko, ed. New York: Foundation Center, 1996

Government Research Directory: A Descriptive Guide to More Than 4,300 U.S. and Canadian Government Research and Development Centers, Institutes, Laboratories, Bureaus, Test Facilities, Experiment Stations, Data Collections and Analysis Centers, and Grants Management and Research Coordinating Offices in Agriculture, Commerce, Education, Energy, Engineering, Environment, the Humanities, Medicine, Military Science, and Basic and Applied Sciences
Jacqueline Barrett & Monica Hubbard, eds. Detroit: Gale Research, 1996

Research Centers Directory
Detroit: Gale Research, 1996

Social Work Education and Graduate Studies

Directory of Colleges and Universities with Accredited Social Work Degree Programs: Baccalaureate and Master's Programs
Alexandria, VA: Council on Social Work Education (annual)

Statistics on Social Work Education in the United States: 1996
Todd M. Lennon. Alexandria, VA: Council on Social Work Education, 1997

Career Planning and Professional Development

The Academic Job Search Handbook (2nd ed.)
Mary Morris Heiberger. Philadelphia: University of Pennsylvania Press, 1996

The Business Plan Guide for Independent Consultants
Herman Holtz. New York: John Wiley & Sons, 1994

Can They Do That? A Guide to Your Rights on the Job
M. A. Zigarelli. New York: Lexington Books, 1994

Career Change: Everything You Need to Know to Meet New Challenges and Take Control of Your Career
David P. Helfand. Lincolnwood, IL: VGM Career Horizons, 1995

Career Choices for the 90's for Students of Political Science and Government
New York: Walker, 1990

Careers for Dreamers and Doers: A Guide to Management Careers in the Nonprofit Sector
Lilly Cohen & Dennis Young. New York: Foundation Center, 1989

Careers in Social Work
Leon H. Ginsberg. Boston: Allyn & Bacon, 1998

Changing Hats: From Social Work Practice to Administration
Felice Davidson Perlmutter. Silver Spring, MD: NASW Press, 1990

The Complete Guide to Consulting Success
Howard Shenson & Ted Nicholas. Dearborn, MI: Enterprise, 1993

The Consultant's Manual: A Complete Guide to Building a Successful Consulting Practice
Thomas Greenbaum. New York: John Wiley & Sons, 1990

The Curriculum Vitae Handbook: Using Your CV to Present and Promote Your Academic Career
Rebecca Anthony & Gerald Roe. Iowa City, IA: Rudi Publications, 1994

Doing Well by Doing Good: The Complete Guide to Careers in the Nonprofit Sector
Terry McAdam. Rockville, MD: Fund Raising Institute, 1993

Electronic Job Search Revolution: How to Win with the New Technology That's Reshaping Today's Job Market
J. L. Kennedy & T. J. Morrow. New York: John Wiley & Sons, 1995

Electronic Resume Revolution: Create a Winning Resume for the New World of Job Seeking (2nd ed.)
Joyce Lain Kennedy & Thomas J. Morrow. New York: John Wiley & Sons, 1995

Electronic Resumes: A Complete Guide to Putting Your Resume On-Line
James C. Gonyea & Wayne M. Gonyea. New York: McGraw-Hill, 1996

Every Employee's Guide to the Law
L. G. Joel. New York: Pantheon Books, 1996

Finding a Job in the Non-Profit Sector
William Wade. Rockville, MD: Taft Group, 1991 (biennial)

The Five-Minute Interview
Richard H. Beatty. New York: John Wiley & Sons, 1986

Getting to Yes
Roger Fisher & William Ury. Boston: Houghton-Mifflin, 1992

Good Works: A Guide to Careers in Social Change
Donna Calvin, ed. New York: Barricade Books, 1993

Graduate School Funding Handbook
April Vahle Hamel. Philadelphia: University of Pennsylvania Press, 1994

Great Careers: Fourth of July Guide to Careers, Internships, and Volunteer Opportunities in the Nonprofit Sector
Devon Smith, ed. Garrett Park, MD: Garrett Park Press, 1990

Great Connections: Small Talk and Networking for Businesspeople
A. Baber & L. Waymon. Manassas Park, VA: Impact Publications, 1992

The Guide to Internet Job Searching
Margaret Riley, Frances Roehm, & Steve Osernnan. Lincolnwood, IL: VGM Career Horizons, 1996

It's Negotiable: The How-to Handbook of Win/Win Tactics
P. B. Stark. San Diego: Pfeiffer, 1994

The Job Seeker's Guide to Socially Responsible Companies
K. Jankowski. New York: Visible Ink Press, 1995

Job Shift
William Bridges. Reading, MA: Addison-Wesley, 1994

Making a Living while Making a Difference: A Guide to Creating Careers with a Conscience
Melissa Everett. New York: Bantam Books, 1995

The 1997 National Job Hotline Directory
M. P. Williams & S. A. Cubbage. New York: McGraw-Hill, 1997

Negotiating Your Salary: How to Make $1,000 a Minute
Jack Chapman. Berkeley, CA: Ten Speed Press, 1996

The New Rules of the Job Search Game: Why Today's Managers Hire . . . And Why They Don't
Jackie Larson & Cheri Comstock. Holbrook, MA: Adams, 1994

New Social Entrepreneurs: The Success, Challenge and Lessons of Non-Profit Enterprise Creation
J. Emerson & F. Twersky. San Francisco: Roberts Foundation, Homeless Economic Development Fund, 1996

The New Social Worker: The Magazine for Social Work Students and Recent Graduates (serial)
Harrisburg, PA: White Hat Communications

The Non-Profit Handbook: National Edition
Gary Grobman. Harrisburg, PA: White Hat Communications, 1997

A Non Profit Organization Operating Manual
A. J. Olenick & P. R. Olenick. New York: Foundation Center, 1991

Non-Profits' and Education Job Finder
Daniel Lauber. River Forest, IL: Planning/Communications, 1997

The Perfect Cover Letter
Richard H. Beatty. New York: John Wiley & Sons, 1997

Peterson's Grants for Graduate and Post-Doctoral Study
Princeton, NJ: Peterson's Guide, 1995

Profitable Careers in Nonprofit
William Lewis & Carol Milano. New York: John Wiley & Sons, 1987

Put Your Degree to Work: The New Professional's Guide to Career Planning and Job Hunting
Marcia R. Fox. New York: W. W. Norton, 1988

The Smart Woman's Guide to Interviewing and Salary Negotiation
Julie Adair King. Franklin, NJ: Career Press, 1995

Social Work in Private Practice: Principles, Issues, and Dilemmas
Robert L. Barker. Silver Spring, MD: NASW Press, 1992

Social Work Laws and Board Regulations: A Comparison Study
Culpeper, VA: American Association of State Social Work Boards, 1996

Student Advantage Guide to America's Top Internships
Mark Oldman. New York: Random House, 1996

Surviving Your Dissertation: A Comprehensive Guide to Content and Process
Kjell Erik Rudestam & Rae R. Newton. Newbury Park, CA: Sage Publications, 1992

Sweaty Palms: The Neglected Art of Being Interviewed
H. Anthony Medley. Berkeley, CA: Ten Speed Press, 1993

The Upstart Guide to Owning and Managing a Consulting Service
Dan Ramsey. Chicago: Upstart Publishing, 1995

We Are All Self-Employed: The New Social Contract for Working in a Changed World
Cliff Hakim. San Francisco: Berrett-Koehler, 1994

What Color Is Your Parachute? A Practical Guide for Job-Hunters and Career-Changers
Richard Nelson Bolles. Berkeley, CA: Ten Speed Press, 1997

What Social Workers Do
Margaret Gibelman. Washington, DC: NASW Press, 1995

Who We Are: A Second Look
M. Gibelman & P. H. Schervish. Washington, DC: NASW Press, 1997

Zen and the Art of Making a Living: A Practical Guide to Career Design
Laurence G. Boldt. New York: Arkana, 1993

Information Specific to Fields

Appendix 4 is a reference for those looking for positions in the fields of

- aging and health care
- children, family, and school services
- developmental disabilities
- domestic relations, domestic violence, justice services, and victim services
- macrolevel social work
- mental health, substance abuse, and employee assistance.

Information for each broad field includes work settings (areas in which social workers in that field might find employment), job titles, and suggestions on information to gather about the field. See appendix 1 for associations and appendix 3 for directories of employers. Discussions with people in each field generated this information.

Aging and Health Care

Work Settings
adult day care and respite programs
area agencies on aging
bank trust departments
chemical dependency or substance abuse treatment programs
community health clinics
courts
dialysis centers
family services
geriatric case management agencies and practices
government divisions or departments on aging
guardian programs
guardian services
HMOs (health maintenance organizations)
home health services
hospice programs
hospitals or medical centers
housing (apartments, assisted living, public housing, retirement centers, or campuses)

managed care firms

multiservice agencies (for example, for HIV/AIDS, head injuries, or breast cancer)

national health organizations (for example, American Cancer Society)

nursing homes

physician offices

public health facilities

rehabilitation centers

senior citizen centers and nutrition programs

skilled-nursing centers

veterans' medical centers

wellness programs

women's health services

Job Titles

activity coordinator

clinical social worker

coordinator, managed care program

coordinator of community services

coordinator of geriatric services

director for adult day care

director of geriatric partial hospitalization program

elder-care unit director and case manager

emergency-unit social worker

geriatric care manager

geriatric social worker

geropsychiatric social worker

HIV prevention specialist

home care social worker

home health coordinator

hospice social worker

long-term care administrator

medical social work coordinator

medical social work department director

medical social worker

older-adult specialist

oncology social worker

pediatric medical social worker

program director

resident manager

social work or social services manager

social worker, long-term care

Information to Gather

- How does the community care for its dying people? What hospital and independent hospice programs exist? Do the managed care organizations have their own hospice programs, or do they contract for those services?

- What public, nonprofit, and for-profit organizations provide services (for example, wellness or health promotion programs; primary, acute, trauma, or pediatric care; skilled nursing; residential programs; nursing home care; home health; day care for older adults; geropsychiatric services; dialysis; hospice; and rehabilitation)?
- What organizations provide guardianship or geriatric case management services? Do banks or funeral homes in the area use social workers?
- How do the roles of social workers vary across nursing homes? Are they focused on psychosocial aspects, or on a combination of admissions, discharge planning, and marketing?
- What do the guidelines of funding sources say about the number of allowed social work home visits? Is this number comparable to other regions? Is it changing?
- What do the state regulations require regarding social workers in hospitals? Are changes in the regulations anticipated? Do they require MSWs in all units or in specific units (for example, psychiatric, oncology, rehabilitation, dialysis, burn units)? Are hospitals required to have a social work manager over all social workers on staff, or can they use a consultant?
- Which hospitals are open to or are pursuing new programs or services involving social workers—for example, social workers working in primary care physicians' offices, in outpatient services, in preventive services, or in disease management programs?
- Medical social work departments in hospitals are dismantled and re-created as hospitals cut costs or determine that other staff cannot perform the role. Where do social workers fit into the organizational charts of the local hospitals? Which have social work departments? Does that department director report to a vice president, the head of nursing, or the head of utilization review? Or do social workers individually report to administrators of product lines?
- What is the relationship between the state's department on aging and the area agencies on aging? Is the focus in this community on institutional care or on alternative care for older adults, or both?
- How are home health services funded—through managed care, or a prepayment system, for example?
- All health care organizations are struggling to provide the same quality of care at the lowest cost. How are the local organizations dealing with this challenge?
- Which hospitals have formed networks, and which have recently merged? Where are those hospital groups in the process of streamlining their operations and eliminating duplication?

Children, Family, and School Services

Work Settings

adoption services
chemical dependency treatment center for children

child day care center
child protection services or child welfare
children of divorced families
children's hospital
children's psychiatric hospital
children's (or adolescents') residential treatment center
court-appointed advocates program
family preservation or Families First program
family services
foster care services
gang prevention programs
juvenile court
mental health services for children and families
multiservice clubs or agencies for youths
private schools
public school systems
services for particular populations (such as services for pregnant teenagers or children with autism or children's or youth shelters)

Job Titles

adolescent therapist, alternative school
adoption social worker
assessment specialist, residential center
behavior specialist
case manager, residential treatment center
child care director
child care subsidy services coordinator
clinical manager
clinical supervisor, foster care
coordinator of outreach programs
developmental therapist
director, child abuse program
educational support counselor
executive director
family advocate
family clinician
family preservation worker
family services worker
family support coordinator
family therapist
family unit manager
field executive
home-school liaison
intervention counselor
management analysis specialist, child support enforcement
Medicaid director
parent educator

prevention specialist
program director
residential services program director
school social worker
social worker
support manager, family services program
teen–parent group educator
therapeutic foster care home coordinator
therapist and case manager
therapist, juvenile sex offender treatment program
truancy case manager

Information to Gather

- What is the value base? Social work values are not universally held by social services organizations. Communities differ in practice and politics. For example, in child welfare, is a family-focused, community-based approach used, or is it a law enforcement model?
- If collaboration is taking place, is it at regular meetings among many parties or a multidisciplinary group that has a mission statement; shares resources, funding, and power; struggles with issues; and is culturally responsive?
- What public, nonprofit, and for-profit organizations are providing social services for children, youths, and their families? Where are the services delivered or based: onsite at schools, linked to schools, or in community agencies?
- What types of relationships does the public system have with private agencies? Does the state provide direct services, or does it buy services? How do policies translate into programs and contracts with nonprofit organizations?
- How are terms defined in the state: collaboration, wraparound services, integrated service delivery, family support, family-based services, family-centered practice? What "buzz" phrases are being used in that state?
- Is there a commitment to family-centered practice? How is this approach being integrated into services, funded, and staffed? Are there training funds for it? Is it being integrated into child welfare services only, or across the board in state services (legal, mental health, juvenile justice, aging, community)?
- Are services run through a state system or a county system? That is, are decisions made at a state, county, or regional level? What effect does this decision level have on quality assurance standards?
- Are the family services agencies serving primarily individual clients and families through clinical services, or do they also have community interventions in place?
- Where are social workers involved in schools: truancy programs, family resource centers, guidance offices, Title I or Chapter I reading and math tutoring programs? What roles or titles do social workers have:

counselors, school social workers, family resource coordinators, home and school visitors? How do funding differences among school districts affect school social work services?

- Are there schools that specialize in education for particular populations?
- What is the role of social workers in schools? Are they concerned primarily with basic needs of students and their families, or are they members of interdisciplinary teams focused on academic and behavioral issues of students? Has the role changed recently? Is it expected to change?
- What percentage of services are Medicaid driven? Are services under managed care? If yes, is managed care part of mental health services and family services? If not, when is that anticipated?
- What has been the impact of declassification on hiring in the public sector? What is the background of the beginning-level worker? How much experience do senior staff have?
- How do other public services interact with public child welfare? What is the quality of relations? Is it difficult to get children into the public mental health system? Is it a detention-only service? Does it have an advocacy role?
- What are the programs that schools have, are discussing, or should have (for example, school-to-work initiatives, conflict resolution, peer mediation, character education, parent involvement, parent education, early prevention, and drug prevention or intervention programs)? What innovative education practices and programs are in place or being developed in school districts and private schools?
- Is there a current or recent court order in effect and, if so, how is it affecting hiring, caseloads, salaries, and career paths?
- How are services funded? Are they funded primarily through public dollars? What is the mix of funding dollars, and how does it affect public and private services?
- Has the state legislature guaranteed mental health or managed care mental health services for children?
- What has been the state's investment in social services? How is the state dealing with cutbacks?

Developmental Disabilities

Work Settings

education programs
family support programs (case management services and respite care)
guardianship programs
home care
public and private schools
recreational programs
residential programs
sheltered workshops
small group homes

supported employment programs
vocational programs

Job Titles

advocate
community integration specialist
coordinator, family and infant development program
executive director
human services counselor
human services specialist
job placement counselor
manager, group home
program analyst
program manager or director
supervisor
supported living coordinator
vocational evaluator

Information to Gather

- Does the state organize services by county or region?
- Is there a single advocacy association for all types of developmental disabilities in the community, or does each type have its own organization?
- Which organizations have particular programs for children, adults, and older adults with developmental disabilities?
- Are there residential programs, sheltered workshops, vocational programs, supported employment programs, small group homes, home care, family support programs (including case management services and respite care), or guardianship programs?
- How is education provided to people with developmental disabilities?
- Is there an individual services coordination system?
- Which organizations are developing alternative care programs?
- What is being done for those individuals who are not currently capable of independent living?
- Does the state provide a continuum of services?
- How are ADA and recent welfare reform initiatives affecting services?
- Has the state been operating under a waiver for Medicaid? How has the state changed eligibility and services?
- What changes in eligibility and services are anticipated under the federal and state welfare reform changes?
- Where are developmental disabilities services located in the state government structure? Are they part of the mental health department, or social services department? How does the location affect philosophy, programs, and funding?
- How does the state law define developmental disabilities—that is, which disabilities are covered by state programs?
- How dependent is the state on federal funding?
- What is the potential for fiscal growth in programs?

- Does the state anticipate budget cuts in developmental disability programs?
- What is the funding configuration (Medicaid, state funds, and private funds) for services?

Domestic Relations, Domestic Violence, Justice Services, and Victim Services

Work Settings

advocacy and protective services
child advocacy centers
court-appointed special advocate programs
domestic relations divisions of courts
domestic violence prevention programs
domestic violence programs or shelters
family courts
family violence councils
guardian ad litem programs
juvenile courts
legal aid or legal services
police departments
prisons
public defender offices
victim services councils

Job Titles

alternative sentencing specialist
case manager
children's program coordinator
crime victim advocate or educator
custody evaluator
deputy juvenile officer
detention youth leader
director of client services
director of court services
director of a domestic violence program
evaluator, domestic relations
facilitator of a guardian program
family specialist
family therapist
foster care social worker
juvenile justice youth officer
mediator, domestic relations
parent educator
parenting specialist, domestic relations

parole officer
probation officer
sex crimes case manager
social worker
social worker, domestic relations
training specialist
victim or witness coordinator
victim's advocate
volunteer coordinator

Information to Gather

- Where in the court system are family cases heard?
- Is there a family court system? What types of cases does it hear: divorce, paternity, adult abuse (domestic and elder), domestic violence, juvenile delinquency, criminal cases? Does it hear both civil and criminal cases?
- How do judges get on the family court? Are they appointed, or do they volunteer? How many have law and social work degrees?
- In this state or community, which organizations emphasize services for battered women and children and which organizations emphasize social change targeted at domestic violence?
- What is the range of services for battered women and children: volunteer crisis lines, shelters, multiple services, and advocacy programs?
- What family and domestic relations court services are provided in this state or county? Do they provide education programs for parents; mediation; arbitration; custody evaluations, assessments, and home studies; therapeutic mediation; supervised visitations?
- What services are provided outside the court?
- What victim services or advocacy organizations exist? Are they part of the circuit attorney's office, or are they independent organizations? Do they work with civil and criminal aspects?
- Does the court encourage mediation? Do they have court-affiliated mediators?
- If the state is regulating domestic violence workers, what impact is that regulation having on the scope of services and advocacy for domestic violence programs?
- How has the increased federal funding for domestic violence changed services? What is the mix of funding for these services?

Macrolevel Social Work

Macrolevel social work includes areas such as housing, homelessness, employment, neighborhood stabilization, and economic development. It is closely linked with macrolevel functions, including advocacy, consulting, organizing, policy, research, political involvement, and program planning.

Work Settings

advocacy organizations
citizen groups
community action agencies
community centers
employment projects
family services agencies
foundations
fund-raising organizations
government departments: housing, employment, economic development
homeless shelters
housing corporations
job-training programs
neighborhood centers
policy centers
regional planning offices
religious organizations
research centers
settlement houses
think tanks
university extension services
university research or project offices

Job Titles

budget analyst
county program director, university extension services
director, church division human development program
director of development
director of youth and community services
economic development director
employment specialist
executive director, community group
executive director, foundation
executive director, neighborhood association
family literacy program coordinator
functional analyst, human services department
legislator (and other elected positions)
lobbyist
manager, disaster services
neighborhood coordinator
neighborhood planning and enforcement specialist
program analyst
program director, foundation
program director, neighborhood services
program evaluation administrator
project coordinator
project director, research project for refugees program

public policy specialist
regional developer of community services
research administrator
research analyst
senior program officer, foundation
social science analyst
special-events coordinator
survey researcher
union organizer

Information to Gather

- What organizations are studying and influencing policy, conducting research, or providing consulting and training at an international, national, or state level in your interest area? What are their positions on issues?
- What public, nonprofit, and for-profit organizations are providing multiple services to neighborhoods and at-risk populations? These might be settlement houses, neighborhood centers, or community centers.
- What organizations are the key players in housing, economic development, crime prevention, neighborhood planning, employment, services for homeless people, advocacy, disaster and emergency services?
- What roles are local and state governments playing in the social and economic development of the area? Are public and private initiatives in place?
- What are the relationships among community development corporations, religious institutions, Urban League, United Way, family services agencies, neighborhood centers, universities, the housing authority, and state and local economic development departments?
- What pilot community projects were completed recently? What projects are planned or under way?
- What groups are addressing antidiscrimination, education reform, and welfare reform issues?
- What organizations are evaluating outcomes of community-building projects?
- What organizations are providing technical assistance to community or neighborhood groups?
- How are policies and programs changing at the federal, state, or local level in housing, employment, economic development, and so on?
- Are the family services organizations serving primarily individual clients and families, or do they also have community interventions in place?
- How is the local United Way involved in community initiatives?
- Is the state or local government piloting any projects in urban or rural communities?
- What changes in family services, housing, employment, crime and safety, or welfare are taking place as a result of the policy shift from the national to the state level?
- What is the relationship between social development (or community development) and economic development at the state and local levels?

- What is the approach to community work? Is it from an assets-based development perspective; from a needs-assessment, problem-solving perspective; or from a combination of perspectives?

Mental Health, Substance Abuse, and Employee Assistance

Work Settings

chemical dependency treatment programs: outpatient, inpatient, therapeutic communities
clubs or day programs for people who are chronically mentally ill
community mental health centers
employee assistance firms or programs in companies or agencies
family services agencies
hospital units: inpatient, outpatient, eating disorders, dual diagnosis, stress, forensic
managed care companies
military branches: family services
private practice
psychiatric hospitals
women's services

Job Titles

adult outpatient counselor
case manager
chemical dependency counselor
clinic administrator
clinical case manager
clinical casework assistant
clinical consultant
clinical director
clinical social worker
community mental health services supervisor
community support worker
director for consumer affairs, mental health department
director of evaluation team
director of family development, child psychiatry unit
EAP counselor
mental health administrator
mental health outreach specialist
private practitioner
program coordinator
psychiatric social worker
rehabilitation specialist
social work practitioner
social work supervisor

social worker or program director, club house
substance abuse coordinator
substance abuse counselor
substance abuse treatment specialist
supervisor of supportive care
therapist
triage intake coordinator

Information to Gather

- What public, nonprofit, or for-profit organizations provide mental health services: outpatient services, inpatient programs, managed care companies, employee assistance programs?
- How does the state deliver public mental health services? Does the state own all of its mental health facilities or centers? Are state services organized by catchment or regional areas? Is there a county mental health system?
- If you are interested in EAP work, what is the percentage breakdown of large and small companies in that community? Business needs will differ depending on the size of the organization. Which companies have internal EAPs, and which are outsourcing (that is, contracting with consultants for external EAP services)?
- What organizations or individuals are known for their expertise in addressing particular issues (for example, chronic mental illness, post-traumatic stress disorder, dual diagnosis, sexual abuse, eating disorders, substance abuse, domestic violence, or divorce)?
- Are public and private substance abuse services combined with mental health services? Might this change?
- Where are chemical dependency treatment services offered (in therapeutic communities, outpatient programs, inpatient programs, services in the criminal justice system, employee assistance programs, or managed care programs)? What models do they use? Are there program links between mental health services and primary care or substance abuse treatment?
- Where do clinical social workers work? Are they in individual practice and have subcontracts for individual cases with managed care companies? Do private practitioners join the panel of the managed care companies? Are they employees of nonprofit, for-profit, or public organizations that are subcontractors with managed care companies?
- States are quickly decreasing facilities and size of staff: How is this changing services and positions in the public and private sectors?
- The movement from office-based to community-based services is strong and an indication of organizational growth: What organizations have engaged the community in a partnership to develop community-based services?
- How is managed care affecting services? In what stages of evolution toward managed behavioral health care are the state, county, and local systems?

- What is the profile of the community population, cultures, and ethnic groups? What are the service needs of the population?
- Are services consumer driven? Are consumers and families involved in all aspects of treatment, including program development? Are they on advisory committees?
- What is the mix of funding for public or private mental health? How stable is the funding? How much does the state, county, or local level rely on Medicaid funding?
- What organizations have strategic alliances? Are these short-term arrangements, mergers, or acquisitions?
- What is the political climate? Is the tax base stable or being cut back?
- Traditional block grants for substance abuse prevention and treatment may be replaced with performance partnership grants that depend on achieving outcomes. What changes in services are anticipated?
- What are the state mandates or other legislation affecting mental health in this state?
- Who is the director or commissioner for the state, county, or local system? How long has the person been there? What is his or her professional reputation? How much turnover has there been in the position?
- Look at the state mental health plan. What are the state's philosophy, mission, objectives, and history regarding mental health services?
- Is the state mental health system traditional and conservative, focusing on clinical treatment, or is it progressive, focusing on consumer-driven services? Or is the system in transition?

Reference

Gibelman, M. S. (1995). *What social workers do.* Washington, DC: NASW Press.

Sample Cover Letters and Other Correspondence

The first four sample letters in this appendix correspond to résumé samples 4, 5, and 6 in appendix 6. These are the letters of a fictional social work student, Lisa Denton, who has experience in pediatric medical social work, day treatment, and domestic violence. Lisa is thinking of returning to Dallas and is looking at several possibilities. Her letters emphasize those elements of her background specific to each audience. Letters 5 through 12 are additional samples for various other situations. Topics of the letters are as follows:

Sample 1:   *Letter seeking advice*

Sample 2:   *Unsolicited letter*

Sample 3:   *Letter based on a referral*

Sample 4:   *Letter in response to an ad*

Sample 5:   *Letter of application*

Sample 6:   *Letter requesting an informational interview*

Sample 7:   *Thank-you letter to a contact*

Sample 8:   *Letter following a telephone call*

Sample 9:   *Letter of application*

Sample 10:   *Letter following an application*

Sample 11:   *Thank-you letter following a job interview*

Sample 12:   *Letter of acceptance*

Sample 1: Letter Seeking Advice

Address
City, State, Zip
Phone

October 22, 1996

Mr. James Tolan
Director of Clinical Services
The Children's Home
2343 Any Drive
Dallas, Texas 00000

Dear Mr. Tolan:

I am a graduate student at My University in Anytown with an interest in children and families at risk. At this time, I am exploring my career options for the future and a possible move to Dallas. I am writing to you for information and advice.

Providing therapy for youths and their families is my particular interest. However, because managed care has had a large impact on the field, I am wondering what types of therapeutic services are being offered in the Dallas–Fort Worth area. If I want to pursue a long-term career in clinical social work with youths and families in central Texas, what type of experience should I look for over the next several years? I would appreciate any thoughts you would be willing to share with me.

My clinical experience was at the Children's Center, Anytown, as a therapist intern for youths and families in the day treatment program. My coursework in family therapy and practice, adolescent problems, and clinical interventions complements my training. In addition, I worked with families in crisis at Children's Hospital, Anytown. Before attending graduate school, I was coordinator of the children's program for the Women's Shelter in Dallas.

I would appreciate your advice, and I will contact you soon.

Sincerely,

Lisa Denton

Sample 2: Unsolicited Letter

I am seeking an opportunity to use my medical social work experience in pediatric health care, and I would like to be considered for positions in your department. Dallas was my home for several years; I plan to return there in May when I complete my MSW degree.

My recent experience includes medical social work at Children's Hospital and day treatment at Children's Center in Anytown. As a medical social work intern, I provide services on the neonatal and pediatric intensive care units and handle backup services for all other units in the hospital. I enjoy the fast-paced, team environment of a hospital and understand the complex ethical and managed care issues facing social workers today. At the day treatment program, I primarily provided therapy for children at risk and their families. Previously, I coordinated an effective volunteer service and children's program for the Women's Shelter in Dallas. In all settings, I have been complimented for my work with families in crisis.

The Children's Medical Center is my first choice in work settings. Several of my contacts in the Dallas area have said that your social work department is well integrated with all services in the Center. They also indicated that your staff is respected in the community for their advocacy work on behalf of patients.

If possible, I would like to meet with you during my visit to Dallas the week of March 6; I will give you a call. My résumé is enclosed. Thank you for your consideration.

Sample 3: Letter Based on a Referral

Susan Street, director of the Family Center, suggested that I contact you regarding your opening for a social worker in day treatment. In May I will be returning to Dallas and looking for opportunities to work with children at risk and their families. I would like to learn more about the Day Treatment Center and about the position that is open.

In addition to an MSW education, I have training and experience in day treatment, pediatric social work, and women's and children's services. At the day treatment program for the Children's Center in Anytown, I handled assessments, participated on the treatment team, and provided therapy for youths at risk and their families. This experience expanded my skills in working with emotionally disturbed youths in a culturally diverse setting. Before I began my graduate work, I was the coordinator for an effective volunteer service and children's program for the Women's Shelter in Dallas. In all of these settings, staff have complimented me for my work with families and children in crisis.

Susan Street highly recommended the Day Treatment Center. It is my understanding that your staff have initiated several programs that are considered models for working with culturally diverse populations.

Thank you for considering my application; my résumé is enclosed. You can reach me at home in the evenings at 111-222-3333 or at work on Tuesdays and Thursdays at 111-000-1111. I look forward to hearing from you.

Sample 4: Letter in Response to an Ad

I am responding to your announcement for a program coordinator in the March 22 issue of the *NASW News*. In May I will be returning to Dallas, where I plan to continue my work with women and families in crisis. The work of the Samuelson Women's Center is of particular interest to me.

Before I began graduate work at the Deal School of Social Work, I served as the volunteer coordinator and an advocate for the Women's Shelter in Dallas. As the coordinator, I expanded the volunteer program and created a children's program. This experience included recruiting and supervising staff, working with board members on policies, coauthoring a grant proposal, and managing a budget. As a graduate student, I sought training opportunities to expand my clinical skills and knowledge of services. In all settings, I have been complimented for my work with families in crisis.

I understand that the Women's Center is expanding and seeking additional staff for a second shelter. During my tenure at the Women's Shelter, I enjoyed coordinating advocacy efforts with Alice Sela, at that time with the Women's Center. I learned a great deal about the field from the Center staff; it would be exciting to continue my career with your organization.

If possible, I would like to meet with you during my visit to Dallas the week of March 6; I will contact you in the next two weeks. Thank you for your consideration.

Sample 5: Letter of Application

Jana Smith, specialist with University Extension, and Rochelle Jones, Dean for Extension, recommended that I contact you about openings that you have for the position of Community Development Specialist. My interests lie in the field of rural community development. Since my home is currently in the [city] area, I understand that travel would be necessary for a rural assignment; I would consider relocating.

I had the opportunity to work with Jana Smith and several of her University Extension colleagues in Poverty Project, a statewide group that addresses issues of rural poverty. I am now helping the group develop a project proposal to expand information about services and programs, via the Internet, to rural communities in [state]. My role with the group has been to conduct research, initiate contacts and relationships for collaboration, and write and compile sections of the project proposal. I worked in a quasi-governmental setting at the Community Development Group, forming successful relationships with community leaders. Assisting in developing, implementing, and evaluating the Initiatives Project in [city] gave me the opportunity to use my skills in assessment, planning, and social and economic development for communities; experience with the King Business Association increased my skills in economic development.

After reviewing the mission and programs of University Extension and talking with several staff members, I am interested in investigating how my skills might enhance the progress of University Extension. I would welcome the opportunity to meet with you to discuss my background. Please call to let me know whether such a meeting is possible and to confirm the appropriate next steps. I can be reached at 000-111-2222.

Thank you for your consideration. I look forward to meeting you.

Sample 6: Letter Requesting an Informational Interview

[Note that such requests are usually made by telephone.]

I believe I met you briefly on several occasions, at a breakfast sponsored by the social work school at State University, at a Lincoln Foundation function last summer, and at a Convergence, Inc., education committee meeting.

I am writing you in the hope of getting some advice about planning my next career move. I have had a unique experience as a full-time intern at Jackson Electric for the past 16 months; this internship is unusual for Jackson, because they accepted me not as the usual MBA intern but as a social work intern. I have enjoyed my work at Jackson so much that I would like to continue working in the area of corporate philanthropy and community relations. Would you be willing to meet with me to discuss the qualifications and experience necessary to work in this field?

I will give you a call in the next few days to get your response; if possible, I would like to schedule a brief informational interview with you or, if you are unable to meet with me, with someone you suggest.

Thank you.

Sample 7: Thank-You Letter to a Contact

Thank you so much for taking the time in February to talk with me about my job search. Your advice was helpful and appreciated.

As you suggested, I am in the process of contacting Natalie Jackson at Danes Hospital. I am also looking into the post-masters' program in eating disorders at State College. The program sounds very interesting.

I have enclosed a copy of my résumé. If you think of other ideas or hear of any openings, I would appreciate it if you would keep me in mind.

Thank you again for your help.

Sample 8: Letter Following a Telephone Call

Thank you for taking the time to speak with me on August 20. I am enthusiastic about the current and future job openings available in the Office of Family Assistance.

As I mentioned in our telephone conversation, I have a Master of Social Work degree from [university] in [city]. I am interested in public policy issues regarding children and families. I believe that my experience in direct service with clients is a strong complement to my interest in public policy and program development.

My experience with program planning and development has been quite successful and enjoyable. The most challenging task I have faced was formulating a community development project in [country]. Through a combination of research, interviewing, community meetings, and data analysis, the final project was accepted for funding through the Relief and Development Corporation.

My experience with local programs has been equally successful. While at Family and Children's Service, I completed an intensive program evaluation and, through implementation of my recommended changes, increased the program success rate by 40 percent within a six-month period. I am very interested in contributing to the development of social services programs.

As you suggested, I have enclosed a copy of my résumé. I plan to call you within the next week to answer any questions you may have. If you wish to contact me sooner, my number is 000-111-2222. Thank you again for your time.

Sample 9: Letter of Application

Enclosed please find my résumé in response to your job announcement in the January 1997 issue of *Voice*. This position sounds exciting, and I would welcome the opportunity to discuss it further with you.

I am currently employed by Advocates for Children, a statewide child advocacy organization that focuses on issues of family preservation, foster care, child abuse, substance abuse in families, child day care, and maternal and child health. As a program associate, I have lobbied for family leave and child care safety laws; I also have conducted research and community education on state policy concerning substance-exposed children and day care.

My graduate studies at the World School of Social Work have included coursework in children's policy, family poverty and policy, and the economics of social policy.

I would be most interested in learning more about your organization and your legislative advocacy program. I believe that my employment and academic experience would make me an asset to your organization. You can reach me at my office during the day at 000-111-2222.

Thank you for your consideration. I look forward to hearing from you soon.

Sample 10: Letter Following an Application

After reading the article on the work of Family Services in the August 14 issue of the *Paper*, I decided to send you a second letter. I am again indicating interest in the part-time social work position in the drug prevention program in the county schools.

My five years' experience working with child and family services are pertinent to this position. I have worked with children of various ages in school settings and have run groups on self-esteem and conflict. At The Center, I worked with at-risk teens and their families, individually and in groups, regarding addiction and other at-risk behavior.

I would welcome the opportunity to talk with you about this position. You can reach me by telephone at my part-time position at Focus Center, 000-111-2222, Monday, Wednesday, and Friday. My home telephone number is 000-111-3333.

Thank you a second time for your consideration.

Sample 11: Thank-You Letter Following a Job Interview

I would like to thank both you and Ms. Fox for taking time to meet with me this past Tuesday to discuss the social worker supervisor position. After speaking with you and learning more about Johnson Center, I feel strongly that my background in working with older adults and their families, planning with an interdisciplinary team, and coordinating special services offers the leadership qualities you are seeking.

Enclosed you will find a list of my references, the outline for an in-service training program that you requested, and a report I wrote on long-term care alternatives.

I look forward to hearing from you soon. Again, thank you.

Sample 12: Letter of Acceptance

I am writing to formally accept your job offer and to tell you once again how pleased I am to be coming to work at the Orange Center. After learning more about the Center and its progressive services, I am excited about being able to contribute.

Per our conversation of April 19, I am accepting the Social Worker position you have offered me at Orange Center. I understand that my responsibilities will entail assessments and treatment planning with the interdisciplinary team at an annual salary of $31,800. As agreed, I will begin work on June 12. I look forward to receiving the contract and job description. The contract will be returned promptly.

Between May 20 and 25, I will be moving to Boston, and I will call you with my new telephone number as soon as I arrive. Again, thank you for this opportunity.

Appendix 6

Sample Résumés

These sample résumés are those of actual job seekers; only the names have been changed. The samples demonstrate how experience and education might be presented in various résumé formats.

The sample résumés illustrate the points made in chapter 3. For example, a paragraph format is used in samples 2 and 3 (written for a fictional

BSW student, James Teal) to save space. Sample 2 is a straightforward presentation of Mr. Teal's experience. Note that both a current and a permanent address are listed, because he will be using this résumé while he is in the process of moving (he could instead have indicated a moving date and new address in a letter, but that letter might not always be attached to the résumé when it is circulating in an agency). The paragraphs about Mr. Teal's experience at Community Hospital and Stevens Foundation describe not only the skills he used but also the knowledge of issues he gained in these jobs. He has made an effort to understand the big picture, to see his work in context. The descriptions of an important asset—his leadership experiences on campus—use quantities ("one of four," "netting $3,500") to express the selectivity or the level of responsibility involved. He could have listed each of his other work and volunteer positions in detail, but he instead summarized them in two statements to keep the résumé brief. These statements still convey the idea that he has work experience in several settings and additional volunteer experience with children. Sample 3 emphasizes Mr. Teal's experience with children and families to support the objective he states at the top of this résumé.

Samples 4, 5, and 6 illustrate three different formats for résumés: chronological, functional, and combination-target. All are written for the same fictional MSW student, Lisa Denton. These samples are straightforward, simple, one- or two-page presentations of the highlights of Ms. Denton's experience. If she wanted to create a résumé specifically for positions in medical social work, she could describe her hospital experience in greater detail and her day treatment, shelter, and professional development work in less detail. She could eliminate the description of her work as research assistant altogether, letting the title suffice. She could also add a specific objective—for example, "Seeking a medical social work position using skills in discharge planning, assessments, and crisis intervention." She could even add a second sentence to the objective: "Particularly interested in pediatric and teaching hospitals."

Sample 7 describes someone with beginning technical expertise in a software program with applications for social services and community development. The highlights of Ms. Edward's experience, when put in priority order, happen to be in reverse chronological order, so she is able to use this simple style. If an earlier experience supported her current search objective, which is to find a position in social services or community development using her technical expertise, then she probably would create a separate section on the résumé for her most important qualifying experiences. Because her position titles convey her specific background more powerfully than do the names of the organizations where she worked, the titles lead off each entry. At the end of the résumé she lists specific computer skills.

Sample 1: Chronological Format for a BSW Graduate with Prior Experience

MARIA GONZALEZ
Address
City, State Zip
Phone

OBJECTIVE To secure a position as a case manager in a service delivery setting. Interested in services for youths, families, and homeless people.

EDUCATION Bachelor of Social Work, May 1996, Magna Cum Laude
University of South State, Anytown, State
Dean's List, Honors Convocation, 4.0 GPA in Major, 3.9 overall

EXPERIENCE
Social Work Intern, 1/96–4/96
Social Services, Anytown, State

- Introduced to probations, grant-writing, volunteer programs, emergency shelter and transitional-living programs, food and clothing services, FEMA and SHARE financial-aid assistance programs for families at risk of homelessness.
- Conducted home visits. Interviewed and built rapport with clients to assess needs.
- Assisted clients in goal setting and conducted goal reviews.
- Made appropriate referrals and followed up with clients and resources to evaluate the effectiveness of referrals.
- Collaborated with the employment counselor to overcome obstacles to clients' employment.
- Participated in community case conferences to optimize services for a homeless population and to reduce duplication.

Resident Apartment Manager, 4/89–9/93
Management, Inc., Anytown, State

- Managed a 352-unit bond-financed property with a staff of 12.
- Interviewed, hired, trained, motivated, supported, and evaluated staff.
- Collaborated with HUD to ensure guidelines were being followed.
- Collaborated with retained attorney to ensure landlord complied with the law regarding contracts and compliance procedures.
- Prepared annual budgets and monitored monthly expenses.
- Assessed community functions, made recommendations, and implemented change.
- Assessed community's place in the market to create and implement appropriate marketing strategies.
- Promoted community spirit through organized activities and a monthly newsletter.
- Established and maintained detailed record-keeping procedures.

Volunteer Service

Senior Home Improvement Project, Anytown, State, Summers 1991–1993

• Worked effectively as a team member to completely paint individual senior citizens' homes in one day.

The Center, Anytown, State, 9/93–2/94

• Consoled individuals over the telephone who had lost a loved one.

Theatre Company, Anytown, State, 4/89–1/91

• Worked as a team member on set construction, props, lighting, sound, costumes, and special effects on 10 productions. Required teamwork, quick problem-solving during performances, creativity with limited budgets, organizational and negotiation skills, and technical knowledge.

Affiliations	National Association of Social Workers
	Beta Sigma Phi
Skills	American Sign Language (minimal)
	Basic computer skills

Sample 2: Chronological Format for a BSW Student

JAMES TEAL

Present Address (until June 15, 1994)   **Permanent Address**
Address   Address
City, State Zip   City, State Zip
Telephone   Telephone

EDUCATION
Bachelor of Social Work, 1997, State College, Phoenix, Arizona
Dean's List, G.P.A. 3.2/4.0, Major G.P.A. 3.3

EXPERIENCE
Community Hospital, Anytown, State
Social Work Intern, January 1997–present

Work directly with chronically mentally ill individuals. Assist clients with daily living skills, social and recreational skills, and employment needs. Conduct home visits. Co-facilitate a support group; led two sessions independently. Observe supervisor in individual client sessions. Have developed a broad understanding of social policies, public and private service delivery, advocacy efforts, individual needs, and medical terminology related to this population. Complimented for efforts to integrate classroom knowledge and practice.

Stevens Foundation, Inc., Anytown, State
Trainer (paid position), September 1996–present

Teach independent-living skills and provide support to people with developmental disabilities. As part of a team provide assessments and evaluations. Serve as liaison with local employers. Assist in preparing new trainers. Served on a committee that successfully expanded employment sites. Familiar with issues facing families, agencies, and employers.

Camp Frost, Anytown, State
Lead Counselor (paid position), Summer 1996

Supervised a staff of four counselors serving 40 children in a residential camp. Planned and monitored activities, safety, supplies, and maintenance. Hired and trained two new counselors.

Counselor (paid position), Summers 1994, 1995

Worked with a group of ten children. Organized activities, taught swimming, led hikes, and provided support. Intervened in crises; resolved disputes among campers.

1992–1993. Held part-time and summer jobs in a hospital, retail store, and restaurant.

LEADERSHIP and VOLUNTEER EXPERIENCE
Freshmen Orientation Leader, State College, January–May 1996, August 1996

One of four students out of 20 applicants selected for the freshmen orientation committee. Planned a week-long series of events for 500 incoming students. Led a team of five volunteers, gave presentations to students and parents, and coordinated peer advising sessions.

Philanthropy Co-Chairperson for social fraternity, State College, September 1995–April 1996

Organized three fund-raising events netting $3,500 to benefit three local nonprofit organizations.

Other volunteer work includes tutoring and organizing activities for a children's program.

Sample 3: Combination-Target Format for a BSW Student

JAMES TEAL
Address
City, State Zip
Telephone

OBJECTIVE: Seeking a position serving children and families in low-income neighborhoods.

SKILLS AND KNOWLEDGE
Oversaw planning for children's activities in an after-school program and a camp.
Knowledgeable about child development and cultural diversity issues.
Hired, trained, and supervised counselors for a residential camp.

EDUCATION
Bachelor of Social Work, 1997, State College, Anytown, State
Dean's List, G.P.A. 3.2/4.0, Major G.P.A. 3.3
Studies included child development, family issues, and social policy. Wrote papers on child abuse, low-income family issues, and teen violence.

RELATED EXPERIENCE
Camp Frost, Anytown, State
Lead Counselor (paid position), Summer 1996
Supervised a staff of four counselors serving 40 children in a residential camp. Planned and monitored activities, safety, supplies, and maintenance. Hired and trained two new counselors. Learned about the daily responsibilities of running a residential camp.

Counselor (paid position), Summers 1994, 1995
Worked with a group of ten children. Organized activities, taught swimming, led hikes, and provided support. Intervened in crises; resolved disputes among campers.

State College Volunteer Corps, Anytown, State
Volunteer, Academic years 1995–1997
Tutored elementary school children in an after-school program. Organized and supervised athletic activities. Provided support and encouragement to children in the program. Became familiar with the needs and concerns of children living in a low-income community.

LEADERSHIP EXPERIENCE
Freshmen Orientation Leader, State College, January–May 1996, August 1996
One of four students out of 20 applicants selected for the freshmen orientation committee. Planned a week-long series of events for 500 incoming students. Led a team of five volunteers, gave presentations to students and parents, and coordinated peer advising sessions.

Philanthropy Co-Chairperson for social fraternity, State College, September 1995–April 1996
Organized three fund-raising events netting $3,500 to benefit three local nonprofits.

ADDITIONAL EXPERIENCE
Community Hospital, Anytown, State
Social Work Intern, January 1997–present
Assisted individuals with daily living skills, social and recreational skills, and employment needs. Conducted home visits and co-facilitated a support group. Observed supervisor in client sessions.

1992–1997. Held part-time and summer jobs in a center for people with developmental disabilities and in a hospital, retail store, and restaurant.

Sample 4: Chronological Format for an MSW Student

LISA DENTON
Address
City, State Zip
Telephone

EDUCATION

Master of Social Work, My University, Anytown, State
Anticipated graduation: May 1997. Emphasis: Children and youths, health, and mental health care.
Scholarship recipient, Student Council vice president, teaching assistant for family therapy.

Bachelor of Arts in Psychology, 1993, The College, Anytown, State
Dean's List. Admitted to two honorary societies.

PROFESSIONAL TRAINING

Children's Hospital, Anytown, State
Medical Social Work Intern, September 1996–present
- Provide services on the neonatal and pediatric intensive care units.
- Handle back-up services for all units, including the emergency room.
- Complete assessments and discharge planning; deal with crises.
- Provide emotional support to families; lead weekly parent support group.

Children's Center Day Treatment Program, Anytown, State
Graduate Social Work Intern, January 1995–June 1995; Volunteer, July 1995–present
- Assess needs of emotionally disturbed youths with behavior and learning problems.
- Provide individual, group, and family therapy.
- Expand knowledge of community resources; make referrals.

WORK AND VOLUNTEER EXPERIENCE

Family Center for Autism, Anytown, State
Respite Provider, May 1996–August 1996
- Provided respite care for youths with autism; learned about developmental disabilities.

Women's Shelter, Anytown, State
Volunteer Coordinator, March 1994–August 1995
Advocate, August 1993–February 1994
- Recruited, trained, and supervised eight volunteers providing support for clients.
- Designed and implemented a children's program staffed by volunteers.
- Provided support and advocacy for clients dealing with the legal system.

Crisis Intervention Center, Anytown, State
Hotline Volunteer, September 1993–August 1994

The College Psychology Department, Anytown, State
Research Assistant–Domestic Violence Project, September 1992–April 1993
- Conducted a literature review; collected data through interviews; entered data using SPSS.

PROFESSIONAL DEVELOPMENT

Certificate in Play Therapy, The Institute, Anytown, State, 1994
1994–1996 attended seminars on impact of domestic violence on children, divorce and children, crisis management, and fund-raising.

Sample 5: Functional Format for an MSW Student

LISA DENTON
Address
Anytown, State Zip
Telephone

OBJECTIVE
Seeking a clinical social work position in a pediatric health or mental health care setting working with children, adolescents, and families.

SKILLS
Direct Services
- Provided medical services on the neonatal and pediatric intensive care units.
- Handled back-up services for all hospital units, including the emergency room.
- Completed assessments, dealt with crises; provided emotional support to families.
- Led weekly parent support group in a hospital setting.
- Provided individual, group, and family therapy in a day treatment center.
- Assessed needs of emotionally disturbed youths with behavior and learning problems.
- Have knowledge of various developmental disabilities.
- Trained to handle crises and make appropriate referrals.
- Provided support and advocacy for clients dealing with the legal system.

Program and Project Implementation
- Recruited, trained, and supervised eight volunteers for a women's shelter.
- Designed and implemented a children's program staffed by volunteers.
- Co-chaired a committee that held a successful orientation event for 130 students.
- Collected data for a study through interviews; used the SPSS computer package.

EDUCATION
Master of Social Work, My University, Any Town, State
Anticipated graduation: May 1997. Emphasis: Children and youth, health, and mental health care. Scholarship recipient. Elected to Student Council vice president and curriculum committee.

Bachelor of Arts in Psychology, 1993, The College, Anytown, State
Dean's List. Admitted to two honorary societies.

EXPERIENCE
Children's Hospital, Anytown, State, Medical Social Work Intern, September 1996–present.
My University School of Social Work, Teaching Assistant for family therapy course, 1996.
Children's Center Day Treatment Program, Anytown, State, Graduate Social Work Intern, January 1995–June 1995. Volunteer, July 1995–present.
Family Center for Autism, Anytown, State, Respite Provider, May 1996–August 1996.
Women's Shelter, Anytown, State, Volunteer Coordinator, March 1994–August 1995. Advocate, August 1993–February 1994.
Crisis Intervention Center, Anytown, State Hotline Volunteer, September 1993–August 1994.
The College Psychology Department, Anytown, State, Research Assistant–Domestic Violence Project, September 1992–April 1993.

PROFESSIONAL DEVELOPMENT
Certificate in Play Therapy, The Institute, Anytown, State, 1994.
1994–1996 attended seminars on impact of domestic violence on children, fund-raising, divorce and children, and crisis management.

Sample 6: Combination-Target Format for an MSW Student

LISA DENTON
Address
Anytown, State Zip
Telephone

OBJECTIVE
Seeking a clinical social work position in a pediatric health or mental health care setting working with children, adolescents, and families.

QUALIFICATIONS
- Direct practice experience with children and families in an intensive care pediatric hospital environment.
- Individual and group clinical experience working with severely emotionally disturbed youths.
- Experience designing and implementing services for women and children in a shelter.
- Knowledge of impact of illness on families, child development, developmental disabilities, youth at risk, domestic violence, and interdisciplinary collaboration.

EDUCATION
Master of Social Work, My University, Any Town, State
Anticipated graduation: May 1997. Emphasis: Children and youth, health, and mental health care. Scholarship recipient. Elected to the curriculum committee.

Bachelor of Arts in Psychology, 1993, The College, Anytown, State
Dean's List. Admitted to two honorary societies.

PROFESSIONAL TRAINING
Children's Hospital, Anytown, State
Medical Social Work Intern, September 1996–present
- Provide services on the neonatal and pediatric intensive care units.
- Handle back-up services for all units, including the emergency room.
- Complete assessments, deal with crises; provide emotional support to families.
- Lead weekly parent support group.

Children's Center Day Treatment Program, Anytown, State
Graduate Social Work Intern, January 1995–June 1995
- Assessed needs of emotionally disturbed youths with severe behavior and learning problems.
- Provided individual, group, and family therapy.
- Expanded knowledge of community resources; made referrals.

Volunteer, July 1995–present
- Worked with the recreation program; tutored preteens.

WORK AND VOLUNTEER EXPERIENCE
Family Center for Autism, Anytown, State
Respite Provider, May 1996–August 1996
- Provided respite care for youths with autism.
- Gained knowledge about various developmental disabilities.

Women's Shelter, Anytown, State
Volunteer Coordinator, March 1994–August 1995; Advocate, August 1993–February 1994
- Recruited, trained, and supervised eight volunteers providing support for clients.
- Designed and implemented a children's program staffed by volunteers.
- Provided support and advocacy for clients dealing with the legal system.

Crisis Intervention Center, Anytown, State
Hotline Volunteer, September 1993–August 1994
- Trained to handle crises and make appropriate referrals.

The College Psychology Department, Anytown, State
Research Assistant–Domestic Violence Project, September 1992–April 1993
- Conducted literature review; collected data through interviews; entered data using SPSS.

PROFESSIONAL DEVELOPMENT
Leadership
Vice President, Student Council, My University School of Social Work, 1995
Orientation Leader, selected position, The College, 1992

Training
Certificate in Play Therapy, The Institute, Anytown, State, 1994
1994–1996 attended seminars on impact of domestic violence on children, fund-raising,
divorce and children, and crisis management.

Teaching
Teaching Assistant for family therapy course, My University School of Social Work, 1996

Sample 7: Chronological Format for an MSW Graduate with a Technical Background

KATHRYN EDWARDS
Address, Apt. #, City, State Zip
Telephone; E-mail: name@place.org

EDUCATION

The School of Social Work
Candidate for MSW, Expected Graduation December 1996
Concentration: Social and Economic Development
Specialization: Management

The University, School of Arts and Sciences
Bachelor of Arts, 1994. Majors: Biology and Psychology

PROFESSIONAL EXPERIENCE

Geographic Information Systems (GIS) Developer, 5/96–Present
Division of Family Services (DFS), Department of Social Services, Anytown, State

- Create a customized geo-mapping computer program for use by DFS caseworkers in identifying resources and other community characteristics.
- Train DFS and community workers in the use of the customized program.
- Coordinate a statewide DFS committee whose purpose is to explore the potential use of GIS and present the findings in a report to the director of DFS.
- Teach the DFS committee members how to use ArcView, a GIS program.

Citizen Participation Intern/GIS Intern, 5/96–Present
Regional Planning Council, Anytown, State

- Writing user guides for staff of information analysis software programs.
- Creating GIS maps for a variety of policy and programming projects.
- Conducted a community survey of 253 residents and analyzed the results in a report for the Interim Board of the Cornerstone Partnership Initiative.
- Organized a town hall–style meeting for residents of City and County, to learn about and discuss a variety of issues related to individual and community revitalization.

Geographic Information Systems Instructor, 8/96–Present
The University, Anytown, State

- Developed the course "GIS for Social Services and Community Development."
- Teach approximately 25 social work and architecture master's students and professors.

Computer Lab Instructor, 8/96–Present
The University, Anytown, State

- Developed a one-session "Introduction to Microsoft Word" class.
- Teach and assist several introductory computer classes offered to MSW students.

Kathryn Edwards, page 2
Telephone

Community Development Intern, 8/95–5/96
Catholic Social Ministry, Anytown, State

- Planned a community celebration event for 200 people, resulting in positive sense of community.
- Designed a computer membership system for the volunteers and financial contributors.
- Assisted the Business Association in a beautification project.

PRESENTATIONS
Geographic Information Systems: A Tool for Community Development

- Discussion and demonstration of geographic information systems and how that tool can be of use in social services and community development. Presented at the following meetings:

NASW Conference, Anytown, State, date
Child Abuse and Neglect Conference, sponsor, Anytown, State, date
Community Consortium Conference, sponsor, Anytown, State, date

SKILLS
GIS: ArcView, Maptitude
Word Processing: Microsoft Word, WordPerfect
Spreadsheet: Excel, Quattro Pro
Presentation/Graphics: PowerPoint, Harvard Graphics

Sample 8: Combination Format for an MSW Graduate with Policy and International Interests

MADELINE MATTHEWS

until July 15, 1997	*after July 15, 1997*
address, city, state zip	address, city, state zip
telephone	telephone
E-mail address	

EDUCATION
Master of Social Welfare, Great University, Anytown, State, May 1997
Bachelor of Arts, Community Studies/Latin American Studies, First University, 1994
Senior Thesis: "El Salvador: Critical Issues"
Honors/Societies: (Names of those *specific* to her interests)

PROGRAM SKILLS
Languages: English and Spanish
Computer: Excel, Microsoft Word, Geographic Information Systems
Program: Development, implementation, evaluation
Writing: Grant proposals, evaluation reports

AREAS OF POLICY STUDY/INTEREST
Policy Areas: immigration, international development, foreign policy, housing, HIV/AIDS
Interest: implications of policy for low-income persons at the local community level
Experience Abroad: Dominican Republic, Mexico, El Salvador, Panama, Honduras, Guatemala, Nicaragua

CIVIC AND COMMUNITY EXPERIENCE
International Projects, Anytown, State
Latin American Program Intern, January 1997–May 1997

- Anticipated functions include evaluation of sustainable microenterprise projects in Guatemala, project development in Nicaragua, coordination of annual meeting for affiliated organizations in Central America, facilitation of relationships between City area public schools and development projects in Central America.

The Garden Project, Anytown, State
Graduate Research Intern, community development/garden agency, July 1996–December 1996

- Evaluated survey results of urban gardening program aimed at stabilizing low-income neighborhoods. Coded and analyzed data.
- Wrote final report on survey results.
- Used computerized census data from Geographic Information Systems to create informational maps.

Pathways, Anytown, State
Direct Service/Fund-raising Intern, January 1996–July 1996

- Applied Housing and Urban Development (HUD) low-income housing policies to HIV/AIDS client issues.
- Worked with various groups: tenants, neighborhood associations, and government agencies (HUD).
- Conducted client intakes and assessments for a low-income, HIV/AIDS housing program.
- Researched and wrote grants. To date, 30 percent of proposals have been successful.

Madeline Matthews, page 2
until July 15: telephone
after July 15: telephone

Amigos, City, State
Tutoring Chairperson and Board Member, October 1995–June 1996

• Organized volunteer bilingual tutoring program involving 25 volunteers and 90 students from three local elementary schools.
• Collaborated with other board members on fund-raising events.

Refugee Committee, City, State
Project Coordinator, April 1995–April 1996

• Assisted refugees with applications for temporary protected status.
• Planned, fund-raised, and led committees for material-aid projects.
• Prepared and co-led a delegation to El Salvador.
• Organized City area speaking tour of Salvadoran psychologists.

County Immigration Project, Anytown, State
Immigration Law/Rights Intern, March 1994–June 1995

• Translated client documents.
• Assisted lawyer in explaining rights to immigrants.

Amigos, City, State
Route Leader, Volunteer, September 1992–August 1993

• Trained new volunteers for summer projects in public health in Latin America.
• Supervised, evaluated volunteers during the summer in City, Mexico.
• Solicited funds for summer projects in public health for rural Latin America.
• Organized community members to carry out latrine construction in City, Mexico, cement floors in the Dominican Republic.

Mary School, Anytown, State
Junior High Girl's Basketball Coach, January 1990–March 1990

• Led team practices and taught skills to team members with various abilities.

KXXD Public Radio and Television, Anytown, State
Volunteer Fund-raiser, September 1991–June 1994

WORK EXPERIENCE
Senior Customer Service Representative, Sports, Inc., Anytown, State, July 1995–July 1996

Assistant Manager, Mexican Food Restaurant, Anytown, State, November 1994–May 1995
Supervised up to ten staff, communicated in Spanish

Bilingual Substitute Teacher for two school districts in State, September 1994–May 1995

Sample 9: Chronological Format for an MSW Graduate with Community Development Experience

ROCHELLE SMITH
Address
Anytown, State Zip
Telephone
E-mail

Education
Name University, Anytown, State
Master of Social Work, December 1996
Focus: Social and Economic Development, and Management

University of State, Anytown, State
Bachelor of Social Work, Minor in Psychology, December 1993
Magna Cum Laude

Community Development Experience
Rural Community Development Intern, September 1996 to present
Center for Community Development, Anytown, State

- Provide staff support to the *Pathways* team
- Assist in developing a proposal for a program designed to address rural poverty issues by making program and service information more accessible via the Internet
- Expand information and data on rural community resources for use on the Internet
- Use the Internet to research community resources and grant opportunities

Community Development Intern, Full-time, May 1996 to September 1996
Community Development Agency, Anytown, State

- Gathered data, information, and necessary support for grant proposals
- Wrote components for grant proposals
- Worked on budgeting and fiscal management, community relations, marketing, planning, problem-solving, and board development
- Assisted in developing and implementing the *Enterprise Community* initiatives; completed site visits and written evaluations
- Collected and prepared data on economic trends and activities
- Expanded community resource information for the Community Information Network on the Internet
- Assisted in writing and publishing an issue of the program newsletter
- Researched topics on the Internet

Social and Economic Development Intern, August 1995 to March 1996
Social Ministry, Anytown, State

- Co-coordinated a Community Celebration
- Provided staff support in developing a Community Center at Smith Branch
- Co-developed a membership program, which the agency continued
- Provided staff support to the King Business Association
- Organized a commercial area clean-up involving five community organizations and 30 volunteers
- Researched building ownership for the King Business Association

Direct Service Experience
Social Service Coordinator, Full-time, December 1993 to July 1995
Memorial Home, Anytown, State

- Managed a staff of social workers
- Assisted families and residents through the admission process
- Met with residents/family members on a regular basis and addressed problems as they arose
- Completed social history and progress notes on each resident
- Led the plan of care for each resident and participated in quality assurance
- Facilitated an Alzheimer's support group

Case Management Intern, August 1993 to December 1993
Regional Center, Anytown, State

- Supported clients with developmental disabilities and mental retardation
- Engaged in social work practice with individuals, families, task groups, community resources, and team relationships
- Completed social history, assessments, and monthly reviews on clients
- Co-facilitated a support group for supportive employment workers
- Developed a community integration project for several individuals receiving residential services from Central Regional Center

Computer Proficiency Skills
- Microsoft Word
- WordPerfect
- Microsoft Excel
- SAS
- Internet

Sample 10: Functional Format for an Experienced MSW Graduate with Program Interests

JENNIFER BLACK, ACSW, LCSW

Address

Anytown, State Zip

Telephone

SUMMARY OF QUALIFICATIONS

Ten years' experience in program development and community organization entailing start-up, promotions, and fund-raising; all positions have been in management or leadership capacities. More than eight years of social service experience in clinical and administrative functions, including counseling, training, and supervision.

PROGRAM DEVELOPMENT/COMMUNITY ORGANIZATION SKILLS

- Successfully initiated Healthy Initiative, a comprehensive, multi-agency partnership providing health services and wellness education to four day schools serving 700 students; program is currently allocated a $100,000 budget by The Hospital.
- Established first local intergenerational program at older-adult housing project; identified appropriate facility and participants and organized activities for more than five years.
- Planned elementary school fund-raiser generating more than $1,000 in sales of projects created by students; recruited parents and vendors to donate time and services.

CLINICAL SKILLS

- Provided clinical services to people age 60 and older as part of multidisciplinary team in a hospital setting; treatment included initial assessment, therapy, and discharge planning.
- Conducted short- and long-term therapy for older adults and facilitated support groups for family members on issues concerning aging.
- Supervised students working on Master of Social Work degrees.
- Solely staffed senior citizen employment office by canvassing local businesses with needs matching applicants' abilities.

LEADERSHIP SKILLS

- Recently appointed to Older Adult Committee, The Foundation; assist in decision making regarding grant appropriations.
- Serving on Board of Directors, Academy; provide guidance and direction setting for school policy and practices.
- Member of Advisory Committee, Healthy Initiative; recommend program enhancements and mediate difficulties.
- Selected by National Council of Jewish Women to interview citizens for oral history using questionnaire.

WORK HISTORY

Primary Clinician, Community Mental Health Clinic, Anytown, State	1985–1986
Clinical Therapist, Family and Children's Service, Anytown, State	1981–1984
Social Worker, Vocational Service, Anytown, State	1979–1980

EDUCATION

Master of Social Work, The University, Anytown, State	1978
Bachelor of Science in Social Welfare, State University, Anytown, State	1976

Sample 11: Combination-Target Format for an Executive Director

CARL JEFFERSON
Address
Anytown, State Zip
Home telephone; Work telephone

Innovative social work/healthcare administrator with proven expertise in strategic planning, business development, continuum-of-care services, fund development, contract negotiations, and operations management for a social service program, medical center/research institute, home health services program, physical medicine/rehabilitation, and physician medical groups. Outstanding record of improving profit by increasing volume, extending market penetration, developing new programs, and managing costs. Directed multiple departments with more than 175 employees, improving patient outcomes and productivity.

PROFESSIONAL EXPERIENCE

January 1996– **THE HOSPITAL,** Anytown, State
Present Executive Director, Clinical Services
Responsibilities include operational oversight of Social Services, Discharge Planning, Employee Assistance Program, Outpatient Case Management, Neurosciences Institute, Neurosurgical Physician Practice, Neurology Laboratory, Physical Medicine, Continuum-of-Care services (Home Health), Respiratory/Pulmonary, and Orthopedic Institute. Additional responsibility for business development, contracting, marketing, and fund development. Supervise 175 employees, combined budgeted expenses of $12 million, revenue of $36 million.
- Created comprehensive Movement Disorders program (increased rehabilitation, skilled nursing unit, and out-patient therapy census by 20 percent).
- Established community case management liaison service (grant funded).
- Reduced operating expenses with integration of new skill mix and elimination of purchased labor and overtime ($2 million).
- Developed Huntington's disease neurotransplant program (first in the United States).
- Created physician/social work practice partnership program (integration of social work and physician private practice).

October 1992– **THE HOSPITAL,** Anytown, State
January 1996 Director Social Work Services/
                        Neuroscience Institute
In this capacity, responsibilities included managerial oversight of Social Work Services, Discharge Planning, Community Case Management, The Neuroscience Institute, Neurology Lab, and Epilepsy Research Center. Supervised 45 employees, combined budgeted expenses of $6 million, revenue of $9 million. Main accomplishments:
- Obtained 14 grants for Out-Patient Case Management ($1.5 million).
- Established Epilepsy Research Center (physician recruitment).
- Developed community/physician/hospital continuum-of-care program (community outreach program, grant funded).
- Created Parkinson and Brain Tumor Information & Referral Centers (17 community support groups, three chapters).
- Provided leadership/coordination for continuum-of-care quality improvement team (95 percent JCAHO survey outcome).

August 1988–   **THE HOSPITAL,** Anytown, State
October 1992   Director Social Work Services
Responsibilities included management of Social Work/Discharge Planning, Utilization Review, Employee Assistance Program, Senior Partner Program, and Respite Care Services. Supervised 15 employees. Provided clinical supervision of social work staff, coordinated department quality improvement program. Main accomplishments:
- Developed Community Outpatient Case Management Program.
- Established computerized High-Risk Screening Program, cost savings $1.9 million.
- Revitalized hospital/community respite program (community board).
- Created clinical social service revenue program.
- Improved productivity by 25 percent (high-risk and intern programs).
- Established two community/hospital partnerships to reduce LOS and improve quality of care (DE and psychiatric services).
- Developed hospital Employee Assistance Program.
- Reduced average length of stay hospitalwide by 2.5 days (physician profiles, education).

April 1986–   **HOSPITAL HOME HEALTH CARE AGENCY,**
July 1988   Anytown, State
                Director Rehabilitation/Social Services
Responsibilities included management of rehabilitation services (physical therapy, occupational therapy, and speech therapy) and social services staff of 50 clinicians for three offices. Recruited, hired, and oriented qualified staff. Responsible for revenue of $2 million and quality assurance program.
- Established home health/University MSW internship program.
- Increased revenue by 50 percent through business development and department re-engineering.

July 1983–   **THE HOSPITAL AND REHABILITATION CENTER,**
April 1986   Anytown, State
                Clinical Social Worker
Responsibilities included clinical social work (assessment/therapy) and discharge planning services to acute rehabilitation and emergency department patients.
- Developed rehabilitation support groups.
- Created community rehabilitation resource guide.

EDUCATION   MSW—State University, Anytown, State
                  BA—Sociology, Anytown, State
                  Licensed Clinical Social Worker

PROFESSIONAL ACTIVITIES
Adjunct Professor, University of State
Member: NASW, Society for Social Work Administrators in Health Care
Healthcare consulting services: Skilled Nursing Facilities, Acute Care Hospitals

Sample 12: Combination-Target Format for an MSW Graduate with Managed Care Experience

NICOLE STEVENS
Address
Anytown, State, Zip
Telephone

OBJECTIVE

Seeking a behavioral healthcare management position in a medium-sized corporate healthcare setting in the [geographic] area.

QUALIFICATIONS AND BACKGROUND

A Licensed Clinical Social Worker with more than six years' experience in Behavioral Healthcare Management. Extensive expertise in developing and implementing client-specific managed care policies and programs; on-call policy development; contract negotiation; public speaking; clinical and administrative supervision; quality management; utilization and concurrent review; and pharmacological review, including ECT.

ACHIEVEMENTS

- **Developed** national leadership consultation program for the senior executives of select clients. **Result:** Established a national network of highly specialized professionals to provide client-specific services.

- **Conceptualized** a "Care Management Program" that identified beneficiaries who had reached 70 percent of their lifetime benefit. **Result:** Intensive planning among patients, their families, and provider(s) maximized the remaining benefits and transition into community resources with minimal stress.

- **Designed** client-specific clinical criteria and policies to be used for six [type] accounts. **Result:** Improved satisfaction and compliance among beneficiaries and management. Able to address client-specific needs and blend "medical necessity" protocols with the client culture. This criterion is used in the national sales and marketing division and has identified a niche market.

- **Public speaking,** including presentations at workshops and symposia to mental health practitioners and clients on managed behavioral healthcare issues. **Result:** Company is seen as a leader in client-specific behavioral healthcare programs.

- **Troubleshooting** with third-party payers to reduce pended claims. Designed a numerical coding system, allowing case managers to authorize care using a code number, ensuring a consistent interpretation by commercial carriers with a reduction in claims processing time to two weeks.

- **Supervise and manage** daily operations of six clinical and seven support staff. **Result:** Customer satisfaction at 90 percent; quality assurance protocols are maintained for computer training and troubleshooting, policy implementation.

- **Negotiation** of contracts with specialized individual providers and facilities. **Result:** Special rates and cost savings to the client while meeting managed care goals.

- **Risk management program** developed and implemented. **Result:** Decreased lawsuits by 60 percent in one year; increased stable labor force by 72 percent; improved insurability by commercial carriers, thus reducing placement in risk pool.

CAREER EXPERIENCE

Health Plans, Anytown, State, Psychiatric Disability Case Manager, 1995–Present

Health, Inc., Anytown, State, Senior Clinical Case Manager, Team Leader, 1991–1995

Great Health Plans, City, State, Psychiatric Reviewer, 1989–1991

The Children's Center, Anytown, State, Senior Clinician, 1987–1989

Task Corporation, Anytown, State, Risk Manager/Operations Manager, 1980–1987

Private Clinical Practitioner, 1991–Present

PROFESSIONAL AFFILIATIONS

National Association of Social Workers, State Chapter
- Board of Directors, elected; 1996–Present
- Executive Committee, appointed by president; activities include policy, development, and budgeting; 1995–Present
- Member, Managed Care Committee; 1993–Present

EDUCATION

University, Master of Social Work, 1986
University of State, Bachelor of Arts in Psychology, 1984

COMPUTER SKILLS

Microsoft Works for Windows; MS Word; MS Excel; MS Access

Sample 13: Chronological Format for an Experienced MSW Graduate with Direct Service and Policy Experience (includes keyword summary for electronic scanning)

MELISSA JONES
Address
City, State Zip
Telephone

KEYWORDS

Child Welfare Policy Specialist. Social Policy Development. Policy Analysis. Regulation Development. Guidelines for States. Child Protective Services Supervisor. MSW, My University.

EDUCATION

MSW, My University School of Social Work, Anytown, State, 1983.

SOCIAL WORK and PSYCHOLOGY BS, The College, Anytown, State, 1980.

EXPERIENCE

DEPARTMENT OF HEALTH AND HUMAN SERVICES, The Capital

Child Welfare Policy Specialist (March 1994–Present): Develop regulations, policies, procedures, and guidance materials related to child welfare services programs for the use of state and federal staff; provide consultation to regional, central office, and state staff as well as other federal agencies in program areas related to child welfare; represent the Division of [name] as requested, with respect to public child welfare services in group and individual conferences with other divisions, bureaus, and federal agencies.

COUNTY DEPARTMENT OF SOCIAL SERVICES, Anytown, State (December 1985–March 1994)

Child Protective Services Supervisor (January 1992–March 1994): Supervised the Sexual Abuse Treatment Services Unit staff of five, provided clinical and casework consultation regarding the treatment of sexual abuse victims and their families.

Foster Care Supervisor (March 1988–January 1992): Supervised a unit of seven foster care workers, provided casework/clinical consultation regarding family reunification and adoption preparation, provided policy/procedures training for new staff, managed the foster care supportive services budget, served as Foster Care Review Board liaison to coordinate monthly case reviews, monitored and reviewed cases for compliance with federal and state regulations, reviewed and edited all written documents such as court reports and case plans, handled crises in workers' absence, and supervised MSW student.

Social Worker (December 1985–March 1988): Managed a caseload in both foster care/adoption services and independent-living/adolescent foster care services. Handled individual and family casework, home and school visits, counseling with foster parents, written court reports, and court appearances. Supervised BSW student.

CORRECTIONAL CENTER FOR WOMEN, Anytown, State

Social Worker (December 1984–December 1985): Conducted initial admission and re-entry to community groups for incarcerated women, wrote psychosocial assessments completed upon admission through inmate and family interviews, developed group protocols for ongoing and specialized population groups, handled crisis intervention with inmates, completed daily written group process reports and individual evaluations for each group member at termination, participated in multidisciplinary team meetings, and developed interagency contacts and agreements for referrals for inmates at release.

GROUP HOUSE, Anytown, State

Social Worker (August 1983–December 1984): Provided individual, group, and family counseling with emotionally disturbed adolescents in a group home setting; formulated treatment plans; organized preadmission interviews; led treatment team meetings and monthly evaluations on each resident; provided supervision to child care staff; and acted as administrator on duty once a month.

ADOLESCENT CENTER, Anytown, State

Mental Health Associate (August 1982–August 1983): Handled individual counseling and crisis intervention with emotionally disturbed adolescents in a residential treatment facility, led group meetings, and participated in planning and implementing the adolescent independent-living program.

TOWN HOSPITAL, ADOLESCENT CLINIC, Anytown, State

Graduate Social Work Intern (January 1981–December 1981): Provided individual counseling, casework, psychosocial assessments, group counseling, family therapy (co-leader), and home and school visits. Provided services to pregnant adolescents and sexual assault victims.

CERTIFICATION

State Licensed Certified Social Worker

Sample 14: Curriculum Vitae

DEA JONES
Address
Anytown, State Zip
Home Telephone
Work Telephone
E-mail

EDUCATION
PhD Social Work Candidate
Name School of Social Work
Name University, Anytown, State
Dissertation topic: Effects of Poverty Wages on Health
Advisor: Name

Master of Science in Social Work, 1990
Administration and Planning Concentration
University of State, Anytown, State

Bachelor of Arts: Major-Sociology, Minor-History, 1988
University of State, Anytown, State

TEACHING INTERESTS
Analysis of Practice
Evaluation of Programs and Services
Social Welfare Policy, Policy Practice
Child and Family Policy and Advocacy

RESEARCH INTERESTS
Poverty Wages and the Working Poor
Health Care Policy and Health Status Research
Homelessness
Program Evaluation and Policy Practice

HONORS
1986–88   Liberal Arts Scholarship, University of State, City
1988   Name Honor Society, University of State, City
1986   Phi Theta Kappa, City Community College

PROFESSIONAL EXPERIENCE

Teaching Experience
Name School of Social Work, Name University
Instructor, 1996–1997
Master's-level Evaluation of Programs and Services

Co-Instructor, 1995
Master's-level Analysis of Practice
Co-instructor: Name

Lab Instructor, 1995
Master's-level Social Work Statistics
Course Instructor: Name

Teaching Assistant, 1994
Master's First Semester Social Policy Course
Course Instructor: Name

Research Experience
Program Evaluation Consultant, 1996–1997
   Name, Project Director
   Development Corporation, Anytown, State
   Survey development, interview training, statistical consultant

Research Assistant, 1995–1996
   Name, Assistant Dean
   Name University
   1996 Advisor Evaluation Survey
   Data entry and statistical analysis

Research Assistant, 1994–1995
   Name, Director
   Name University
   Reaccreditation Alumni Survey and Annual Placement Surveys
   SAS programming, design, and statistical analysis

Research Assistant, 1993–1994
   Name, Associate Professor
   The Transitional Housing Project, Anytown, State
   Computer programming, manual preparation, statistical analysis

Practice Experience
1990–1993   Director of Homeless Services
              Agency, Anytown, State
Worked with homeless women and children in locating temporary and permanent housing.
Experienced in crisis intervention, resource development and referral, volunteer training,
and program planning. Managed a budget.

1989–1990   Social Work Intern
                Agency, Anytown, State
Worked with people with mental retardation in groups and individually, and with their families as a liaison between the institution and client and family to advocate for client needs.

PRESENTATIONS

1997 Leadership Initiative on Cancer, city, state/country
Guest Speaker: "Challenges and Benefits of Community Development"
Coauthors

1997 HUD Regional Conference, city, state/country
Panel: "Building Partnerships to Build Communities"
Coauthors

1996 Conference on Social Welfare, city, state/country
Workshop: "Advocacy and Community Organizing for Human Service Providers"
Coauthors

1996 Council on Social Work Education, Annual Program Meeting, city, state/country
"Predictors of Permanent versus Temporary Housing"
Coauthors

1995 American Association Annual Meeting, city, state/country
Oral Presentation, International Section
"Indicators of Health and Interaction Effects on Health Status"
Coauthors

1994 American Association Annual Meeting, city, state/country
Committee on Homelessness
"A Decade of Homeless Families"
Coauthors, city, state/country

1994 Field Instructor Seminar, Program Evaluation Section
Name School of Social Work
Name University

PUBLICATIONS
Journal Article
Authors (1996). Title, Journal, volume number, pages

Papers under Review
Title, author(s)

UNIVERSITY AND CIVIC SERVICE

1996	Academic Adviser and Field Liaison, Name University
1990	Graduate Student Committee, Name University
1988–89	Volunteer instructor for English as a Second Language classes
1988–89	Volunteer reader for the blind with the Commission.
1987	Volunteer for the physically handicapped.

AFFILIATIONS

Council on Social Work Education
National Association of Social Workers

SPECIAL SKILLS AND TALENTS

Language skills: bilingual, English and Spanish. Have translated in both medical and educational environments. Extensive travel in rural and urban Latin America.

Computer skills: SAS statistical package, SPSS statistical package, Excel Spreadsheet, Lisrel structural equation modeling, Rbase, Microsoft Word, WordPerfect, QuattroPro.

Research skills: Have worked on several research projects, in both academic settings and in the community. Have worked as a research assistant and consultant; have taught statistics, research methods, and program evaluation.

Sample Interview Questions

The following are questions that have been asked in interviews for social work and related positions. It is important to note that employers are increasingly using the behavioral interview format. Behavioral interview questions are often phrased as follows: "Tell me about a time when . . . ." The focus is on specific situations. Preparing responses, which should include examples from your experiences, to the following questions will enable you to respond effectively regardless of the interview format used. Tailor your responses to the specific position for which you are interviewing. Note that you will sometimes encounter vague questions; several are included below. At the end of this appendix is a sample list of information you might want to gather about an organization. Some of the items would be appropriate to ask in an interview. Discussions with employers and candidates generated these lists.

Generic Questions

1. What are your career goals?
2. Are you where you thought you would be in your career?
3. How does the work in this organization fit your professional mission?
4. What is your experience in working with diverse staff? What did you find difficult and easy about that?
5. What is your experience with diverse ethnic groups?
6. Why do you think you can work well with people who are [ethnic group]?
7. How do you work?
8. Tell me about a time when you had to juggle your regular responsibilities and deal with a sudden priority.
9. How do you evaluate your work?
10. What would most intimidate you?
11. What would you dislike most in a position?
12. What do you need to hear about this organization and position that will tell you this would be a good match for you?
13. What is your knowledge of regulations [Medicare or Medicaid, for example]?
14. What issues might you have with [adoption, for example]?

15. I am getting the impression that you really do not know what it is like [to work in that community with the drug situation or to be poor, for example]. Do you have a comment?

16. What is the biggest obstacle you found in working with [a particular issue or population]?

17. What did you not like about your work?

18. How would your coworkers describe you? How would your supervisor describe you?

19. What kind of people rub you the wrong way?

20. Describe a situation in which you feel you could have done a better job with a [project, patient, or client, for example]?

21. How do you plan?

22. What qualities do you feel are most important in a supervisor?

23. What do you do to cope in a fast-paced work setting?

24. What makes you think you would be good at this job?

25. What do you think will work and why [in a particular situation]?

26. How do you take care of yourself?

27. Why do you want this job?

28. Is this job still something that you are interested in now that you have heard about it?

29. Tell me about yourself.

30. Why do you want to leave your present position?

31. What do you see as the most difficult aspects of working in this field [or with this population]?

32. What do you want to be doing in five years?

33. What are your qualifications?

34. Why should I hire you?

35. How would you approach [a particular problem or situation]?

36. What are your clinical strengths; what are your administrative strengths?

37. What are your weaknesses?

38. What did you learn from your field-training experiences?

39. What has been your greatest accomplishment?

40. Tell me what you know about our agency.

41. How do you see yourself in the role of [school social worker, advocate, clinical supervisor, or legislative aide, for example]?

42. Talk about your view of [hospices, family life education, or community development, for example].

43. What experience and/or training have you had in the area of [a particular field or function]?

44. How do you deal with hostility, anger, or stress?

45. Describe the process you go through in developing [a case plan, budget, workshop, contract, or marketing plan, for example].

46. What kinds of things are important to you in a job? What has been satisfying?

47. What kinds of things do you like or not like in a job? What has been a hassle in your work?

48. What do you have to offer as a [clinician or administrator, for example]?
49. Why are you in social work? Why did you study social work?
50. What brought you into social work?
51. How is social work different from what you expected?
52. What would your friends say about you?
53. What could you offer to this job?
54. How would you handle a situation in which you had a disagreement with a coworker?
55. Have you ever been perceived as not doing something correctly and how did you handle it?
56. What are your questions?
57. In what areas do you prefer not to be involved?
58. What about this position is most attractive to you? What are the disadvantages or concerns you have about this job?
59. What was the most adverse situation with which you have had to deal in your professional life? How did you deal with it? What was the outcome?
60. Have you made any mistakes in your career? If so, what were they? How did you fix them?
61. What was the most difficult ethical decision you have had to make and what was the outcome?
62. If we hired you next week, what unfinished business would you leave in your current work?

Direct Practice Questions

1. Service delivery has been changing for several years away from long-term services delivered in offices to intensive services delivered in homes, schools, and other settings. What skills can you bring to these services?
2. What is your understanding of service delivery in [a particular field]?
3. What is your experience with targeted case management?
4. Tell me about a time you were in a disagreement over a treatment plan.
5. Describe your favorite and least favorite clients.
6. What is your experience in working with clients who are different from yourself?
7. Why were you successful working with clients who are different from yourself, and why were you unsuccessful?
8. How do you assess for suicide risk?
9. What are your technical skills [or diagnostic skills or treatment skills]?
10. Tell me about a time when you advocated for more services for a client, but funding or policies did not allow you to provide the services you thought were appropriate.
11. Why do you think you can work with [for example, parents, older adults, substance abusers, clients with low incomes, survivors of rape

or incest] when you haven't been there yourself? What could hinder your work with this population?

12. How is practice different from what you expected?
13. What do you think produces change?
14. What is your philosophy on [a particular issue or treatment]?
15. What is your theory base? What is your theoretical approach? How has your theoretical approach changed?
16. Describe one of your cases. Describe a particularly challenging case for you.
17. What types of client issues have you dealt with?
18. Give some examples of treatment choices that you made and explain why you made those choices.
19. With what client issues are you most comfortable working?
20. How would you work with families living in different communities?
21. What has been your experience with agency paperwork and how do you feel about it?
22. What does [family therapy, for example] mean to you?
23. What are your expectations of both individual and group supervision?
24. How do you protect your personal boundaries when responsibilities demand your time, attention, and energy?
25. How do you think court intervention might be useful in a case?
26. What other populations have you worked with?
27. Clinically, what is the most difficult experience you have had?
28. Identify some boundary issues that may confront someone in this position and describe the way you would handle them.
29. In which job did you have the most responsibility? How many employees were under your management authority? Explain your management style. Give a specific example of your management experience in resolving staff conflict. Describe any innovative way you resolved a major problem that resulted in a change in how the organization did business.
30. Describe your management style specifically as it relates to setting direction, creating an environment, and changing organizational cultures in a complex organization.
31. Describe your experience in managing a diverse work force and highlight experiences you have had in forming partnerships or coalitions with diverse community groups.
32. Describe your experiences in setting priorities and allocating and managing resources, including budgets and staff.
33. Describe your experience and identify specific strategies you use to provide quality assurance and continuous quality improvement.

Administrative and Policy Questions

1. Since this is a newly created position, how would you proceed?
2. What are examples of work you have accomplished by facilitating [or organizing] the work of others?

3. What projects [or programs] have you run? What challenges did you face?
4. What is your experience with preparing and using a budget?
5. Have you written grant proposals? Were they successful?
6. Tell me about your involvement in collaborative efforts.
7. If you developed a coalition, whom did you decide to include?
8. How would you address tension in a group?
9. How do you work under pressure?
10. What was the most tense situation you experienced, and how did you handle it?
11. What is your experience with writing quickly, under pressure?
12. Tell me about your research skills.
13. What are the pitfalls of extrapolating data, particularly from the local to the national level?
14. Give an example of a situation in which you had to set aside your beliefs on a particular issue and work toward a politically and financially feasible goal?
15. Have you been involved in projects or efforts that took more than a year? How did you maintain your enthusiasm and organize your work?
16. Have you been involved in an effort that failed? Did you attempt to resurrect it? Why or why not? Did you make changes the second time?
17. Tell me about a time you found it difficult to work with a team.
18. What is your experience in working with people with opposite viewpoints on policy?
19. What is your experience in working with people from other disciplines? What did you bring to the discussion?
20. Tell me about a time when you had responsibility for a complex project. How did you ensure that it was completed?
21. How do you approach negotiation? What are some examples?
22. As the new CEO of an agency, what steps would you take to assess its strengths, weaknesses, and opportunities?
23. What kinds of financial information do you need to make decisions?
24. How would you handle the press if a negative situation developed in the agency and became public knowledge?
25. How would you develop and maintain the commitment and motivation of the staff [or board]?
26. What criteria should the board use in evaluating your performance?
27. What are the primary issues facing this type of agency?
28. How would you approach the process of making key contacts in this community?
29. What is your experience with writing fact sheets, option papers, and sound bites?
30. What is your experience with legislative advocacy?
31. What is your experience with policy advocacy?
32. Who is in your congressional delegation? Who are your state representatives?

If you do not have frontline experience, how will you be an effective [program manager or policy analyst, for example]?

34. How does your particular policy interest fit into the big picture?
35. What experience do you have in analyzing the opposition's viewpoint?
36. Describe how you resolved a major problem.
37. What would your priorities be in the first three months of this position?
38. Based on what you know about our organization, what ideas do you have for future developments of the program?
39. How would you describe your supervisory style?
40. If you have a staff member who isn't following through on something he or she had promised to do or change, what would you do?
41. How would you resolve a problem between a clinician and a case manager who disagreed on the handling of a case?
42. How do you build a team under you?
43. Tell me how your approach to managing an organization has changed from the way it was 10 years ago.

Teaching and Research Questions

1. What are your teaching interests?
2. What are your research interests?
3. Tell us about your research experience.
4. Tell us about [a particular] project. What was your role? How was it accomplished? What were the results?
5. What are you looking for in a work environment?
6. What texts would you use to teach a course on [a particular subject]?
7. What can you teach?
8. How would you go about teaching [a particular subject]?
9. Why are you interested in our school?
10. Do you like to work collaboratively, or independently?
11. What is your dissertation topic?
12. How did you collect your data?
13. Why did you choose this topic for your dissertation?
14. What are the implications for [policy or practice, for example] in reference to a research project?
15. How would you describe yourself as a teacher?
16. Do you know how our curriculum differs from other programs?

Sample Information to Collect Regarding a Position

Note that not all of these questions are ones you would actually ask in an interview.

1. What are the responsibilities and scope of the position? Why is the position open?

2. Where does this position fit in the organizational structure? Is it in a social work department?

3. What is the organization's philosophy? For example, in a children's facility, is the focus on developing empathy in children, or on behavior modification?

4. What structures support the philosophy? If you are told that the staff work as a team, ask how often they meet. You can also ask, "How does that work [or work out]?" Look for inconsistencies.

5. How does the agency encourage excellence in staff? How is staff morale?

6. How do staff describe the work environment?

7. Is the organization a single entity or part of a local, regional, or national system? If the agency is part of a parent company or umbrella organization, what is that relationship? If it is part of a larger organization, how easily do people transfer to other positions in the system?

8. Take a tour. How well is the building maintained?

9. What are the characteristics of the population, and how severe are their problems?

10. What is the organization's approach to working with clients who threaten staff?

11. What is the typical caseload? When a worker is swamped, can another worker be asked to open a case?

12. Are staff on-call, and how is that handled?

13. Who is on the board, and what are their strengths?

14. What is the relationship of the board to the staff?

15. What are the goals of the board? Where do they want to take the agency? Does the agency have a strategic plan?

16. What are the agency's funding sources, and how successful has the agency been in securing new sources? What is the budget and how does it compare to similar organizations?

17. How stable is the staff? Or, what is the turnover rate?

18. What are the strengths and weaknesses of the agency?

19. What are the critical issues facing this organization?

20. If this agency uses public funds, what are its relationships with public agencies?

21. Who are the key people in the organization that ensure its success or make it work?

22. What accounting procedures are in place? Is there a financial plan?

23. What is this agency's reputation among the public, its peers, its funders, its clients?

24. Is the organization contracting, expanding, rebuilding, or stabilizing?

25. What is the organizational structure? Is it centralized or decentralized? How long has this structure been in place?

Appendix 8

Job Information: Online Sources, Publications, and Referral Services

Online Job Information and Career Services

Online information is expanding daily. You can use an Internet browser such as Netscape to explore some of the sites listed here, but your own exploration and information gleaned from discussion groups will be your best approaches to the Internet.

There are a wide variety of career services available online, including

- job listings
- résumé databases
- career and job-hunting information
- organization information
- discussion groups.

Social Work and Other Career Services

The Web sites listed below are good jumping-off points if you are looking for job announcements and researching organizations or if you just want to learn more about using the Internet for career purposes. Many of these sites have links to other Web sites listing jobs and to home pages of specific organizations.

Association for Advanced Training in the Behavioral Sciences
http://206.215.148.4/socialwork
Provides information on independent study programs for the social work licensing exams.

InterAction (American Council for Voluntary International Action)
http://www.interaction.org/
This site has information about the work of this coalition of nonprofit organizations, which focuses on international efforts such as relief and social development.

Internet Nonprofit Center's Nonprofit Locator
http://www.nonprofits.org/library/gov/irs/search_irs.shtml
There is a searchable database on nonprofit organizations at this site.

The Internet Online Career Center
http://www.occ.com/occ
You can search all jobs by key words or search jobs alphabetically. You can also look through lists of Online Career Center members, by industry, state, or city; you may also find display ads and agency or search firms.

JobTrak
http://www.jobtrak.com
In addition to posting your résumé, this page lists job-search tips and access to jobs if your college is a member.

JobWeb
http://www.jobweb.org
This site has a searchable job and employer directory, job-search and industry information, and career planning resources.

National Association of Social Workers (NASW)
http://www.naswdc.org
The home page of the NASW national office provides links to related Web sites, including state chapters.

The New Social Worker Online
http://www.socialworker.com
This is the home page of *The New Social Worker*, a professional development publication for social work students and recent graduates. It lists some jobs in addition to other resources.

Philanthropy Journal Online
http://www.philanthropy-journal.org/
This site has extensive links to Web pages of nonprofit organizations.

PRAXIS (Resources for Social and Economic Development)
http://caster.ssw.upenn.edu/~restes/praxis.html
This site has links to international organizations, employment opportunities, and other Web sites related to international social development.

The Riley Guide
http://www.dbm.com/jobguide/
Social workers who want to post their résumés on the Internet should follow the recommendations outlined at this site, which lists employment opportunities and job resources on the Internet; there is a category for social sciences.

Social Work Access Network (SWAN)

http://www.sc.edu/swan/

SWAN has links to many resources of interest to social work job hunters, including national organizations, global organizations, U.S. government departments, schools of social work, listservs, and newsgroups.

Social Work and Social Services Jobs Online (SWSSJO)

http://www.gwbssw.wustl.edu

SWSSJO is a social work–specific career resource. It includes a jobs database, links to other job databases, and links to career resources, including cost-of-living and online résumé information.

Social Work Examination Services Web Site

http://www.tiac.net/users/swes/

The site offers information on licensing review and study guide publications.

State Social Work Boards

http://www.tiac.net/users/swes/boards.htm

Browse course descriptions, view sample questions, peruse a list of review lectures, request fee information, or order a home-study course. This site also includes the addresses and telephone numbers of state licensing boards.

What Color Is Your Parachute: The Net Guide

http://www.washingtonpost.com/wp-adv/classifieds/careerpost/parachute/parafram2.htm

This guide outlines uses of the Internet for job hunting and provides links to related sites.

Organization Home Pages

Many large nonprofit organizations, government entities, associations, and corporations have their own Web sites—for example, American Red Cross, United Nations, American Society on Aging, and various departments of the U.S. government. You will find links to these home pages at several of the Web sites listed above. You can also use search engines to search for specific organizations.

Social Work–Related Listservs

Listservs, which are online discussion groups, are a good way to stay current on trends and to find some job announcements. You can go to the following location online for a directory:

http://www.sc.edu/swan/listserv.html

Social Work–Related Web Sites on Social Issues

If you are searching for information on a social issue or field of practice, you will find extensive links to Web sites at the following locations:
http://www.sc.edu/swan/
http://www.gwbssw.wustl.edu
http://caster.ssw.upenn.edu/~restes/praxis.html

Online Résumé Databases

Résumé databases enable employers to search a candidate pool using specific criteria such as geographic target, skills, and job titles. Some databases are free—that is, candidates may submit résumés without charge. Look carefully at these services, especially if you are considering a service that does charge a fee. Find out which employers use the service and whether, given the search options, potential employers can find you. For example, one service allows searches using single-word titles, which means that an employer would not be able to search for "social worker."

Social Work Job Hotlines

NASW JobLink, 303-221-4970, provides toll-free, 24-hour access to a comprehensive selection of social work job opportunities available nationwide. Job listings can be searched according to geographic preference. Job seekers can express interest in a job listing immediately by recording a confidential minirésumé, which is transmitted to the prospective employer the next day. Contact NASW (Attention: NASW JobLink), 750 First Street, NE, Suite 700, Washington, DC 20002-4241; 202-408-8600 (TTD 202-336-8396), fax: 202-336-8310.

   Social Work DirecTree, 573-884-TREE [8733], provides 24-hour telephone access to a network of social work job opportunities nationwide. Job listings are sorted by state and job type and are never more than two weeks old. Contact Social Work DirecTree at 706 Clark Hall, Columbia, MO 65211-1000; 573-882-8697, fax: 573-882-8926; e-mail: swtree@showme.missouri.edu; Internet: http://www.missouri.edu/~swtree.

Publications That List Jobs

The publications described below routinely list various positions of interest to social workers. Some of these publications are available in public or university libraries. See also appendix 1 on associations, some of which publish job listings in their newsletters.

   The Chronicle of Higher Education, a weekly publication, lists positions in teaching, student services, fund-raising, and research in colleges and in some nonprofit organizations, such as foundations and research centers. About 100 jobs (most of them teaching positions) are listed in each issue. Job titles for positions also include admissions counselor, alumni relations representative, counselor, career services coordinator, child welfare academic coordinator, coordinator for students with disabilities, director of leadership education, director of a black cultural center, and executive director. The *Chronicle* also prints position-wanted ads. For further information, write to P.O. Box 1955, Marion, OH 43305-1955; fax: 202-296-2691; Internet: http://chronicle.merit.edu.

Each issue of the *Chronicle of Philanthropy*, which is published twice a month, lists about 100 fund-raising and development jobs for health, university, religious, and other nonprofit institutions. Job titles include assistant development director, consultant for capital campaign, corporate gifts director, development writer, director of alumni affairs, director of annual giving, director of grant resources, endowment director, executive director of an agency, project manager, senior development researcher, staff associate for corporate relations, and telemarketing account executive. *Chronicle of Philanthropy* also prints position-wanted ads. For further information, write P.O. Box 1989, Marion, OH 43305-1989; fax: 202-296-2691.

Community Jobs, published twice a month, lists administrative, executive, fund-raising, organizing, marketing, and some direct-service positions nationwide; about 80–100 jobs are advertised in each issue. Sample job titles include community organizer, development director, family program coordinator, human resources director, program associate, staff director, and supervising counselor. Position-wanted ads can also be posted. The organization that publishes *Community Jobs* also publishes *Community Jobs/D.C.* (about 10–15 jobs listed in each issue), and *Community Jobs/N.Y.-N.J.* (17–25 professional-level jobs listed each issue). For further information, contact ACCESS, 1001 Connecticut Avenue, NW, Suite 838, Washington, DC 20036; 202-785-4233, fax: 202-785-4212.

Current Jobs for Graduates offers six job lists. Those that seem most applicable to social work are Current Jobs International and Current Jobs in Management and Business, which include government jobs and management positions in nonprofit organizations. Positions are primarily for new graduates. For further information write to P.O. Box 40550, Washington, DC 20016; 703-506-4400.

Human Services & Liberal Arts Careers, a weekly publication, lists 330–350 positions nationwide in each issue. Among the job titles advertised are eligibility coordinator, HIV case manager, mental health counselor, social work therapist, and substance abuse counselor; some internships are listed as well. For further information, contact KB Enterprises/NHSE, 1317 Penndale Lane, Fairfax, VA 22033; 703-378-0439.

International Career Employment Opportunities, published twice a month, lists about 500 openings in the United States and abroad. Job titles include analysis manager, associate program officer, development coordinator, field office director, program consultant and coordinator, project assistant, regional director for a foundation, and senior program officer. Many of these openings, but not all, are for senior-level candidates. For further information, contact International Employment Opportunities, Route 2, Box 305, Stanardsville, VA 22973; 804-985-6444, fax: 804-985-6828.

Jobs Bulletin, a publication of the California chapter of NASW, lists 50–60 openings in each issue for direct practice and administrative positions in California. Job titles for these positions include case manager, child and family therapist, director, executive director, program director, and senior psychiatric social worker. For further information, write Jobs Bulletin, NASW California Chapter, 1016 23rd Street, Sacramento, CA 95816; 916-442-4565; Internet: http://naswca.org/main.html.

The Management Opportunities Bulletin, a monthly publication, lists primarily executive- and administrative-level positions nationwide, about 12–15 each issue. Sample job titles include administrator, area director, chief financial officer, executive director, and president/CEO. These positions are listed also in the *Personnel Information and Referral Bulletin* (see below). Contact Management Employment Representative, Family Service America, Inc., 11700 West Lake Park Drive, Milwaukee, WI 53224; 1-800-221-3726, fax: 414-359-1074.

NASW News lists 45–60 social work positions nationwide in each monthly issue. It also publishes private practice opportunities and position-wanted ads. Among job titles are assistant professor, clinical social worker, director of research, executive director, mental health clinician, public health social worker, social work supervisor, therapist, and utilization review or case manager. For further information, write to NASW, 750 First Street, NE, Suite 700, Washington, DC 20002-4241. Members may call 1-800-742-4089; nonmembers should call 202-336-8377.

Opportunities in Public Affairs lists mostly public affairs and public relations positions (about 100 every two weeks) in the Washington, DC, area and in other parts of the country. Positions include Capitol Hill, government affairs, legislative, and public policy jobs and internships. Among job titles for the positions are legislative assistant, policy analyst, program assistant, program director, project assistant, and research associate. Contact Brubach Publishing Company, Opportunities in Public Affairs, P.O. Box 15629, Chevy Chase, MD 20825; 301-986-5545, fax: 301-986-0658.

Opportunity Nocs, published in Atlanta, Dallas, Los Angeles, Philadelphia, and San Francisco, lists a few direct-practice jobs, but mostly administrative, fund-raising, and program positions; about 40–50 jobs are listed biweekly or monthly, except in San Francisco, which lists about 100 weekly. Job titles include administrator, advocate, clinical coordinator, community outreach coordinator, community planner, development director, grant writer, and program coordinator. For further information, contact The Management Center, 870 Market Street, Suite 800, San Francisco, CA 94102-2903; 1-800-344-6627, fax: 415-362-4603.

Personnel Information and Referral Bulletin lists in each monthly issue about 13–15 executive, chaplaincy, and counseling positions in Lutheran agencies nationwide. The bulletin also reprints jobs advertised in the newsletter of Family Service America. Job titles include chaplaincy director, counselor, director of development, director of pastoral care, executive director, and nursing home administrator. Position-wanted ad space is available at $5.00 for three successive issues. Contact the Evangelical Lutheran Church in America, 8765 West Higgins Road, Chicago, IL 60631; 312-380-2689, fax: 312-380-2702.

Social Service Jobs lists in each issue more than 150 direct practice, supervisory, program management, and executive positions nationwide (more than half of the openings are located in eastern states, however). Among the job titles listed are case manager, executive director, program director, social worker, social work supervisor, and therapist. For further information, contact *Social Services Jobs*, 10 Angelica Drive, Framingham, MA 01701.

Social Service Employment Bulletin advertises a range of positions in social services nationwide. The bulletin is published twice a month. You can get further information about *Social Services Employment Bulletin* by contacting P.O. Box 50303, Provo, UT 84605, or calling 801-423-2546.

Y National Vacancy List advertises positions available nationwide with YMCAs; 60–70 jobs are listed in each monthly issue. Job titles for the positions include branch program manager, child care director, executive director, program executive, resident camp director, and senior program director. For further information, write YMCA of the USA (Attention: National Vacancy List), 101 North Wacker Drive, Chicago, IL 60606; 312-977-0031.

Referral and Information Services

A few organizations offer résumé referral or information services to candidates and employers. These services are not online. Details about these associations are in appendix 1.

- Association of Jewish Family and Children's Agencies
- Council of Jewish Federations
- Evangelical Lutheran Church of America
- Family Service America
- Jewish Community Centers Association
- National Association of Child Advocates.

Special Opportunities: Fellowships, Internships, Training, and Loan Forgiveness Programs

Postgraduate and predegree training opportunities are described in this appendix. These programs are very competitive, and many of them serve as springboards for exciting careers. Before applying for these programs, ask for names of current program participants and consult with them on the quality of the experience and strategies for making a successful application. Always address the interest of the program in every aspect of your application, and ask several people with knowledge of the subject to critique your essays. Many programs pay a salary or stipend, but some charge participants.

Postgraduate-Degree Opportunities: Administrative and Policy

AFL-CIO Organizing Institute

815 16th Street, NW
Suite 216
Washington, DC 20006
202-408-0700
fax: 202-408-0706

A three-step program in which participants are recruited, trained, and then placed in union-organizing positions across the country. The first step is a three-day training program. If completed successfully, the trainee moves on to an internship/apprentice program for organizers. In the final step, trainees are placed in a union-organizing job with an affiliated union. The AFL-CIO is committed to the rights of workers and to their collective voice.

Requirements: Each stage has a set of selective criteria that vary; the three-day training program looks for applicants with strong social justice values and aspirations.

Where: Washington, DC

When: Starting dates vary, as does duration of the program.

Stipend: Individuals who complete the training program become salaried employees.

Deadline: None—open enrollment

Congressional Research Service Internship

Congressional Research Service (CRS)
Administration Office, LM-208
Library of Congress
Washington, DC 20540-7110
202-707-7641

A volunteer position aimed at providing research, analysis, and reference experience and skills. CRS is a department of the Library of Congress, which supplies information services exclusively to members of Congress and their staffs.

Requirements: Good research and writing skills; open to graduates, undergraduates, postgraduates, and professionals

Where: Washington, DC

When: Three months to a year

Stipend: None

Deadline: None—submit applications 4–8 weeks in advance of proposed starting date.

Coro Fellows Program in Public Affairs

Coro Eastern Center
One Whitehall Street, 10th Floor
New York, NY 10004
212-248-2935

Coro Midwestern Center
1730 South 11th Street, Suite 102
St. Louis, MO 63104
314-621-3040

Coro Northern California
690 Market Street, Suite 1100
San Francisco, CA 94104
415-986-0521

Coro Southern California
811 Wilshire Boulevard, Suite 1025
Los Angeles, CA 90017-2624
213-623-1234
E-mail (for all centers): coro@inlink.com
Internet: http://www.coro.org

This professional program focuses on the structure and functions of government agencies, political campaigns, community-based organizations, labor unions, and businesses. The program is an intensive array of field assignments, projects, and seminars, with the aim of understanding how people function and organize themselves to meet social, political, economic, and religious needs in society.

Requirements: Must be a bright, self-motivated risk taker with a commitment to public service

Where: New York, St. Louis, San Francisco, and Los Angeles

When: September–May

Stipend: Tuition to participate: $3,500; up to $6,000 available, based on need

Deadline: February

County of Los Angeles Management Trainee Program

Chief Administrative Office
713 Kenneth Hahn Hall of Administration
500 West Temple Street
Los Angeles, CA 90012
213-893-0355

A two-year management trainee program for careers in local government. Program includes extensive orientation, a mentoring program, and work experience in county departments such as human services, budget offices, and regional services. After completing the program, participants are placed in administrative or managerial positions in Los Angeles County.

Requirement: BA or MA, preferably in public or business administration or a related field, and demonstrated managerial potential

Where: Los Angeles

When: July–June

Stipend: Salary ranges from $27,000 to $33,000, plus health coverage, pension, and vacation

Deadline: March

Fellowship in Public Policy

Congressional Hispanic Caucus Institute
504 C Street, NE
Washington, DC 20002
1-800-392-3532

A fellowship program for people of Hispanic origin to study and participate in public policy at a national level. Fellows are encouraged to spend half their time in congressional committees and subcommittees.

Requirements: Recent college degree (granted within the past year). Hispanic origin. See application for additional requirements.

Where: Washington, DC

When: August–May

Stipend: Approximately $1,200 a month, plus health coverage and transportation to and from Washington, DC

Deadline: April

Ford Foundation Program Assistant Position

The Ford Foundation
320 East 43rd Street
New York, NY 10017
212-573-5000
Internet: http://www.fordfound.org

Program assistants handle research and special projects, draft grant recommendations, and monitor field developments in one of nine programs: urban poverty, rural poverty, rights and social justice, media, reproductive health and population, governance and public policy, education and culture, international affairs, and program-related investments.

Requirements: Recent master's or law degree (granted within the past two years), excellent writing and research skills, demonstrated interest in a program area. See application for details on eligibility.

Where: New York City, with possible travel opportunities

When: September–August

Stipend: Salary plus benefits

Deadline: Fall; see application for current deadline

Governor's Policy Fellows Program

Maryland Higher Education Commission
16 Francis Street
Annapolis, MD 21401
410-974-2971

This fellowship program offers an opportunity to work with policy-making officials in the executive branch of Maryland state government. The program is tailored to fellow's needs and professional aspirations.

Requirements: Recent graduate from a master's or doctoral program in policy or administration

Where: Location varies

When: Two-year commitment

Stipend: Salaried position does not include health insurance or other benefits

Deadline: February

James H. Dunn, Jr., Memorial Fellowship Program

Director
2 ¹/₂ State House
Springfield, IL 62706
217-782-4921

This fellowship focuses on state government, including the budget, legislative, and scheduling offices. The goal of the program is to give practical experience in state government for fellows with aspirations toward policy-making positions.

Requirements: Bachelor's degree and demonstrated commitment to excellence in community or public service areas

Where: Chicago and Springfield, Illinois

When: August–July

Stipend: $22,248 plus benefits

Deadline: February

Jesse Marvin Unruh Assembly Fellowship Program

Legislative Office Building
California State University
Center for California Studies
6000 J Street
Sacramento, CA 95819-6081
916-324-1761

This fellowship program offers work experience in the California legislature. The fellowship strives to give practical knowledge and experience concerning legislative procedures. Program includes work in both houses, as well as seminars with an academic adviser. *Note:* The Assembly Fellowship is one of several programs offered by the center.

Requirements: BA or BS, no preferred major. People with advanced degrees and those in mid-career are encouraged to apply.

Where: Sacramento, California

When: October–August

Stipend: $1,707 per month

Deadline: February

The Millender Fellowship

Associate Vice President for Academic Programs
Wayne State University
4116 Faculty-Administration Building
Detroit, MI 48202
313-577-2424

This fellowship is designed to assist minorities in achieving public service careers. Fellows are assigned to high-level responsibilities with executives of public, private, and nonprofit organizations in the Detroit area.

Requirements: Most applicants are completing a master's program or have equivalent experience

Where: Detroit

When: August–May

Stipend: $20,000, plus benefits

Deadline: March

Presidential Management Intern (PMI) Program

U.S. Office of Personnel Management
Philadelphia Service Center
William J. Green, Jr., Federal Building
600 Arch Street
Philadelphia, PA 19106

A management training program aimed at attracting high-caliber graduates to the federal government. The program focuses on analysis and management of public policy.

Requirements: Master's or doctoral degree. Must be nominated by your academic program in your final year

Where: Washington, DC

When: Two years, usually beginning between June and September

Stipend: Regular GS-9 level employee (high $20,000s)

Deadline: Academic departments select nominees in the early fall. Finalists are announced in the spring.

Ralph I. Goldman Fellowship in International Jewish Communal Service

American Jewish Joint Distribution Committee (AJJDC)
711 Third Avenue
New York, NY 10017
212-687-6200

A fellowship program that focuses on international Jewish communal affairs and international social welfare. The program provides one year of work-study in a field office of the AJJDC.

Requirements: Master's degree

Where: Main office in New York, but field offices vary; includes international settings

When: September–August

Stipend: Salaried position (mid-$20,000s)

Deadline: November

Social Work Congressional Fellows Program

Council on Social Work Education (CSWE)
1600 Duke Street, Suite 300
Alexandria, VA 22314-3421
703-683-8080

Fellows serve as legislative assistants on the staff of members of Congress
or a congressional committee. Program is intended to increase effectiveness of social work knowledge and values in government.

Requirements: Must be a member of CSWE or NASW; accredited degree
in social work; two years of post–social work degree experience

Where: Washington, DC

When: 11 months, beginning in August

Stipend: $31,000, subject to annual review

Deadline: November

United Way of America Internship Program

Human Resources
United Way
701 North Fairfax Street
Alexandria, VA 22314-2045
703-836-7100
fax: 703-683-7811

Internship program designed to give experience in various United Way
of America departments. Program can be used for credit.

Requirements: Current student or recent graduate

Where: Alexandria, VA

When: January, June, or September (one semester)

Stipend: Salary and benefits, plus travel expenses ($1,000–$2,000)

Deadline: Not specific

The White House Fellowship

President's Commission on White House Fellowships
712 Jackson Place, NW
Washington, DC 20503
202-395-4522

Very competitive program that offers a first-hand look at the process of
governing the nation. Fellows work in the Executive Office of the President or a related office. Opportunities include working with the vice president, traveling to meet foreign dignitaries, and taking part in other official meetings.

Requirements: Must be a U.S. citizen and cannot be a federal employee

Where: Washington, DC

When: September–August

Stipend: Paid on appropriate educational level, not to exceed $63,000

Deadline: December

Postgraduate-Degree Opportunities: Clinical

Advanced Clinical Social Work Fellowship

Cedars-Sinai Medical Center Fellowship
Thalians Mental Health Center
8730 Alden Drive, E-33
Los Angeles, CA 90048-3811
310-855-3567

Program offers 1,600 hours of supervised clinical experience plus seminars and conferences. Wide range of clients and social problems are addressed with dynamic therapeutic approaches to individual and family evaluation and treatment.

Requirement: MSW

Where: Los Angeles

When: One year, July–June

Stipend: None at this time

Deadline: Check with the program

Clinical Post-Master's Social Work Fellowship

Children's Hospital Medical Center
Division of Adolescent Medicine
3333 Burnet Avenue
Cincinnati, OH 45229-3039
513-559-4681

Fellowship provides interdisciplinary training in adolescent health care for social work, medicine, psychology, nursing, and nutrition. Direct services, community consultation, developmental disabilities program, and continuing education and development are all components of the program.

Requirements: MSW and clinical experience with adolescents

Where: Cincinnati

When: July–June

Stipend: A liberal stipend, plus benefits

Deadline: March

Minority Post-MSW Fellowship and Post-MSW Fellowship

Yale Child Study Center Fellowship
Director of Outpatient Services
Yale Child Study Center
P.O. Box 207900
New Haven, CT 06520
203-785-6252

The program includes theory and practice in assessment and treatment of children and families, seminars and teaching conferences, intensive supervision, opportunity for exploration in special interests such as research. These are NIMH-funded fellowships.

Requirement: MSW

Where: New Haven, Connecticut

When: July–June

Stipend: Available

Deadline: March

Post Graduate Clinical Social Work Fellowship

University of New Mexico
Children's Psychiatric Hospital
1001 Yale Boulevard, NE
Albuquerque, NM 87131
505-272-2977

Fellowship is designed to enhance the clinical skills in working with children, adolescents, and families.

Requirement: MSW (with preference given to applicants with postgraduate experience in child development and family therapy)

Where: Albuquerque, New Mexico

When: July–June

Stipend: $15,000 a year

Deadline: February

Post-Master's Program in Clinical Social Work

The Menninger Clinic
P.O. Box 829
Topeka, KS 66601-0829
913-350-5836

Fellows have primary placements in one of four programs. Fellowship provides supervision and training in family and individual therapy. Conferences, team meetings, and education programs are included. Ten hours of coursework each trimester and a publication-worthy paper by May are required.

Requirement: MSW

Where: Topeka, Kansas

When: September–August

Stipend: $16,000 a year

Deadline: February

Post-Masters Social Work Internship

University of California, Berkeley
Counseling and Psychological Services
University Health Services, Tang Center
2222 Bancroft Way
Berkeley, CA 94720
510-642-9494

Internship offers comprehensive training in mental health services to a diverse student body. The intern participates in crisis intervention, assessment and referral, brief psychotherapy, group counseling, outreach, and consultation.

Requirements: Master's degree in social work from an accredited program which included coursework in personality development, psychopathology, and theories and techniques of psychotherapy, plus two years of supervised clinical experience

Where: Berkeley, CA

When: August–August

Stipend: $15,000, plus medical insurance

Deadline: April

Social Work Fellowship

Department of Psychiatry
Kaiser Permanente Medical Center
280 West MacArthur Boulevard
Oakland, CA 94611
510-596-6704

Fellowship offers supervision and training in child, adolescent, and adult outpatient services, alcohol and drug abuse treatment, family and group therapy, crisis intervention, and short-term therapy.

Requirements: MSW and clinical experience

Where: Oakland, California

When: September–August

Stipend: Hourly, plus health benefits

Deadline: March

Training Program for Clinical Social Workers

Reiss-Davis Child Study Center
3200 Motor Avenue
Los Angeles, CA 90034

Fellowship program combines psychodynamic and developmental theory with opportunities to work with children and parents performing long- and short-term therapy.

Requirement: MSW

Where: Los Angeles

When: Two-year commitment

Stipend: $4,200 first year, $4,800 second year

Deadline: March

Student Opportunities

Congressional Fellowships on Women and Public Policy

Women's Research and Education Institute
1700 18th Street, NW, Suite 400
Washington, DC 20009
202-328-7070

The fellowship is aimed at giving practical policy-making experience and college credit. The program is designed to encourage more effective participation by women in public policy-making and to increase understanding of how policies affect women and men differently.

Requirements: Current enrollment in a graduate program and proven commitment to equality for women

Where: Washington, DC

When: September–May

Stipend: Paid tuition and living expenses

Deadline: February

Doctoral Fellowships in Social Work for Ethnic Minority Students

Council on Social Work Education
1600 Duke Street, Suite 300
Alexandria, VA 22314-3421
703-683-8080

There are two fellowships available for students interested in doctoral programs. The MFP clinical fellowship is for MSWs preparing for leadership roles in mental health or substance abuse. The MRFP (research) fellowship is for MSWs interested in a research career related to mental health and mental illness.

Requirements: MSW, U.S. citizenship or permanent residency status, full-time doctoral student

Where: Doctoral programs with faculty involved in funded mental health research

When: Awards are renewable

Stipend: Monthly, for limited period; some tuition support is possible

Deadline: February

The Everett Public Service Internship Program

These summer internships for undergraduate and graduate students are offered by several organizations, including the Advocacy Institute, Asian Americans for Equality, Center on Budget and Policy Priorities, and Child Welfare League of America. For a brochure on all participating organizations and contacts, write to

The Everett Public Service Internship Program
Public Allies
1511 K Street, NW, Suite 330
Washington, DC 20005

Internships in Congress

The Washington Center
1101 14th Street, NW, Suite 500
Washington, DC 20005-5601
202-336-7600

Intended to help interns acquire Capitol Hill experience, develop contacts, and expand knowledge on public issues and the legislative process. Interns will attend hearings, write press releases, maintain constituency relations, research issues, and draft legislative histories.

Requirements: Current enrollment in an undergraduate or graduate program; U.S. citizenship

Where: Washington, DC

When: One semester, with starting dates year round

Stipend: None, although $2,000 scholarships are available, based on need and merit

Deadline: None—open enrollment

Junior Commissioned Officer Student Training & Extern Program (JRCOSTEP)

Public Health Service Recruitment
Division of Commission Personnel
ODB, Room 4a-07, Parklawn Building
5600 Fishers Lane
Rockville, MD 20857
1-800-279-1605

The U.S. Public Health Service offers this program to students of medicine, nursing, pharmacy, and other health professions.

Requirements: Current enrollment in a master's or doctoral program

Where: Appointments all over the country

When: One- to four-month appointments, year-round positions

Stipend: Available, plus benefits and travel expenses

Deadline: None—apply three months before anticipated starting date

Minority Leaders Fellowship Program

The Washington Center
1101 14th Street, NW, Suite 500
Washington, DC 20005-5601
202-336-7600

Intended to help interns acquire Capitol Hill experience, develop contacts, and expand knowledge on public issues and the legislative process. Interns will attend hearings, write press releases, maintain constituency relations, research issues, and draft legislative histories.

Requirements: Current enrollment in an undergraduate or graduate program; U.S. citizenship; must be person of Asian American, African American, Pacific Islander, or Native American descent

Where: Washington, DC

When: One semester, with starting dates year round

Stipend: Available

Deadline: None—open enrollment

New York State Senate Fellowships

Senate Student Programs Office
New York State Senate, Room 401
90 South Swan Street
Albany, NY 12247
518-455-2611
fax: 518-432-5470

Program places fellows in senator's offices in order to gain first-hand knowledge and experience in the area of their fellowship.

Requirements: U.S. citizen; New York State resident or enrolled in a college or university in New York; current enrollment in a master's or doctoral program

Where: Albany, New York

When: September–July

Stipend: $22,575 yearly salary, plus health insurance

Deadline: May

Washington Internship Program

National Academy of Social Insurance
1776 Massachusetts Avenue, NW, Suite 615
Washington, DC 20036
202-452-8097

Internship focuses on furthering knowledge and understanding of policy issues centered on social security and related programs and on health care financing. Internship includes working with leading experts in the field, seminars, discussion, and individual projects.

Requirements: Students studying economics, gerontology, journalism, health policy, and social work

Where: Washington, DC

When: January–May

Stipend: $2,000

Deadline: December

Loan Forgiveness and Repayment Programs

Action (VISTA)

Federal Office Building
911 Walnut, Room 1701
Kansas City, MO 64106-2009
816-426-5256

Requirements: The Perkins loan must have been taken out on or after July 1, 1987.

Benefits: For the first and second years of service, 15 percent per year of a volunteer's total loan obligation, including interest, will be canceled. For each of the third and fourth years of service, 20 percent of a volunteer's Perkins loan, including interest, will be canceled. For some Stafford loans, there is a loan deferment during service but no loan cancellation.

Head Start

Administration for Children, Youth, and Families
U.S. Department of Health and Human Services
Washington, DC 20201
816-426-3981

Loan forgiveness is made for both teaching and administrative positions.

Loan Cancellation for Federal Perkins Loan

Individuals working for early intervention services or services for high-risk children from low-income communities may be eligible. Only those who took out loans in 1992 or after are eligible. Check your university financial aid office and employer's personnel office for details.

National Health Service Corps Loan Repayment Program

2070 Chain Bridge Road, Suite 450
Vienna, VA 22182
1-800-221-9393

Licensed clinical social workers provide services for two years in areas with a shortage of health professionals, in exchange for loan repayment. The assignment can be extended beyond two years. Only a few positions are available nationwide.

Requirements: State licensure or certification in the state where you plan to serve; U.S. citizenship
Benefits: A competitive salary and benefit package is offered in addition to loan repayment.

Peace Corps

1990 K Street, NW, 9th Floor
Washington, DC 20526
202-606-3000

Requirement: Students must have received a loan disbursement on or after July 1, 1987.
Benefits: For the first and second years of service, 15 percent per year of a volunteer's total Perkins loan obligation, including interest, will be canceled. For each of the third and fourth years of service, 20 percent of a volunteer's Perkins loan, including interest, will be canceled. For some Stafford loans, there is a loan deferment during service, but no loan cancellation.

Teach For America

P.O. Box 5114
New York, NY 10185
1-800-TEA-1230

Teach For America places corps members in schools where they often are eligible to defer or cancel certain student loans.

Appendix 10

Sample Skills by Function

This appendix lists skills related to the following functions: direct practice, community development and community organizing, consulting, management, policy, research, supervision, and teaching. It also lists skills common to several functions and some general performance skills. Skills specific to presentations, writing, and information management are listed separately.

No list is exclusive. Use these lists to generate ideas about your skills. If you use one of the phrases listed here, be sure that you "own" that skill—think of at least one example that demonstrates that skill. Edit the items to fit your language and experience or the language of your field of practice. Each skill is described actively—that is, each phrase begins with a verb in the present tense. You will convert these to past-tense verbs for descriptions of previous experience. You may wish to change verbs to noun phrases—"analyze data" can become "data analysis." Some of these phrases would not be used in written communication but would serve you well in a face-to-face interview.

Cross-Cutting Functions

When stating a skill that cuts across functions, try to give it more meaning by attaching it to a specific knowledge area (for example, "conduct needs assessments for low-income housing, transportation, and employment for three communities").

- advise clients, patients, families on accessing services
- advocate for particular groups, consumers, clients, patients
- analyze class differences regarding service access and policies
- articulate connections across disciplines
- assess and respond to ethical issues
- build consensus
- conduct assets and needs assessments
- demonstrate a high tolerance for frustration
- demonstrate a sense of professional mission
- demonstrate realistic expectations of self and others
- educate and collaborate with people from other disciplines
- evaluate practice

- facilitate groups: clients or consumers, families, staff, task forces, collaborations
- follow protocols
- function as part of a multidisciplinary team
- guide and monitor volunteers
- identify and resolve ethical issues
- identify group dynamics
- incorporate knowledge of theory with research and practice experience
- maintain confidentiality in oral and written communications
- manage crises
- navigate a bureaucracy
- network with local, regional, national organizations
- think from a generalist perspective, think clearly about problems
- tie immediate work, problems, solutions to a long-term vision
- use comprehensive systems thinking

Direct Practice

- analyze social support networks
- assess for substance abuse, nutrition status, support systems, physical functioning, financial situation, safety, and so on
- assist clients, consumers, and families with developing coping skills
- assist clients in processing information and issues
- build effective client relationships
- collaborate with a treatment team
- complete detailed assessments of clients
- conduct intake interviews
- conduct psychosocial assessments, social histories
- construct genograms and family maps
- contract with clients or consumers
- deal with angry, violent, or suicidal clients
- deal with client resistance
- design treatment to achieve short-term outcomes in a cost-conscious context
- determine client eligibility
- develop and implement intervention plans, treatment plans, care plans, discharge plans
- educate clients, consumers, and patients about health risks, pre-retirement planning, chemical dependency issues, medical compliance, compensation for sensory deficits, and so on
- educate, train family members, care providers, staff
- empower clients, consumers
- evaluate practice
- follow up treatment
- identify, evaluate, compile list of, develop links with, refer to community resources
- identify and intervene with clients who are at risk

- identify outcomes measures
- interview clients, consumers, patients, families
- lead a treatment team
- manage family and client involvement
- manage permanency planning
- measure caregiver strain or stress
- monitor changing functional levels
- organize and run a support group, educational group
- provide case consultation
- provide case management
- provide culturally appropriate services
- recruit, select, train, prepare foster or adoptive parents, guardians, respite care providers
- set and collect fees
- shape the context with diagnostic expertise
- understand an individual in context
- use different treatment approaches: brief therapy, family therapy, play therapy, solution-focused therapy, and so on
- use DSM criteria
- use theory for diagnosis

Community Development and Community Organizing

- acquire and develop abandoned and vacant space
- acquire financing for a community project
- build consensus with community coalitions, grassroots groups, collaborations
- communicate with diverse neighborhood residents
- compile a community resource list
- connect residents with other resources in the community for starting businesses
- construct a community map
- coordinate and train volunteer groups to staff projects
- counsel homeowners and small business owners in the loan acquisition process
- demonstrate the effects of social development on the community and economy
- design a campaign strategy for social change
- develop community, neighborhood, social networks
- develop policies and plans that integrate social and economic development efforts
- educate community members on the intent of outside groups
- educate corporate staff and other groups on how their messages are received in the community
- engage community members in leadership training; identify local leaders

- establish a plan of incremental goals that can sustain a long-term collaborative effort
- evaluate assets of the community: individual, organizational, physical
- evaluate physical assets of a community: land, buildings, transportation
- evaluate target community's or population's strengths, interests, needs
- examine formal and informal service delivery systems
- facilitate a community-building effort
- facilitate the shaping of a vision for the community
- foster a commitment among organizations and individuals to improving the community
- function as a liaison with the business community and local institutions
- gain acceptance in the community
- identify and work with potential sources of capital and credit, investors
- identify barriers to starting businesses and making improvements in the community
- identify tactics: media events, public hearings, elections
- manage conflict among community groups
- manage varying interests of coalition, collaboration members
- provide technical assistance and training to neighborhoods, community groups
- staff a community organization, coalition, collaboration, neighborhood association
- start community development banks, microlevel loan funds, community development loan funds, community development credit unions
- work effectively within a local political system
- work with groups: chamber of commerce, small business owners, neighborhood associations, religious institutions, recreation programs

Consulting

- analyze client resources, strengths, problems, needs
- deliver products, reports, by deadline
- determine fees
- develop a network
- direct, troubleshoot implementation and evaluate solutions
- draft and negotiate contracts
- educate client staff on issues, terminology
- establish rapport with clients
- facilitate discussions with clients on problem clarification, solution options
- identify and package specific services to offer
- identify and research potential clients
- identify potential, future consulting needs of clients
- prepare a marketing plan
- research, develop, and recommend solutions
- train client staff to use new solutions

Management

- access and work with the media
- analyze an annual report
- analyze unit costs
- anticipate and deal with change
- assess risk, liability, legal issues
- change an organization's culture
- collaborate with board members in strategic planning, directing the organization
- communicate with outside groups: funders, governments, consumer groups, media
- conduct feasibility studies
- coordinate multicommittee events and projects
- create a vision for the organization
- create and facilitate interorganizational entities: partnerships, networks, collaborations
- design and evaluate services that meet varying funders' requirements
- design services, programs, and projects that produce measurable outcomes
- develop a board: select, train, direct
- develop a high profile in the community
- develop a network of contacts
- develop and monitor budgets
- develop and oversee a marketing plan
- develop policies and procedures
- develop quality assurance measures
- evaluate programs, projects, services, agency structures
- formulate and direct a fund-raising strategy: special events, capital campaigns, annual funds, volunteer programs, grant writing
- formulate and follow a project work plan
- formulate and implement public relations strategies
- identify tangible results that measure outcomes for objectives
- implement a system for collecting and reporting outcome measures
- interpret federal, state, and local policies and regulations
- make the difficult decisions regarding agency priorities
- manage a complex composition of funding sources and reporting requirements
- manage large volumes of information: organization statistics, outside data
- manage multiple departments, programs
- move a pilot project to a mainline service
- negotiate and secure contracts
- organize committees, groups, special events
- prepare cost–benefit analyses
- provide data and testimony for law and policymakers
- reconcile conflicting values among multidisciplinary teams, agency and funders, agency and regulators

- recruit, supervise, evaluate, promote, and terminate managers, supervisors, staff
- recruit, train, organize, and motivate volunteers
- represent the organization in public arenas
- secure financing
- secure funding to sustain projects
- set agendas, organize and run meetings
- stay current on policy and service delivery trends
- understand financial impacts on services
- weigh alternatives: service delivery, staffing, funding

Policy

- access and use governmental publications
- advocate for particular aspects of policies and regulations
- analyze and interpret statutes, regulations, policies, programs
- analyze community strengths, assets, resources, and needs
- analyze federal policy impacts at local and state levels and state policy impacts at the local level
- analyze policy in political and financial terms
- appreciate the complexity of the larger system
- approach policy with a win–win rather than all-or-nothing attitude
- articulate connections across disciplines
- articulate opposite viewpoints
- build consensus and coalitions, develop relationships
- convey a compelling picture of what might be done
- define the agenda
- develop legislative strategy
- formulate policy recommendations
- get beyond passion and process to make difficult decisions and complete tasks
- handle the frequent and extensive critiquing, editing, and rewriting of one's work
- identify common ground to advance the agenda
- lobby for or against legislation
- locate, explain, and apply relevant statistical data
- prepare action alerts and legislative fact sheets
- prepare and deliver testimony to legislative committees
- prepare proposals for technical amendments to a law
- present options and defend positions orally
- see connections across the big picture rather than focus on a single issue
- take a long-term view
- think agilely about public policy
- think from a generalist perspective, think well about a lot of problems
- tolerate frustrating political situations
- understand current public policy issues
- understand the language of other players, opponents

- use data accurately; understand pitfalls of extrapolating data from the local to national level
- work in political and bureaucratic environments
- write in a quick, concise, clear style

Research

- analyze an issue
- analyze data using quantitative and qualitative techniques
- assess and document intervention outcomes
- clarify, define problems, issues
- collect, clean, code, input, analyze, manage data
- conceptualize areas of knowledge
- conduct structured and unstructured interviews
- conduct surveys
- coordinate research and evaluation projects
- create graphic presentations of data
- critique, assess data, articles, reports
- design a research study
- design and conduct needs assessments, feasibility studies, program evaluation, clinical practice evaluation
- design, improve, critique questionnaires
- develop data profiles
- develop measures
- develop research proposals, write grants
- frame questions
- generate hypotheses
- interpret quantitative and qualitative empirical results
- locate, review, and summarize literature
- run general statistical packages: SAS, SPSS, Harvard Graphics; specific packages for structural equation modeling, network analysis, cluster analyses
- secure and analyze consumer feedback
- use descriptive, inferential, multivariate statistics
- work with institutional review boards to satisfy criteria for protection of human subjects

Supervision

- collect organization, services statistics
- consult with, inform management about progress; crisis situations; personnel issues; staff, client, community assets and needs
- critique oral assignments: case or project presentations, public speeches, in-service training
- differentiate tasks and supervision for professional, paraprofessional, student, and volunteer staff
- draft, make recommendations on content for job descriptions

- edit written assignments: documentation, reports, treatment plans, proposals, grants, assessments, articles
- evaluate staff work: interventions, treatment plans, documentation, projects, programs
- fine-tune services, procedures, and staff performance to meet outcome objectives
- handle staff development: identify training preferences and needs, provide training
- interpret organization objectives, policies, procedures, and outside trends and issues affecting the agency
- make decisions: crisis situations, ethical dilemmas, reduced or expanded resources, changing demands
- manage the conflicting needs of management, staff, and clients/consumers/communities
- match staff abilities with work assignments
- motivate and direct staff performance
- organize, delegate, and schedule work
- orient new employees
- review résumés and interview job candidates, make recommendations on hiring
- serve as liaison between staff and management
- set performance expectations
- suggest changes in services, policies, and procedures

Teaching

- analyze student learning difficulties and recommend action
- command knowledge of the subject area
- compare courses for overlap and continuity
- create assignments that develop critical thinking, practice, creative skills
- create electronic assignments
- create syllabi
- define parameters of a course
- design course lab components: videotaping, community projects
- design distance-learning courses
- evaluate learning, assign grades or credit
- evaluate teaching techniques and seek outside consultation on teaching style
- facilitate discussions, debates
- facilitate self-directed, independent learning
- identify appropriate theoretical and practice literature
- incorporate at-risk population and cultural diversity material in courses
- incorporate technology and presentation options in teaching
- manage disagreement, conflict
- orchestrate coteaching units
- provide constructive criticism
- select course readings, books, visiting speakers

- think conceptually about educational curriculum design
- update course content, format, readings, assignments
- write exams that measure levels of learning and evaluate knowledge and skill mastery

Presentations

- conduct informative, educational presentations: public forums, workshops, seminars
- conduct in-service training
- debate issues effectively
- defend an opinion, argument
- deliver an extemporaneous speech or presentation
- facilitate town meetings, focus groups, neighborhood meetings
- interview effectively: listening, reframing, reflecting, attending
- lobby in person, by telephone, and by mail
- make case presentations
- persuade different audiences on the same topic
- persuade diverse groups: neighborhood associations, small and large businesses, local and state governments, school systems, health care providers, funders, social services agencies
- present in front of a camera: videotaping, live coverage
- present testimony to legislative bodies
- provide court testimony
- respond to impromptu questions: points of information, controversial issues
- serve as liaison among agencies, organizations, and the community
- serve as point person handling questions about issues, projects
- serve as spokesperson with media and other audiences
- speak to large and small audiences
- use effective interpersonal communication: active listening, open-ended questions
- use multimedia technology for presentations: computer, audio, and visual
- use negotiation techniques
- use parliamentary procedure accurately
- "work" a room

Writing

- create education materials
- edit written material quickly, provide constructive criticism
- prepare briefings on issues, meetings, legislation, and so on, for an executive or leader
- prepare case plans with interdisciplinary teams
- prepare talking points on an issue for leaders, groups

- script an executive or leader to conduct a meeting or event (written and oral step-by-step preparation)
- summarize a large volume of information
- write affidavits, documentation, case notes, executive summaries, reports, mission statements, sound bites, treatment plans, minutes, legislation, regulations, press releases, brochures, newsletters, letters, journal articles, op-ed pieces, business plans, project reports, memos, direct-mail pieces, marketing plans, option papers, proposals
- write appropriate material for Internet, video, audio, CD-ROM, and multimedia projects
- write in particular styles: grants, academic, persuasive, promotional, journalistic (features and news), technical, legal, regulatory
- write in styles appropriate to a leader, a purpose of a project, culture of the organization or situation
- write quickly, concisely, clearly
- write technical material and reports using statistics and financial data

Information Management and Computer Technology

- access information on the Internet
- address issues of confidentiality and information management
- design and maintain home pages
- develop and maintain an office intranet
- develop management information systems
- link systems across organizations
- manage a listserv discussion group or newsgroup on social or clinical issues
- market services through the Internet
- produce computer-based presentations
- provide services through remote access links
- serve as a Web master
- train staff and managers to input and retrieve data
- use computer packages: word processing programs, databases, spreadsheets, desktop publishing
- use computer software to record, access, analyze, and report information
- use computers and telecommunications in case management, treatment, and reimbursement
- use decision support tools

Work Characteristics or General Performance Skills

You will often hear people use work characteristics to describe their skills—for example, organized, detail-oriented, assertive, on time, dependable, and thorough. Remember that your specific professional skills are much more vivid and powerful statements of your skills than are general work characteristics. Let your professional skills and examples of your experience speak for your work habits. The same can be said for general performance skills. If you need to use a phrase like one of those below, tie it to an example—"I have taken initiative on several projects, including the resident leadership training program and the intergenerational program, which I established."

- act calm and professional in strained situations and relationships
- anticipate and think ahead
- assert ideas, positions, needs
- identify, analyze, and solve problems
- pick up on cues, read the social context
- take initiative
- work effectively in a team environment
- work with individuals of varied cultural or ethnic and socioeconomic backgrounds
- work with unpredictable schedules

References

Bobo, K., Kendall, J., & Max, S. (1991). *Organizing for social change: A manual for activists in the 1990s.* Washington, DC: Seven Locks Press.

Council on Social Work Education. (1996). *Strategic action plan: Social work and managed care.* Alexandria, VA: Author.

Doelling, C., & Paulsrud, D. (1994). *Preparing for careers in child welfare at the national level: A report on meetings with leaders in Washington, DC.* Unpublished project collaboration report, George Warren Brown School of Social Work, St. Louis.

Kretzman, J., & McKnight, J. (1993). *Building communities from the inside out.* Chicago: ACTA Publications.

Midgley, J. (1995). *Social development: The developmental perspective in social welfare.* London: Sage Publications.

Perlmutter, F. (1990). *Changing hats: From social work practice to administration.* Washington, DC: NASW Press.

Selznik, P. (1957). *Leadership in administration.* Evanston, IL: Row.

Sxiridoff, M., & Ryan, W. (1996). *Prospects and strategies for community-centered family services.* Milwaukee: Family Service America.

Selecting Master's and Doctoral Programs

Planning for Graduate Study at the Master's Level

Identify Your Career Goals

Why do you want a master's degree?

- Must you have the master's degree to do the work you want to do?
- What other disciplines have you considered? Why do you want a master's degree in social work rather than one in policy, gerontology, management, law, or counseling?
- What specific knowledge and skills do you want to develop in a master's program?
- Are you ready for the self-discipline, self-direction, and time management that graduate school requires?

Identify Potential Programs

What is most important to you in selecting a program?

- academic and career advising: within the program or centralized at the institution
- calendar: summer programs
- characteristics of the student body
- cost and financial aid
- curriculum offerings: range of courses, concentrations, specializations, electives, skills training, generalist vs. specialist training
- distance learning
- employment: success of alumni, career services
- faculty: specialties, publications, research interests, teaching emphasis
- interdisciplinary training through electives or joint degree programs
- learning resources: library, computers, multimedia resources, Internet
- location: urban, rural, near family or friends, region, safety, transportation, housing, costs
- physical facilities: skill labs, classrooms, student center, athletic facilities, parking
- practica offerings: settings available, block or concurrent, self-selected, out-of-town or country

- quality of the host institution
- reputation: in the community, among other schools of social work
- special program aspects: training centers, research centers, community projects
- student–faculty ratio

Questions to Consider

Talk with faculty and doctoral students. Where else did they consider applying and why? How selective is the program? Get information about the following aspects of the program:

- Inquire about the average GPA and test scores for applicants at the school.
- Find out whether you need additional coursework or experience.
- Talk with current students and recent alumni. What do they like and dislike about the program? Do the alumni feel prepared for their work and any future directions they might take?
- How well have graduates done in the job market? Does the school collect employment data on new graduates? How long did it take new graduates to find jobs during the past two years? What types of positions, practice, settings, and salaries characterize the employment of last year's class?
- Can you see a profile of alumni? How many are in management, private practice, your interest area? What are the alumni of particular curriculum tracks doing five and 10 years later?
- What percentage of students receive scholarships? How are financial-aid awards determined? What percentage of the students work while going to school?
- What is the expected cost? Will you need to borrow money to attend this school? How much will you need to borrow, and what would be your monthly loan costs after you graduate?
- What choices do you have for practica? Ask to see a list.
- What tradeoffs will you have to make by selecting this program? For whom is this program not appropriate?

Planning Your Academic Experience

- Think of yourself first as a professional who works in the community and second as a student who is expanding her or his knowledge and skills.
- Set goals for what you want to accomplish and learn in courses and in field work. Do not rely on faculty and field instructors to plan your education. Explore the field well enough that you can design a plan for your education.
- Look carefully at the skills lists in appendix 10 and discuss them with social workers, faculty, and others in your field. What skills and knowledge could you demonstrate by the time you leave the program—a field placement, or set of courses? What field work and course projects

will you be able to show in the form of a portfolio?
• Determine what courses you may need for licensure or certifications.

Planning for Graduate Study at the Doctoral Level

This material is based on suggestions from chairs of doctoral programs, an associate dean of a graduate school, and recent PhD graduates.

Identify Your Career Goals
• What do you want to do? Do you want to do research, teach, or practice?
• Do you have enough experience to define the problem you want to address in your work?
• What type of teaching, research, or clinical practice do you want to do?
• What settings interest you: a university, research organization, policy think tank, agency, or private practice? Do you need a doctorate to do this work?
• Do you want to stay in the social work discipline? Do you want to explore other disciplines?
• For what career directions will the degree programs you are considering prepare you?
• Be realistic about your potential and your weaknesses.
• If you are considering a PhD as an additional credential for practice, explore this carefully. The payoff may not be there.
• Do you have the time in your life to devote to a doctoral program?
• Identify strong social work researchers in your interest area and investigate their schools.

Also keep in mind the following advice from faculty:

• If you want to teach practice courses, you will need two years of paid post-MSW experience before you complete your doctoral degree. This is an accreditation requirement of the Council on Social Work Education for schools with faculty teaching practice courses. Some schools of social work hire only faculty candidates who have this experience.
• Get your license. It is a plus and alleviates questions about your practice experience. Of course, you may benefit personally from having a license.
• You need to take debts from your previous education into consideration. How much debt would you incur if you chose to pursue a doctoral degree?

Interests in Research
• Do you consider the doctoral program to be an extension of the MSW program? Study at the doctoral level is qualitatively—not just quantitatively—

different from the MSW level. The types of thinking, tasks, expectations for learning, time required, dedication, and commitment are different.

- Are you interested in and do you have a facility for doing research? Do you have a fear of statistics? Are you comfortable with computers? Do you have an inquiring mind and an interest in theory? Can you translate theory into hypotheses? Do you find that type of thinking exciting?
- If spending a couple of hours browsing through a social work library is your idea of a good time, you will probably enjoy a doctoral program.

Selection of Programs

- Talk with chairs of programs about the fit between the program and your interests.
- For what purpose is the program designed—research, teaching, clinical work?
- How is the program designed? How many courses are required? Are there electives? Can you take courses outside your department? Is interdisciplinary training encouraged?
- Is the conceptual training of the students as strong as the methodological training in research? Do students learn the conceptual foundation of statistical techniques and how to formulate questions?
- What opportunities do doctoral students have to do research?
- Are there teaching opportunities?
- Are there PhD faculty in the program who share your research or practice interests? Are they conducting research in your area? Is that research funded?
- What have faculty published and in what journals? If the faculty are publishing research articles, it is likely that the research training is going to be strong.
- How often do doctoral students publish with faculty?
- Is there an opportunity for mentorship?
- Where are recent graduates working? Where do faculty expect them to find employment? You will be employed at the same level or below the rank of the program if you are looking at faculty positions. It is unlikely that you would be hired by the program from which you graduate.
- Talk with faculty and doctoral students. Where else did they consider applying and why?
- How selective is the program?
- Inquire about the average GPA and test scores for applicants at each school.
- Find out whether you need additional course work or experience.
- What is the average length of time for completion of the program? What percentage of the students do not finish?
- Are there part-time and full-time students?
- What is the expected cost?

Research the Program

Note that as you research doctoral programs, you are in a sense looking at potential employers if you plan to work at a university.

- How strong is the host institution? What is the relationship of the program to the institution?
- Does the PhD program have its own resources and an identity separate from the MSW program?
- What is the formal or informal ranking of the program?
- How well regarded is the program?
- In what part of the development cycle is the program?
- What is the size of the program, the number of students? What are the sizes of the classes?
- How long has the program existed?

Environment for PhD Students

- Does the school value its PhD students? How much autonomy do students have?
- How safe is the campus at night?
- How supportive are the services and environment for PhD graduates? Consider funding for attending conferences, office space, computer access, special purchasing arrangements, housing for graduate students, affordability of the community, and financial-aid services.

Financial Aid

- Learn about funding sources, including the government.
- At least in the past, you could, at a minimum, expect a tuition waiver and fellowship or assistantship. However, in the current funding climate, you can expect less scholarship funding.
- Decisions are made on grades, recommendations, and GREs.
- If you have only partial funding, you need to do very well to get a chance of better funding in the second year.
- Investigate funding from sources other than your specific department.
- External funding gives you a shot at better universities, because it provides admissions leverage.
- Often the deadline for external funding is 1.5 years before you want to start.
- You need to plan for financial aid for a dissertation separately.

Application Process

Generally, you want to apply to schools in each of three categories:

1. two schools that are a reach for admission
2. two schools with 50–50 chance of admission
3. two schools with a high probability of admission.

Ask your former instructors and chairs of doctoral programs to help you realistically assess your chances for admission into particular programs. Find the best social work researcher in your particular field of interest, call that person, talk about his or her work, and apply to his or her school.

Application Preparation

- Do you have references who can speak to your ability to do doctoral work?
- Do all of your transcripts speak to your ability to do doctoral work?
- Address the issue of any poor grades in your statement.
- Have at least one writing sample of 10–15 pages.

GRE and MAT Scores

Keep this information in mind:

- The scores are good for five years.
- If you take the GRE while you are in school, you will probably do better.
- It is best to take the GRE six months before you apply. If you are required to take an area exam in addition to the GRE, take it on a different day.
- Prepare for the math, verbal, and analytical sections. Preparation will make a difference.
- Check the school's policy regarding acceptance of a second set of scores if you are thinking about repeating a test.

Planning Your Career as a PhD Student

After you are accepted to a program, you start the process for tenure if your goal is an academic career. Develop strong relationships with faculty. Manage your time carefully: Set goals to research, publish, present, and teach. Project a time line and try to adhere to it. Plan all term papers, projects, and written coursework to apply to the subject of your dissertation.

Further Reading

American Managed Behavioral Healthcare Association. (1996). *Case manager qualifications in AMBHA member companies.* Washington, DC: Author.

ARC of Northern Virginia, & ARC of the United States. (1993). *Making a difference: Career opportunities in disability-related fields.* Arlington, TX: Author.

Association for Gerontology. (1996). *Careers in aging: Opportunities and options.* Washington, DC: Author.

Berg-Weger, M., & Dent, T. (1992). *Guidelines for professional social work licensure/certification.* Unpublished booklet, Washington University, George Warren Brown School of Social Work, St. Louis.

Berkman, B., Damron-Rodriguez, J., Dobrof, R., & Harry, L. (1995). *A national agenda for geriatric education.* Washington, DC: U.S. Department of Health and Human Services.

Brown, D., Brooks, L., & Associates. (1996). *Career choice and development* (3rd ed.). San Francisco: Jossey-Bass.

Estes, R. (Ed.). (1992). *Internationalizing social work education.* Philadelphia: University of Pennsylvania.

Frey, L., & Edinburg, G. (1983). *Professional growth through continuing education.* In A. Rosenblatt & D. Waldfogel (Eds.), *Handbook of clinical social work* (pp. 345–360). San Francisco: Jossey-Bass.

Germain, C. (1983). Technological advances. In A. Rosenblatt & D. Waldfogel (Eds.), *Handbook of clinical social work* (pp. 26–57). San Francisco: Jossey-Bass.

Granovetter, M. S. (1995). *Getting a job.* Chicago: University of Chicago Press.

Hall, D., & Associates. (1996). *The career is dead—Long live the career: A relational approach to careers*. San Francisco: Jossey-Bass.

Hardcastle, D. (1983). Certification, licensure, and other forms of regulation. In A. Rosenblatt & D. Waldfogel (Eds.), *Handbook of clinical social work* (pp. 826–844). San Francisco: Jossey-Bass.

Kernaghan, S. G. (1994, Fall). *Social work administration, newsletter of the Society for Social Work Administrators in Health Care* (Available from Society for Social Work Administrators in Health Care, American Hospital Association, One North Franklin, Chicago, IL 60606)

Kernaghan, S. G. (1996, June–July, August). *Social work administration, newsletter of the Society for Social Work Administrators in Health Care* (Available from Society for Social Work Administrators in Health Care, American Hospital Association, One North Franklin, Chicago, IL 60606)

Lewis, K. (1981, November). Three approaches to social services. *Contemporary Administrator*, pp. 16–19.

Linsley, J. (1996). Salaries for new social workers: How much will I make? *New Social Worker*, *3*, 14–15.

London, M., & Stumpf, S. A. (1982). *Managing careers*. Reading, MA: Addison-Wesley.

Luna-Idunate, J., & Canon, R. (1997). The electronic connection: Job search @ the Internet. *New Social Worker*, *4*, 12–14.

McFarland, B., Smith, J., Bigelow, D., & MoFidi, A. (1995, September). Unit costs of community mental health services. *Administration and Policy in Mental Health*, *23*, 27–42.

Minahan, A., & Pincus, A. (1977). Conceptual framework for social work practice. *Social Work*, *22*, 347–352.

Mizrahi, T., & Morrison, J. D. (1993). *Community organization and social administration: Advances, trends, and emerging principles*. New York: Haworth Press.

National Association of Social Workers. (1996). *NASW professional social work credentials: Power in the marketplace* (Available from NASW, Office of Quality Assurance, 750 First Street, NE, Suite 700, Washington, DC 20002-4241)

Rogers, J., Smith, M. L., Hull, G. H., Jr., & Ray, J. (1995). How do BSWs and MSWs differ? *Journal of Baccalaureate Social Work*, *1*, 97–110.

Screenivasan, S. (1996, December 2). Web offers an outlet for charitable impulses. *New York Times*, p. C4.

Teare, R., & Sheafor, B. (1995). *Practice-sensitive social work education*. Alexandria, VA: Council on Social Work Education.

Tropman, J., Erlich, J., & Rothman, J. (Eds.). (1995). *Tactics and techniques of community intervention* (3rd ed.). Itasca, IL: F. E. Peacock.

Index

About the Author

Carol Nesslein Doelling, MS, is director of career services at the George Warren Brown School of Social Work (GWB) at Washington University in St. Louis. She provides comprehensive career services for social work students and alumni and information on employment issues to faculty. Ms. Doelling chairs GWB's home page committee and serves as managing editor of *LINKS*, the school's external newsletter.

Ms. Doelling has developed the *Job Market for MSW Graduates* (with Barbara Matz, EdD), an annual report on the job-search experience of new MSWs nationwide. She cofounded and hosted the first Career Development and Social Work Education conference and created *Social Work and Social Services Jobs Online* (with Violet Horvath, MSW), a career Web site especially for social workers.

Ms. Doelling has written for *The New Social Worker* and contributed a chapter on social work to *Great Careers* (edited by Devon Smith; Garret Park Press, 1990). She has made presentations at the annual conference on Career Development and Social Work Education and at conferences of the National Association of Social Workers and the Midwest Association of Colleges and Employers.

Social Work Career Development

Cover design by The Watermark Design Office

Interior design by Naylor Design, Inc.

Composed by Chris Olson and Patricia Wolf, Wolf Publications, Inc., in Janson and Univers

Printed by Graphic Communications, Inc., on 60# Windsor Offset